S0-AXB-091

Received on

Green Lake Library

NO LONGER PROPERTY
SEATTLE PUBLIC LIBRARY

BEST
HIKES
WITH
KIDS
OREGON

BEST HIKES WITH KIDS

OREGON

BONNIE HENDERSON
& ZACH URNESS

2ND EDITION

MOUNTAINEERS
BOOKS

MOUNTAINEERS BOOKS is the publishing division of The Mountaineers, an organization founded in 1906 and dedicated to the exploration, preservation, and enjoyment of outdoor and wilderness areas.

1001 SW Klickitat Way, Suite 201 • Seattle, WA 98134
800.553.4453 • www.mountaineersbooks.org

Copyright © 2018 by Bonnie Henderson and Zach Urness
All rights reserved. No part of this book may be reproduced or utilized in any form, or by any electronic, mechanical, or other means, without the prior written permission of the publisher.

Printed in South Korea
Distributed in the United Kingdom by Cordee, www.cordee.co.uk

First edition, 2007. Second edition, 2018. Earlier versions published as *Best Hikes with Children: Western and Central Oregon.*

Copyeditor: Erin Moore
Design: Jennifer Shontz, www.redshoedesign.com
Layout: McKenzie Long, www.cardinalinnovative.com
Cartographer: Pease Press Cartography
All photos by authors unless noted otherwise

Cover photograph: *Heading out on the Flood of Fire Trail (Hike 117) at John Day Fossil Beds National Monument in Eastern Oregon* (Photo by Zach Urness)
Frontispiece: *A family of backpackers makes their way up Tillamook Head, Hike 77.* (Photo by Bonnie Henderson)

Library of Congress Cataloging-in-Publication Data
Names: Henderson, Bonnie, author. | Urness, Zach, author.
Title: Best hikes with kids : Oregon / Bonnie Henderson and Zach Urness.
Description: 2nd edition. | Seattle, WA : Mountaineers Books, 2018. | Series:
    Best hikes with kids series | Includes bibliographical references and index.
Identifiers: LCCN 2017057619| ISBN 9781680510799 (pbk) | ISBN 9781680510805
    (ebook)
Subjects: LCSH: Hiking for children—Oregon—Guidebooks. | Oregon—Guidebooks.
Classification: LCC GV199.42.O7 H463 2018 | DDC 796.5109795—dc23
LC record available at https://lccn.loc.gov/2017057619

Mountaineers Books titles may be purchased for corporate, educational, or other promotional sales, and our authors are available for a wide range of events. For information on special discounts or booking an author, contact our customer service at 800-553-4453 or mbooks@mountaineersbooks.org.

ISBN (paperback): 978-1-68051-079-9
ISBN (ebook): 978-1-68051-080-5

CONTENTS

EASTERN OREGON

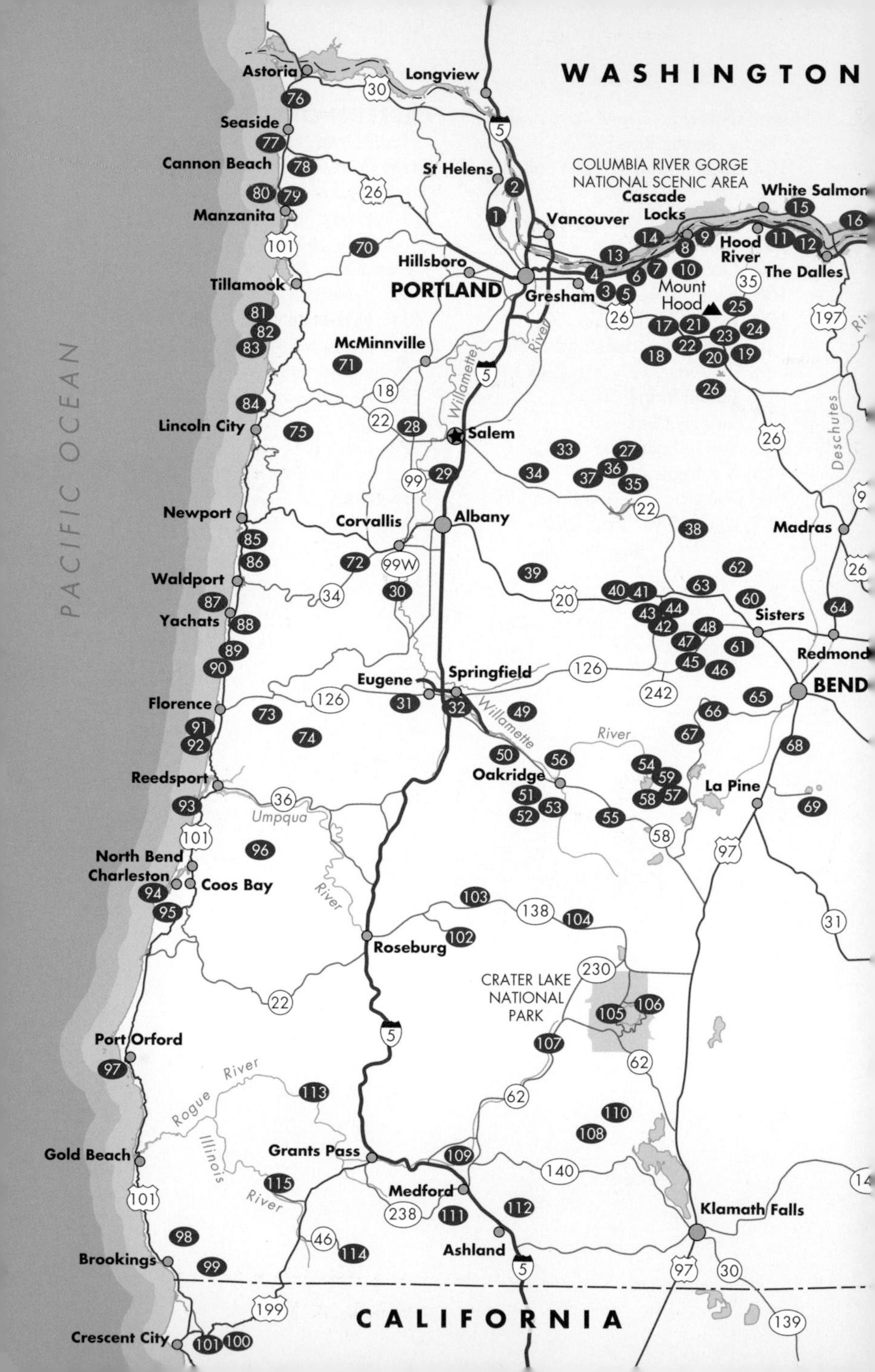

WASHINGTON
CALIFORNIA
PACIFIC OCEAN
COLUMBIA RIVER GORGE
NATIONAL SCENIC AREA
CRATER LAKE
NATIONAL
PARK
Astoria
Longview
Seaside
Cannon Beach
St Helens
Manzanita
Vancouver
Cascade
Locks
White Salmon
Hood
River
The Dalles
Hillsboro
PORTLAND
Gresham
Mount
Hood
Tillamook
McMinnville
Lincoln City
Salem
Newport
Corvallis
Albany
Madras
Waldport
Yachats
Sisters
Redmond
Eugene
Springfield
BEND
Florence
Oakridge
Reedsport
La Pine
North Bend
Charleston
Coos Bay
Roseburg
Port Orford
Gold Beach
Grants Pass
Medford
Ashland
Klamath Falls
Brookings
Crescent City
Willamette
River
Deschutes
Umpqua
Rogue
Illinois

CUTTING TO THE CHASE: A QUICK GUIDE TO OREGON'S "BEST OF" HIKES

For the hiking connoisseur, every adventure description in this guide is worth perusing; that's what earned it a place in this book. But naturally we have our favorites. Note that these lists of the top five hikes in various categories are based solely on our own experience and opinions and are not meant to be exclusive. We simply picked what we happen to remember as our favorite hikes for different occasions and listed them by hike number. After we hike them on another day, with different weather, different companions, and different needs, the list might well be different!

BEST HIKES IN WINTER

- **Multnomah Falls, Hike 7:** Oregon's largest waterfall roars with powerful splendor during the depths of winter. It's also the one time of year when this trek isn't jam-packed with tourists.
- **Niagara Falls, Hike 71:** Each more than 100 feet tall, these two waterfalls are especially spectacular when they're powered by rainfall.
- **Sweet Creek Trail, Hike 73:** This sweet treat of a hike features eleven waterfalls in a mere mile when the creek is flowing high with winter rain.
- **Ecola Creek Forest Reserve, Hike 78:** Almost any hike on the coast is a good choice for winter; this one follows a gravel road into a deep forest of large trees, where a little rain isn't a big problem.
- **Fall Creek and Susan Creek Falls, Hike 103:** You'll feel as though you're exploring a remote rainforest in this narrow canyon where an 80-foot waterfall sprays into a misty grotto at hike's end.

BEST SUPER-EASY WATERFALL HIKES

- **Elowah Falls, Hike 9:** Enjoy visiting a frozen rope of a waterfall in a mossy amphitheater of stone at a trail slightly less packed with visitors than other Columbia River Gorge options.
- **Wahclella Falls, Hike 10:** Although the main attraction is spectacular, it's not just the waterfalls that make this hike special, but also the deep, narrow canyon.
- **Silver Falls State Park, Hike 34:** This iconic park offers Oregon's most breathtaking waterfall hike. Hike behind a waterfall at South or North falls for a short and easy adventure.
- **Spirit, Moon, and Pinard Falls, Hike 51:** Each hike is 0.7 mile or less one-way, and each trailhead is just a short drive from the others; hike one, two, or all three in a day.

▪ **Golden and Silver Falls, Hike 96:** The approach drive is long, but two wondrous waterfalls make this trip worthwhile. You have a choice of two very easy hikes and one slightly tougher, but more rewarding, option.

BEST HIKES FOR FIRST-TIME BACKPACKERS

▪ **Lower Twin Lake, Hike 19:** With a trailhead just off the highway, there is no long forest drive to this popular hike, which features lots of campsites scattered around the lake.

▪ **Pamelia Lake, Hike 38:** Travel along a tumbling creek through old-growth forest to this mountain lake with Mount Jefferson looming overhead. A permit requirement keeps this area less crowded (but requires planning).

▪ **Erma Bell Lakes, Hike 54:** Two easy-to-reach mountain lakes offer scenic views and swimming to those lucky enough to claim a campsite near this chain of wilderness lakes.

▪ **Islet Beach, Hike 59:** A short hike leads to a quiet spot with a shallow, sandy beach for splashing (but wait until the mosquitoes are mostly gone—say, mid-August).

▪ **Blue Canyon Basin, Hike 108:** You'll find lots of camping choices—and decent fishing—at this easily reached series of mountain lakes in a wilderness area of the southern Cascades.

BEST UNIQUE HIKES

▪ **Cascade Streamwatch and Wildwood Wetland Trail, Hike 17:** One highlight of this entertaining interpretive trail is the underwater salmon-viewing station, where you can watch juvenile salmon in their natural habitat (without holding your breath).

▪ **Bagby Hot Springs, Hike 27:** Bathe in a tub carved from a huge tree in water flowing steaming hot out of the earth.

▪ **Little Belknap Crater, Hike 48:** This challenging hike runs through an almost entirely treeless lava flow high in the Cascades. Wear tough shoes (or boots), as the lava rock is rough.

▪ **Lava River Cave, Hike 68:** Rent a lantern at the entrance for your walk into this mile-long lava tube under the high desert.

▪ **Big Obsidian Flow, Hike 69:** Hike on a mountain of black glass! See where obsidian, and obsidian arrowheads, come from on this interpretive trail in Newberry National Volcanic Monument.

BEST HIKES FOR SPRING WILDFLOWERS

▪ **Memaloose Hills, Hike 11:** Views of Mount Hood and a blanket of yellow balsamroot across the hillsides make this less-traveled hike a winner during peak bloom.

▪ **Rowena Crest, Hike 12:** A geologic oddity, this tabletop plateau seems to float over the top of the Columbia River. Come at the right time of year, and it's covered in yellow balsamroot.

Wildflowers bloom in profusion at Columbia Hills State Park (Hike 16) in the Columbia River Gorge.

- **Catherine Creek, Hike 15:** Enjoy a cozy canyon of interesting geology and smaller bites of wildflowers, with camas lilies, lupine, and prairie stars speckled among the rocks.
- **Columbia Hills State Park, Hike 16:** The best overall wildflower hike in spring: entire hillsides turn golden and purple during the peak bloom in late April or early May.
- **Upper Table Rock, Hike 109:** It takes a bit of work to reach the top; but once you do, the flat-as-a-pancake mesa offers a wonderful assortment of wildflowers.

BEST HIKES FOR SUMMER WILDFLOWERS

- **Zigzag Canyon, Hike 23:** Pick a sunny day for this high-mountain hike that starts at landmark Timberline Lodge.
- **Umbrella and Sahalie Falls, Hike 24:** Wildflowers bloom profusely in the ski runs under the chairlifts in mid- to late summer—about the same time the huckleberries are getting ripe!
- **Iron Mountain, Hike 40:** The trailside wildflower display is epic, as is the view from the platform at the top. This relatively short hike climbs steadily, making it a good challenge.
- **Canyon Creek Meadows, Hike 63:** Wildflowers bloom in two meadows during late July below the vertical, multicolored wall of the mountain known as Three Fingered Jack. It's easier than you'd expect to gain such views.
- **Marys Peak, Hike 72:** Bright summer wildflowers festoon the meadows of the highest mountain in Oregon's Coast Range.

BEST BIG-TREE HIKES

- **Old Salmon River Trail, Hike 18:** This nearly flat trail winding among huge old trees is a great way to introduce young children to the ancient forest (and is a good choice for a first backpack trip too).

- **Opal Creek, Hike 35:** The fight to save the giant trees of this enchanted canyon spanned two decades. Visit in the winter, spring, or fall for solitude. Enjoy the swimming holes (but heavy crowds) in summer.
- **Short Sand Beach, Hike 80:** Most of the ancient cedars on the Oregon Coast have been logged off; this short trail to a remote beach passes some very impressive survivors.
- **Redwood Nature Loop, Hike 98:** Visit the world's tallest species of tree on Oregon soil—in one of the few places it's possible—in this emerald glen along the Chetco River.
- **Boy Scout Tree Trail, Hike 101:** Explore the best collection of giant trees along a hike in this book. The largest, the Boy Scout Tree, is a fused redwood with a trunk 40 feet in diameter!

BEST HIKES TO SEE BIRDS

- **Oaks to Wetlands Trail, Hike 2:** Stroll through a wildlife refuge at the edge of the Columbia River. Walk quietly and you'll see even more birds in the sloughs and ponds along the trail, especially in spring and fall.
- **Baskett Butte, Hike 28:** A wildlife refuge designed to lure birds off nearby farms offers one of the richest collections of avian friends in the Willamette Valley.
- **Rail Trail, Hike 29:** The observation blind at this wildlife refuge looks like the turret of a miniature castle and has fun viewing slots for watching every type of bird, from great blue herons to hawks.
- **Woodpecker Loop, Hike 30:** As the name suggests, you'll often hear the sound of woodpeckers here (although actually seeing them is another matter).
- **Sitka Sedge, Hike 83:** Fall through spring, at high tide or low tide, there are almost always water birds in the estuary.

BEST HIKES TO LIGHTHOUSES AND LOOKOUTS

- **Black Butte, Hike 60:** The hike to the summit of Black Butte ends with a close-up view of two very different fire lookouts—one old and one new and still in use.
- **Heceta Head Lighthouse, Hike 90:** This short hike leads past the old lighthouse keepers' home and ends at the picturesque lighthouse itself; if your timing is right, you might be able to take a tour inside.
- **Lake Marie, Hike 93:** Just down the road from this lake-circling hike is Umpqua Lighthouse, more than a century-and-a-half old and open for tours from May to September.
- **Port Orford Heads, Hike 97:** Examine an example of an early coastal lifesaving boat—and the cove where such boats were once launched—from these scenic trails on a tall headland on the southern Oregon Coast.
- **The Watchman, Hike 105:** This lookout tower peers onto what might be the best view in the state—the deep blue of Crater Lake. Visitors aren't allowed into the cabin, but you can explore around it.

Enjoying the view from the summit of Neahkahnie Mountain, Hike 79

BEST HIKES FOR A (BRISK) SWIM

- **Little North Santiam Trail to Elkhorn Falls, Hike 37:** Explore the glorious swimming holes of the Little North Santiam River to cool off during the heat of summer on this easy trek. The hike gets you away from the area's major crowds.
- **Fall Creek, Hike 49:** As a swimming spot, Fall Creek is almost too popular. Visit on a summer weekday (weekends can get a little crazy) to enjoy the pools that form in the rocky creek bed.
- **Bobby Lake, Hike 57:** The big, slanting rock on the western edge of Bobby Lake is ideal for sunbathing and sliding into the water for swimming; but get there early while the rock is still bathed in sunshine.
- **South Waldo Shelter, Hike 58:** From this hike along Waldo Lake, the best place to take a dip is 1.3 miles in, off a spur trail to a peninsula, where the shallow water is (relatively) warm.
- **Lower Sky Lakes Basin, Hike 110:** You'll lose count of the number of lakes encountered on this adventure and the many different places to swim and choices, some better than others.

BEST SUMMIT HIKES

- **Beacon Rock, Hike 14:** Hike up exactly fifty-one switchbacks on a funky, railed trail system to the top of a volcanic plug that rises above the Columbia River. Looking at this rock from a distance, you'll wonder how this trail is even possible.
- **Spencer Butte, Hike 31:** The hike to the top of Spencer Butte, marking the southern end of the Willamette Valley, is a favorite among Eugene families.

■ **Iron Mountain, Hike 40:** A fire lookout used to stand at the top of Iron Mountain; now there's a viewing platform to spy a half-dozen nearby Cascade peaks.

■ **Black Butte, Hike 60:** The hike to the top of this cinder cone—a Central Oregon landmark—is challenging for young children but worthwhile if they're up for it. Avoid it on hot afternoons.

■ **Neahkahnie Mountain, Hike 79:** This coastal-fronting peak rises steeply from the shoreline, but the hike up it is a gradual, steady ascent; from the top, the view to the south (and the ocean stretching west) is stunning.

BEST HIKES TO BRING A FISHING POLE

■ **Veda Lake, Hike 20:** It's a nasty drive in, but as a result there are no crowds at Veda Lake. If you fail to catch any of the brook trout in the lake, try your hand at catching crayfish along the edge.

■ **Doris Lake, Hike 67:** Most of the high lakes in the Cascades require a long access hike; Doris, and neighboring Blow Lake, don't require much of a hike and can reward even young anglers in summer.

■ **Benson Lake (fish at Scott Lake), Hike 47:** At the start of this trail is Scott Lake, one of the few lakes on McKenzie Pass you can reach by car. Scott is best for fishing early in the season, around late June. Naturally, the mosquitoes are heaviest then too.

■ **Detroit Area, Great Getaway:** More than 100,000 trout are stocked at the popular Detroit Lake reservoir each summer and fishing is often excellent.

■ **Anthony and Hoffer Lakes, Hike 120:** Anthony Lake is stocked with thousands of trout every year, making this alpine lake a great place to drop a line when fishing opens in July.

BEST ACCESSIBLE TRAILS

■ **Oaks to Wetlands Trail, Hike 2:** Soar over the railroad tracks on a high footbridge then follow a flat gravel path 0.2 mile to an Indian plankhouse. An asphalt path quickly leads to a turnaround at an ancient oak tree.

■ **Cascade Streamwatch and Wildwood Wetland Trail, Hike 17:** The best parts of this riverside interpretive trail travel on flat or gently sloping asphalt or wooden boardwalk, making them accessible to everybody.

■ **Little Crater Lake, Hike 26:** It's just 0.2 mile on a flat gravel path to this tiny blue lake and the viewing platform at its edge, where the accessible portion ends.

■ **Ray Atkeson Memorial Trail, Hike 66:** The best views on this loop trail are found on the 0.4-mile-long wheelchair-accessible portion, which follows the edge of Sparks Lake.

■ **Sitka Sedge, Hike 83:** Built on an old dike, the first 0.3-mile portion of the compacted gravel trail into Sitka Sedge State Natural Area is level, offering ever-changing views of the estuary and its wildlife.

Hikes are more fun for everyone when kids lead the way.

INTRODUCTION

There's no such thing as the perfect hike for kids, because just like adults, all children are different. Some thrive on a longer adventure—or even a backpacking trip—while others struggle to finish one mile. Some love the idea of a grand multiday adventure to the far reaches of Oregon, while others will tolerate only a short car ride.

This book was written with those differences in mind. Most of the hikes featured here are short, easy, full of interesting attractions, and close to Oregon's largest cities. At the same time, we've included lots of options for longer hikes and first time backpacking experiences. Our "Great Getaways" are designed to guide parents on multiday trips in the state's most beautiful locations. The "Quick Hikes" offer additional options for hiking close to home.

WHY HIKE WITH KIDS?

Kids can get exercise at the gym, and they can learn about nature at a museum or interpretive center. Is hiking even necessary anymore? Yes, now more than ever, we believe. And we have lots of company—among them, pediatricians, psychologists, physicists, biologists, and other parents. Researchers have found that contact with the natural world is essential to our physical and mental health; it may be as important to human health as forming close, personal relationships.

Accustomed as many kids are to the instant gratification of electronic games and devices in general, it's not always easy to get children out the door and onto a trail these days. Some kids love the prospect of an hour or a day on a trail, but more reluctant young hikers will do their best to discourage you. Add to their whining, the gear gathering, the arrangements required to bring friends along, the driving, the logistics, and it's easy to get discouraged.

So why do we drive sometimes an hour or more to spend perhaps only an hour or two on a trail? It gets us out of the city. It gives us time together. It helps us stay healthy. It injects adventure into our lives. It's a relatively inexpensive family activity. It introduces children to nature, to wildlife and wild places. It provides opportunities for children to gain confidence. When the weather takes an unexpected turn and we wind up hunkering down, slogging uncomfortably in the rain for an hour, we learn that we are stronger and more capable than we thought, that our sense of humor needn't disappear when the going gets tough. And when we're back home, we have a great story to tell.

Despite the title, this book isn't just for children; it's for anyone looking for a wide range of interesting, approachable hikes. It's for the adults who go to the trouble of taking kids hiking, not necessarily every weekend, but every now and then; who round up the kids and their friends, gather the gear, pack the lunches and snacks, overcome their own inertia at the end of a busy week, and maintain enthusiasm when the kids' spirits are flagging. What your kids need more than this book is a day outdoors, anywhere, with you.

Hiking along the edge of a wetland in the Willamette Valley (Photo by Leyla Folsom)

WHAT TO TAKE

Planning ahead to meet expectations and knowing the right stuff to bring goes many miles toward ensuring a safe and successful hike. Here's a basic list.

"My Own Pack!"

Particularly with younger children, offering a pack of their own to carry can add excitement to an outing. You don't have to put much in it—the less the better, at first—but you may find you get more cooperation from a child wearing a pack. It seems to signal that you consider the wearer a bona fide member of the party, not just a youngster the adults brought along on their outing.

Small packs sized for children are widely available, but a smallish adult's day pack may get used for more years; just don't overload it. One woman we know adds something special to her grandchild's pack every time they hike: colorful adhesive bandages, a small flashlight, or an emergency whistle.

Boots or Shoes?

Boots used to be the standard footwear for hiking of any kind, but these days a good quality athletic shoe with support and a traction sole is considered quite adequate for most day hikes. If you plan to be on rough terrain, or in snow or on a very wet trail, or if you are carrying heavy packs, you may need more substantial footwear. Just in case, carry moleskin and apply it at the first sign of discomfort. We've found that the best way to avoid blisters is to wear hiking shoes that are on the large size, even a half-size larger than your usual shoe size, but as you gain experience, you will undoubtedly learn what works best for your feet, as well as those of your children.

THE TEN ESSENTIALS

You say you're planning to hike only 2 miles, and the weather's beautiful? It's still a good idea to make sure most, if not all, of these ten essentials items are in your day pack, especially when hiking with children. This list, compiled by The Mountaineers, has become an accepted standard for hikers and other recreationists.

1. **Navigation.** Navigation includes map and compass. Although many of the trails in this book aren't so isolated or complicated that they require a map for routefinding, it's always a good idea to carry one. Older children may enjoy learning to read maps in the field. Maps are often necessary for finding your way on the sometimes complicated network of roads leading to national forest trailheads. A compass is essential in case the fog rolls in or you are otherwise unsure of your path or direction. Be sure to learn how to use it with a map.

2. **Headlamp.** Small and light to carry but powerful, LED flashlights, mini-lights, and headlamps are widely available.

3. **Sun protection.** Sunscreen and sunglasses: children of hiking age usually like to wear sunglasses, especially if they've helped to pick them out. Encouraging kids to wear shades now (especially if they're around water and snow) helps reduce their likelihood of developing cataracts years down the road.

4. **First aid.** Stock and carry a first-aid kit supplied with the basics, plus any special medications your group requires, such as a bee sting kit if someone is allergic.

5. **Knife.** One with various blades and tools is particularly useful (for adults and for kids to use for whittling when they're mature enough).

6. **Fire.** A candle or chemical fire starter of some kind adds little weight to the pack and can be a lifesaver if you wind up bivouacking unexpectedly. To start that fire, waterproof matches, available at sporting goods stores, are safest; keep them in a waterproof container. An inexpensive lighter or two are also handy to have.

7. **Shelter.** Prepare for the unexpected. A tarp and line to hang it and a bivy bag or emergency blanket are useful for tiding over a turn in the weather.

It can be easier to have kids ride in a pack for awhile on the trail rather than expect them to walk the entire way. (Photo by Shannon DePuglia)

Children sometimes need a little help to finish a hike. (Photo by Jeff Green)

8.   **Extra food.** Pack what you plan to eat—and then some, just in case. The traditional hiker's menu consists of high-energy, noncrushable foods that won't spoil too quickly, such as dried fruits, nuts, hard crackers, cheese, and dried meats, and—in limited quantity—candy. Fresh fruit is heavier but refreshing—just remember to pack out cores, peels, etc. Pick foods your children don't ordinarily get, or save certain treats for outings (dried fruit rolls or boxed juices, for example), to make hikes special.

9.   **Extra water.** Since kids don't always say they are thirsty, carrying extra water reminds both you and them to stay hydrated. Flavor packets can add some enticement to drink. Bring a water purifier of some kind if you plan to be out overnight.

10.   **Extra clothing.** Layers of clothing are the secret to hiking in the Northwest and to hiking with children. A little windy? Pull on the windbreaker. Hot spot in the boots? Change to another pair of socks. Kids shivering after dinner? A warm sweater can save the day.

What Else You Might Need

You may wish to have these two other electronic items with you.

Cell phone. Most people use their cell or smartphone and take them along on trips to take pictures and video these days. A smartphone can also be life saving if in range of a signal. But make sure not to allow the phone to overshadow the actual experience.

GPS devices. A handheld GPS device is a great tool, not only for double-checking your route—and finding your way home if you take a wrong turn—but also for mapping. A fun element with kids can be tracking your route, noting statistics like steps taken, top speed, and important spots. A Garmin Oregon is Zach's favorite idiot-proof handheld GPS; Bonnie uses a navigation app called Gaia GPS (one of several available) on her smartphone.

GOOD TRAIL MANNERS

Follow these guidelines to preserve the environment and ensure a good experience for other hikers.

- **Don't litter.** Dispose of waste (including human waste) properly. Better yet, bring an extra plastic bag to bring out others' trash you may find.
- **Leave nature as is.** Develop the habit of leaving what you find in the wild, from flowers to hermit crabs. If you turn over a tidepool rock, put it back exactly where it was. Even dead plants and animals play a role in nature as they decay.
- **Build fires only in established fire rings.** Leave no fire unattended. Make sure your fire is completely out before you go to sleep or hike away.

GOING TO THE BATHROOM—WITHOUT A BATHROOM

The first Murphy's Law of Hiking with Children: Regardless of how many potty stops you make beforehand, someone has to "go" within twenty minutes of leaving the last bathroom. No problem if you're prepared! Do as backpackers do: Carry a small bottle of hand sanitizer, a sturdy, lightweight trowel, and two plastic self-sealing bags, one with dry toilet paper and the other to carry used toilet paper out. Yes, carry TP out like any other litter. Buried paper may get dug up and scattered by animals, and burning it is both ineffective and dangerous in dry weather.

Bury feces at least 6 inches deep, far from the trail and water sources. Even if you pick up a rock, dig a hole under the rock, use the hole, and then replace the rock. If you don't have a trowel, do your best to dig with a stick.

- **Stick to the trail.** Don't cut across switchbacks; they contribute to erosion.
- **Choose campsites carefully.** Avoid camping on lakeshores or other delicate environments.
- **Be considerate of wildlife.** Keep your distance from wild animals, for your own safety and theirs. Don't feed wild animals (even when they "beg").
- **Be considerate of other hikers.** Keep dogs on leash if there are other hikers around (or where it is required). Keep your noise down. If you listen to music, keep it to yourself (use earbuds, not speakers).

SAFETY

The best way to ensure a trip is successful is by doing your homework ahead of time. Check the coordinates of a hike online so you understand the length of the drive. Make a phone call to ask about conditions (see Resources). Have a backup map that shows the surrounding area. Give a friend or family member your itinerary and a time to check in with you when you return. Most of the time, these precautions won't be necessary, but it's always better to have the peace of mind in understanding what you're getting into before you reach the trailhead.

CLOSE TO HOME AND FAR AWAY

It's great to have hikes in your backyard, but it's also nice to get away on a longer trip. With that in mind, we added two new features for this edition: "Great Getaways" and "Quick Hikes."

A NOTE ABOUT SAFETY

Safety is an important concern in all outdoor activities. No guidebook can alert you to every hazard or anticipate the limitations of every reader. Therefore, the descriptions of roads, trails, routes, and natural features in this book are not representations that a particular place or excursion will be safe for your party. When you follow any of the routes described in this book, you assume responsibility for your own safety. Under normal conditions, such excursions require the usual attention to traffic, road and trail conditions, weather, terrain, the capabilities of your party, and other factors. Because many of the lands in this book are subject to development and/or change of ownership, conditions may have changed since this book was written that make your use of some of these routes unwise. Always check for current conditions, obey posted private property signs, and avoid confrontations with property owners or managers. Keeping informed on current conditions and exercising common sense are the keys to a safe, enjoyable outing.

—Mountaineers Books

The petroglyphs at Columbia Hills State Park, Hike 16, offer an excellent educational experience.

QUICK HIKES

Many of the best close-to-home hikes can be found at urban parks. To ensure you don't miss any of these, we've put together a list of the best urban parks with hiking trails for each of western Oregon's largest cities.

GREAT GETAWAYS

This feature spotlights the best family vacation spots around the state for outdoor recreation. You'll find information about hotels, campsites, and fun stuff to do besides hiking. Each getaway is surrounded by featured hikes in its location. The goal is to make multiday adventures just a little bit easier.

SUGGESTIONS?

We've hiked all the trails in this book and checked road names and numbers and directions. But changes do occur; trails fall into disrepair; new roads are built or road numbers and names are changed; and old, abandoned trails are rehabilitated. We would appreciate hearing from readers about discrepancies in the hike descriptions and receiving suggestions of other trails that might deserve inclusion in the next edition of *Best Hikes with Kids: Oregon*. Please write to Zach Urness in care of Mountaineers Books, 1001 SW Klickitat Way, Suite 201, Seattle, WA 98134.

Look for Mount Hood through the trees from the trail to Veda Lake, Hike 20.

HOW TO USE THIS GUIDE

Anything can spoil a hike, especially for youngsters new to the outdoors whose tolerance for cold, heat, fatigue, bugs, and even long car rides can be limited at best. A parent's first job is to choose trails carefully. We selected the hikes in this book for their appeal to kids and for their relative ease. Most of the trails included here go no farther than 1.5 miles without a treat of some kind: a waterfall, bridge, lake, great view, mountain of glass, or tunnel of lava. That way, if hikers go no farther than this turnaround point, everyone can still come away with a sense of accomplishment.

PICKING A HIKE
To help you get around, the book's hikes are grouped by major geographic divisions highlighting the breadth of Oregon's landscapes, from coast to desert, including a few destinations just across the state borders in Washington and California. To help you pick a hike within a region, each description includes the following trail information.

Icons. At the beginning of each hike you'll find symbols that provide a quick-glance way of knowing what that trek is all about. Every hike in this book is short enough to be a day hike, but we also provide a little backpacking icon to let parents know which trails make sense for an overnight experience. Likewise, some of these hikes are best known for wildflower blooms, others for waterfalls, still others for old-growth forest.

A trail leads toward the base of Salt Creek Falls, Hike 55.

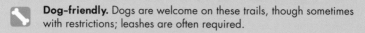

KEY TO ICONS

Dog-friendly. Dogs are welcome on these trails, though sometimes with restrictions; leashes are often required.

Wheelchair/stroller accessible. At least some portion of these trails is designed with wheelchairs and strollers in mind.

Splash zone. These are trails where there's an opportunity to swim—or at least to wade.

Historic site. These trails either played a role in history or take you past a historic structure of some kind.

Backpacking. You'll find campsites on these trails, making them a good choice for backpacking with youngsters.

Waterfall. These trails have one or more waterfalls at the end or along the way.

Old growth. We use the term loosely here to refer to any trail that goes through a noteworthy forest of older, larger trees.

Wildflowers. On these trails you can expect to see lots of wildflowers in either spring or summer.

Wildlife. Birds or other wildlife are frequently spotted, even by kids, from these trails in certain seasons.

Interpretive trail. Signage along these trails helps you better understand the landscape you're walking through.

Season. The goal is to let you know when the trail will be snow-free. Our notes should not be considered the last word, however. The hiking season varies from year to year according to snowpack and weather conditions. Call ahead to the agency listed to check conditions, especially in spring, when valley floors can be 80 degrees and sunny while a mountain hike is still covered in snow. In some cases, road closures dictate a hike's seasonal accessibility.

Difficulty. The designation of a trail as easy, moderate, or challenging is intended for children. Thus, a hike that would be easy for a fit adult might be listed as "challenging." Our book takes into special consideration trail conditions, elevation gain, and distance to the major destination when making these calls. Often children can travel long distances on level trails, especially with interesting distractions along the way. Add some elevation gain and long stretches without much variation in scenery, and the fatigue level quickly goes up.

A hike can bring young children closer together. (Photo by Leyla Folsom)

If a short hike is what you're after, don't limit your choices to those designated "easy": even a trail rated "challenging" may in fact be easy and full of interest for the first mile, making that section a good choice for beginning hikers. Add your own judgment to the formula as well. An exposed ridgeline trail that's a breeze on a balmy June day can quickly turn into a nightmare in blistering heat or persistent rain, especially with very young, tired, or inexperienced hikers.

Round-trip. For each hike, the total mileage for the outing is listed, the total distance to the destination and back or to complete a loop. A loop hike is often truly a "lollipop-loop" and includes an out-and-back section. One-way hikes are those with trailheads accessible by car at either end, but there aren't many of those featured in this book.

Elevation gain. This figure is the total elevation rise (rounded off to the nearest ten) on a given hike, whether it's to the top of a mountain, the return from a trip down to a lake basin or beach, or all the elevation gain on an up-and-down trail.

High point. This number indicates the height above sea level of the highest point on the featured trail section or sections described. Use it as a clue to how cold or exposed the trail might be, or how early or late in the year it might open up.

Walking along a sandy path to Short Sand Beach, Hike 80, on the Oregon Coast

KNOW BEFORE YOU GO

Here's a heads up on what you will want to know before you pack up the car and hit the road.

Map. This guide provides a simple map with every hike (but one: Lava River Cave has no map because it is all underground). But if you want to do more exploring or have some perspective about what's around you, we encourage you to use a supplemental map. Many maps can be downloaded online. When that's the case, search out the website of the agency listed in "Contact." In cases where the map is on a web source other than the contact listed, we'll note as much. In some cases, it's best to buy the US Forest Service map of a given area, especially if you're planning to spend some time there. See Resources for the National Forest Map Store.

Contact. This category denotes the agency that manages the land where the hike is located; or in some cases an alternate, more accessible local agency. (Consult the Resources in the back of the book for details.) They will have the most up-to-date information about trail and road conditions, as well as hours of operation or seasonal closures. It's always helpful to call in advance, especially in the spring, to ask about snow levels, mosquitoes, and crowds. This knowledge can make or break a trip.

Notes. If there's a fee at the trailhead or dogs aren't allowed, this is the place you'll find that information. It also contains information about steep drop-offs or exposure along a trail that could disqualify it for some families; or other warnings, for example the possible presence of poison oak for hikes (see side-

MAP LEGEND

(5)(84)	Interstate highway	(12)	Hike number
(26)(101)	US highway	■	Building of interest
(22)(138)	State route	•	Point of interest
1790	Forest road	♠	Tree of interest
24	County route	▲	Campground or campsite
------	Main trail	→	Direction of travel
....	Continuation or alternate route	⊶	Gate
....	Other trail	↷	Good turnaround point
═══	Paved road	▲	Peak or mountain
▭▭▭	Gravel road	🛆	Picnic table
-≠-	Bridge	⊕	Restroom or privy
-⊣⊢-	Underpass or tunnel	℗	Parking
------	Boardwalk	⊤	Trailhead
⬭	Body of water	ⓣ	Alternate trailhead
∼	River or stream	ⓥ	Viewpoint
▨	Park, forest, or wilderness area	----	Ski lift
▬▬	Boundary	-•-•-	Power line
▨	Private land	+++	Railroad
⋱	Wetlands	⤙	Waterfall
▨	Tide flats	◌	Glacier
		▨	Lava

bar, "Poison Oak Myths and Facts" in Hike 114). Knowing whether bathrooms are available on a particular hike is often particularly important for families; the notes let you know if a privy is available at the trailhead or nearby.

These hikes cross land managed by several different agencies. Figuring out permits can be quite tricky. The notes indicate whether a permit is necessary for a particular trailhead; check the agency's website or call them (see Resources) before you go to find out the current rates. In Oregon, you will need a Northwest Forest Pass from the US Forest Service to park at trailheads in many national forests. An annual federal lands pass, available from the National Park Service, is useful if you plan to visit any national parks or national wildlife refuges in a given year. Some Oregon State Parks require a fee; if you visit often, you may want to purchase an annual pass. Most Washington State Parks require a Discover Pass. Some Bureau of Land Management districts and regional and local parks charge a day-use fee for parking; the notes indicate whether you'll need to have some cash or perhaps a checkbook with you. Popular Pamelia Lake, Hike 38, requires an additional limited entry permit from the USFS; for summer weekends especially, you'll want to plan ahead.

GPS coordinates. In each information block, you'll see a section called "GPS" with corresponding coordinates. This is a helpful way to guide you to the trailhead. In most mapping systems on your smartphone—including Google Maps—you can just plug in the coordinates and it will show the trailhead in question. You can navigate right to it. If you're using a stand-alone GPS device, make sure it is set to WGS84, the datum used by Google Maps. The format used for this book is degrees and decimal minutes, for example, N45° 49.498' W122° 44.536'.

Don't rely exclusively on coordinates and a digital mapping system—especially in more remote locations. A road may be closed or the route snowed-in. Rather, use the coordinates as a tool that combined with the book's directions, and a hard copy map, will guide you to the trailhead safely.

Directions. The directions in this book are given from the closest major city or town, or from the most logical jumping-off point. Given today's mapping technology, most people have little trouble navigating even to smaller towns.

PERMITS

A permit is required to park at many trailheads. County parks, state parks, national forests and refuges all have their own permit systems. In most cases you can purchase day-use permits on site, but not always. If you have a season pass that applies where you're headed, be sure to bring it—or bring cash (typically $5 or less) to buy on site if possible.

Opposite: Taking a winter walk on the Oaks to Wetlands Trail, Hike 2

PORTLAND AREA

1 WAPATO ACCESS GREENWAY

BEFORE YOU GO
   MAP Map posted at trailhead
   CONTACT Wapato Access Greenway State Park
   NOTES Privy available along trail at Hadley's Landing (not at trailhead)
   GPS N45° 39.618' W122° 50.311'
ABOUT THE HIKE
   SEASON Year-round
   DIFFICULTY Easy
   ROUND-TRIP 2.5-mile loop
   HIGH POINT 70 feet
   ELEVATION GAIN 250 feet

GETTING THERE

From downtown Portland, take US Highway 30 about 10 miles to the Sauvie Island Bridge. Cross it and drive north on Sauvie Island Road for 2.5 miles until you see the signed trailhead on your left; there is parking for perhaps ten cars.

ON THE TRAIL

A pastoral island of farms and fields, much of it protected by the state as a wildlife refuge, Sauvie Island lies at the meeting of the Willamette and Columbia rivers, northwest of Portland. This trail around Virginia Lake, which fills with

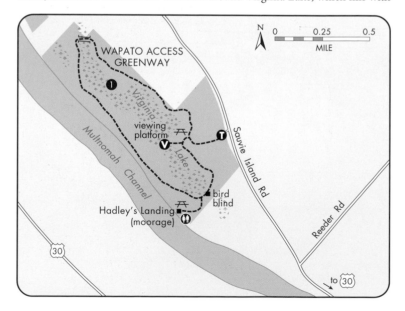

water only in winter, is a quiet beauty all year long. You may see resident and migratory birds on the lake; a blind helps you hide while you watch. You will see boats on the river where the trail cuts back toward Multnomah Channel. Bring a picnic and, in July and August, containers for the blackberries you'll pick. While you're on the island, stop at a farm stand for fresh produce or, better yet, u-pick berries with the kids in season.

Walk around the gate and down the trail heading out from the parking area. At 0.2 mile you'll reach a rise with the covered picnic shelter. For a clockwise hike, bear left, past the shelter; immediately you'll hit a spur trail that leads a short distance to a large viewing platform. Return to the main trail to slowly

QUICK HIKES IN PORTLAND

Portland justifiably prides itself on its access to the wild in the city. Every corner of the greater Portland area has open spaces with trails. Some are part of the "40-Mile Loop" of trails around Portland, a project under development for more than a century and now stretching some 140 miles.

Forest Park. The 30-mile Wildwood Trail (a national scenic trail) is the longest of the many trails in this park hugging the wooded ridge northwest of downtown Portland. Trails wind among trees, follow creeks, and hook up with more paths leading to such attractions as the Oregon Zoo, Portland Japanese Garden, and Pittock Mansion.

Mary S. Young State Natural Area. Walk along the river or follow a trail through the forest at this park on the Willamette River in West Linn, south of Portland. The 5-plus miles of trail offer lots of options for short loop hikes.

Mount Tabor Park. A network of short trails wind around a volcanic cinder cone in the middle of the city. There's also a paved bike path, playground, and other amenities.

Oaks Bottom Wildlife Refuge. Great blue herons are among the many kinds of birds you might witness from the paths at this urban preserve on the east side of the Willamette River. It's a good spot for short walks with youngsters.

Powell Butte Nature Park. This park has it all: moist wetlands, shady forest, and open meadows with views in all directions, including east to Mount Hood. Eight miles of trail include a paved, all-abilities path.

Tryon Creek State Natural Area. Logged long ago, the forest along Tryon Creek is now a lush Douglas fir forest. A lacework of trails includes eight footbridges and a paved, all-abilities trail. Young hikers can listen for woodpeckers, watch for squirrels, and try to spot evidence of beavers at work on the water. Start your visit with a stop at the interpretive center.

Tualatin Hills Nature Park. A lush nature preserve surrounds the confluence of Beaverton and Cedar Mill creeks in the heart of suburbia west of Portland. Its 5 miles of trails include dirt paths as well as paved, all-access routes. Check out the exhibits at the interpretive center near the entrance, which also has restrooms.

circle the lake. At 0.5 mile you'll reach a wooden bird blind; it's 0.1 mile farther to a spur trail to Hadley's Landing on Multnomah Channel, where boaters can tie up and hikers can sight-see or picnic with a water view.

Continuing on the loop, the trail veers away from Virginia Lake's edge, following close to Multnomah Channel with frequent views of the water. Emerging from the trees, the trail crosses the north end of the lake at 1.5 miles and ascends a short rise, offering views of neighboring farms. The trail returns you to the picnic shelter at 2.3 miles; return to the trailhead as you came.

2 OAKS TO WETLANDS TRAIL

BEFORE YOU GO
    MAP Download from refuge website
    CONTACT Ridgefield National Wildlife Refuge
    NOTES NWR entrance fee; dogs prohibited; first 0.4 mile wheelchair accessible;
      privy available
    GPS N45° 39.618' W122° 50.311'
ABOUT THE HIKE
    SEASON Year-round
    DIFFICULTY Easy–moderate
    ROUND-TRIP 2.1-mile loop
    HIGH POINT 40 feet
    ELEVATION GAIN 80 feet

GETTING THERE

From Portland, take Interstate 5 north to exit 14 (Ridgefield, Washington). Head west on Pioneer Street for 3 miles, through two roundabouts, to downtown Ridgefield. Turn right on North Main Avenue and follow it 1 mile. At the sign to Ridgefield NWR, turn left onto NW 291st Street and park in the gravel parking area near the trailhead kiosk.

Cathlapotle Plankhouse sits near the water's edge off the Oaks to Wetlands Trail.

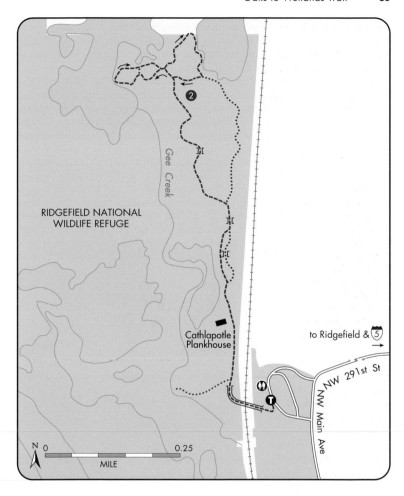

ON THE TRAIL

Less than a half-hour's drive north of Portland, Ridgefield National Wildlife Refuge in Washington preserves a portion of the Columbia River floodplain. Swans, geese, and ducks stop here in the fall on their way south from breeding grounds farther north; some continue south, and some stay for the winter. This trail winds through wetlands and uplands forested with rare white oaks.

You'll likely encounter two kinds of visitors on the Oaks to Woodlands Trail: adult birdwatchers and young children with their adults. Families are drawn in by the large curving footbridge at the trailhead, the traditional Chinookan plankhouse a short distance down the trail, and the variety of birds that even kids without binoculars can often spot, from osprey to Canada geese and even migrating sandhill cranes in spring and fall. With several spur trails, the route can get a little confusing, but the distances here aren't great, and all trails ultimately loop back to the main trail.

Cross the long, high footbridge (the highest ascent on the trail) and head down the gravel path alongside Gee Creek 0.2 mile to Cathlapotle Plankhouse. In 2005, local Chinookan people built this replica of the type of multifamily house their ancestors lived in here and at other sites on the lower Columbia. The plankhouse is typically open to the public on weekends from April through September and on special occasions.

Here the path turns to asphalt and continues north another 0.2 mile to the site of a 400-year-old white oak. Continue north on the trail (on dirt now). For a 2.1-mile loop, stick to the main trail, bearing left at trail junctions; it runs north and loops around the edges of the lakes and sloughs that dot this marshy refuge at the edge of the Columbia River. After reaching the end and looping back past another large lake arm, you'll reach another trail junction; turn right to return to the main trail. Alternately, a left turn leads to a narrow, rocky spur trail that eventually connects to the main trail. Return via the main trail or an alternate path through the trees on your left.

3 OXBOW REGIONAL PARK

BEFORE YOU GO
   MAP Download from park website or pick up at entry booth
   CONTACT Oxbow Regional Park
   NOTES Park entry fee; open 6:30 am to sunset; privy available
   GPS N45° 30.069' W122° 18.369'
ABOUT THE HIKE
   SEASON Year-round
   DIFFICULTY Easy
   ROUND-TRIP 3.8-mile loop
   HIGH POINT 241 feet
   ELEVATION GAIN 300 feet

GETTING THERE

From Portland, take Interstate 84 east to exit 16 (Wood Village). Drive south on 238th Street (which becomes Hogan Drive) for 2.7 miles to Division Street and turn left, continuing 5.5 miles to a four-way junction. Turn left onto Oxbow Parkway at a sign pointing toward the park and continue 1.6 miles to a tollbooth and office at the park's entrance.

ON THE TRAIL

The Sandy River takes center stage at this 1000-acre natural area just outside the hustle of Portland's metro area. Fishing, camping, swimming, rafting, and horseback riding are all popular here, and the park's 13 miles of trail allow

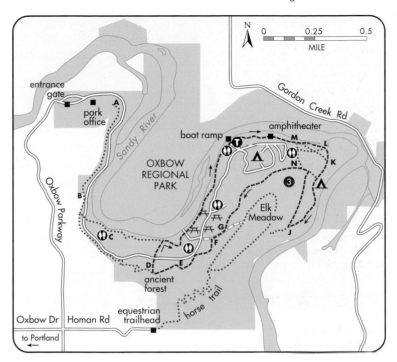

families to enjoy a close-to-home adventure year-round. One important point to remember before getting started is that while the trails are well marked by a system of letters, these are only decipherable with a park map: so make sure to print one off in advance from the park's website or grab one at the entrance.

There are countless options at this park. But one in particular allows families to combine the park's best assets—its riverfront and old-growth forest—on a 3.8-mile loop. If it's summer, bring a swimming suit. If it's winter, bring a fishing rod and maybe you can reel in one of the river's famed winter steelhead. The loop can feel somewhat confusing due to the park's many intersections, but if you have a map, you should be OK.

Start at the main campground and boat launch parking area at the end of the main entry road. To get started, hike to the right, above the river at first and past the campground, to a stretch of trail with 0.6 mile of rocky-beach river access. This stretch is marked as "M" on the park map. Your route follows the curve of the river southwest. Swim or fish here and explore numerous curiosities. Next, the trail turns inland and passes a few gravel road markers for 1 mile before entering the park's "ancient forest." Large, hundred-year-old trees rise in this most scenic section of the park.

Stay on the trail for more old growth, arriving at the junction with the trail marked "D" on the park map. Turn right and cross back over the entry road,

The Sandy River takes center stage at Oxbow Regional Park.

turning right again at the intersection with the riverfront trail. The final stretch follows high above the river and past several group picnic areas, before dropping down as you approach the boat ramp and the loop's conclusion.

Following the many intersections of trail can make this hike feel like a route-finding adventure—and can be confusing—but it's a nice way to explore all the charms that make this park so beloved.

4 SANDY RIVER DELTA

BEFORE YOU GO
  MAP Download from scenic area website
  CONTACT Columbia River Gorge National Scenic Area
  NOTES Possible USFS day-use fee; Trail closes at night; dogs on leash on
    Confluence Trail; no shade, avoid on hot days; privy available
  GPS N45° 32.780' W122° 22.439'
ABOUT THE HIKE
  SEASON Year-round
  DIFFICULTY Moderate
  ROUND-TRIP 2.6 miles out and back
  HIGH POINT 30 feet
  ELEVATION GAIN 20 feet

GETTING THERE

From Portland take Interstate 84 to exit 18 for Lewis and Clark State Park and Oxbow Nature Park. Follow signs a short distance to Sandy River Delta, just north of the freeway. The large parking area is often full, but be patient; people come and go, and you may not have to wait long for a spot to open up. Parking may be easier if the proposed entry fee goes into effect.

ON THE TRAIL

It seems like everyone on the trails at Sandy Delta has a dog; they're allowed off-leash everywhere but on or within 100 feet of the Confluence Trail, a rule that seems to be rarely enforced. Few visitors trek all the way to the end of the Confluence Trail, where an elegant bird blind, designed by esteemed sculptor and architect Maya Lin, is perched above the confluence of the Sandy and Columbia rivers.

Look for the start of the Confluence Trail at the far end of the parking area, toward the right. Many trails, both official and unofficial, crisscross the area; the Confluence Trail is the only 6-foot-wide gravel trail, which helps with wayfinding.

The trail traverses a wide, open meadow, crossing the Meadow Trail at 0.7 mile and the Meadow Road 0.9 farther before crossing the Old Channel Trail and going under a powerline 0.25 mile farther. Here the trail nears an old channel of the river and enters a riparian area under restoration, with stately cottonwoods and tall native shrubs providing shade. Just past the final trail junction (with the Boundary Trail) at 1.3 miles you'll reach the end of the curving boardwalk leading up and into the remarkable bird blind at hike's end.

Should your children not spy any birds from the blind, there's an understated lesson to be learned from the words etched there. Each slat names an animal encountered by the Lewis and Clark Expedition on its trip across the continent from St. Louis from 1804 through 1806. Each animal is identified by the name

A bird blind at the end of the Confluence Trail conceals visitors while teaching them about history and conservation.

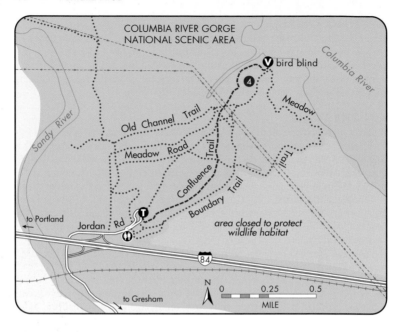

by which it was known to Lewis and Clark, the common and scientific name by which it is known today, the date the expedition first encountered the species, and the bird's current conservation status, whether threatened or endangered or in one case extinct.

Happily, since the blind was completed in 2008, several species' conservation status has improved. The words highlight how our understanding of nature changes over time and how fragile some wildlife populations are today. Protecting wildlife habitat is the reason for all the restoration activities along this hike. (For more information about the bird blind and the ambitious public art project it is part of, visit www.confluenceproject.org.)

Return as you came for a 2.6-mile walk or, using the map above, pick another route back to extend your hike and see more of the delta, which is being restored to enhance wildlife habitat.

Opposite: Multnomah Falls, Oregon's tallest cascade and Hike 7, drops in splendor into the Columbia River Gorge.

COLUMBIA RIVER GORGE

Latourell Falls roars in the early summer from a viewing platform you reach quite early on the hike.

5 LATOURELL FALLS

BEFORE YOU GO

MAP Download from park website

CONTACT Guy W. Talbot State Park

NOTES To avoid crowds, weekdays are best; arrive early to park or use Columbia Gorge Express; trail is within area affected by 2017 Eagle Creek Fire; privy available

GPS N45° 32.328' W122° 13.054'

ABOUT THE HIKE

SEASON Year-round

DIFFICULTY Easy–moderate

ROUND-TRIP 1 to 2.2-mile loop

HIGH POINT 700 feet

ELEVATION GAIN 270 to 550 feet

GETTING THERE

From Portland, take Interstate 84 east for about 28 miles and take exit 28 (Bridal Veil). Drive a short distance to the Historic Columbia River Highway. Turn right and drive 2.8 miles to the parking area at the base of the falls.

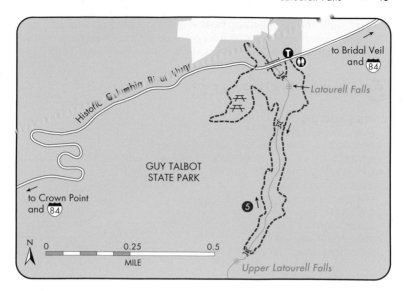

ON THE TRAIL

As magical as most waterfall-blessed Gorge trails are, this one seems even more like a path through a fairyland. The trail was not heavily impacted by the 2017 Eagle Creek Fire—unlike many of the pathways in this area—meaning the trail should still be bright with butterflies, bleeding hearts, and white trilliums on green hillsides. Little footbridges and a huge natural amphitheater make the Gorge at the falls' base particularly impressive. The trail is formed like a figure-eight, with trails on both sides of Latourell Creek and a footbridge in between the main and upper falls. For a shorter hike, follow just the lower loop; hike it clockwise to save the best for last.

From the parking lot and left of 249-foot Latourell Falls, an asphalt path leads up the hill a short distance to a viewpoint. From here, the trail turns to dirt, leading to a second overlook near the top of the falls. Drop down (passing under a tree overhanging the trail) to a footbridge not far above the falls. Stand on the bridge and close your eyes, not only to hear but also to feel the rumbling falls in your feet. If your party is game, backtrack a few steps to a trail junction, turn right, and follow the trail up along the east side of the creek about 0.5 mile to the footbridge at the base of Upper Latourell Falls, then recross the creek to continue down the west side of the creek to meet the lower trail just west of the lower falls footbridge.

From this middle bridge the trail drops down to the highway at a picnic area 0.2 mile west of the parking area. Rather than return on the road, cross it, drop down some steps and a couple of switchbacks, then bear right, following an asphalt path under the highway and over a footbridge at the base of the falls.

Linger a while in this magnificent basalt amphitheater before continuing up to the parking area. Consider a stop at Vista House, 2.3 miles west on the historic highway, before heading home (more details in description for Hike 6).

6 BRIDAL VEIL FALLS

BEFORE YOU GO
   MAP Use map below
   CONTACT Bridal Veil Falls State Scenic Viewpoint
   NOTES Trail is within area affected by 2017 Eagle Creek Fire; privy available
   GPS N33° 12.279' W122° 10.983'
ABOUT THE HIKE
   SEASON Year-round
   DIFFICULTY Easy
   ROUND-TRIP 0.7 mile
   HIGH POINT 200 feet
   ELEVATION GAIN 150 feet

GETTING THERE
From Portland drive east on Interstate 84 and take exit 28 (Bridal Veil). Drive a short distance and turn right onto the Historic Columbia River Highway (US Highway 30). Follow it about 1 mile and turn right into the parking area for Bridal Veil State Scenic Viewpoint.

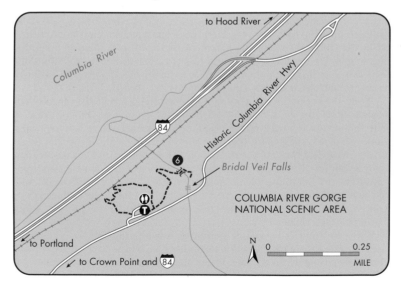

WILDFIRE IN THE GORGE

In 2017 a devastating wildfire swept through the Columbia River Gorge, turning lush green forest into steep hillsides of blackened snags. It was started by a teenager playing with fireworks along Eagle Creek Trail, one of the Gorge's most beloved trails; that trail is expected to be closed until at least 2019. Several other trails in this book were also closed because of this fire's effects but are expected to reopen sooner.

Fire is a natural part of the forest lifecycle, and this forest—like others you'll see from trails in this book—will recover. But wildfire also threatens lives and damages property (historic Multnomah Falls Lodge was saved only by heroic work of firefighters). Climate change is expected to make fires—whether caused by humans or natural events such as lightning—more frequent and more intense. Do your part to prevent wildfires by being extremely careful with fire yourself. Don't use fireworks in the forest or anywhere they are prohibited. Observe seasonal restrictions on campfires. Never leave a campfire unattended, and make sure your campfire is completely out before leaving it.

ON THE TRAIL

Bridal Veil Falls is less than 100 yards from the freeway, but because it's tucked around a corner, you can't see it as you pass in a car. For hikers, the roar of the freeway is drowned out by the roar of the 130-foot, two-tier falls, sheeting over cliffs like a fine white veil. This short hike wasn't heavily impacted by the 2017 Eagle Creek Fire and makes a good choice for very young children or as an add-on to fill out a day in the Columbia River Gorge. Lengthen it a bit with a walk on the park's paved interpretive trail.

To reach the falls, follow the paved trail northeast out of the parking lot, and at the Y, bear right. The pavement soon gives way to gravel and starts switchbacking down the hill, crossing a short bridge in the process. Look for the mill pond and bits of a wooden log flume—remnants of the lumber mill that functioned here from the 1880s to 1937. At Bridal Veil Creek cross the gently arching wooden footbridge and follow steps back uphill a short distance to a viewing platform in front of the falls. Return as you came.

Back at the Y, a left turn leads onto a mostly flat, 0.5-mile paved interpretive trail along the bluffs overlooking the Gorge. It circles a large field of camas, a tall, blue wildflower that blooms mid-April to early May. Look for wild lilies, irises, and lupine blooming here in spring as well. The path ends back at the parking area.

Extend your outing by driving 2.5 miles west on the Historic Columbia River Highway to reach the Vista House at Crown Point, with perhaps the most dazzling views in the Gorge. The octagonal, copper-domed Vista House opened in 1918. Browse the gift shop and the interpretive displays, telling of the Gorge's history and geology. It's open daily March through October. To return to Portland, wind west on the old highway another 4 miles to return to I-84 at exit 22.

7 MULTNOMAH FALLS

BEFORE YOU GO
MAP Download from lodge website
CONTACT Multnomah Falls Lodge
NOTES Upper trail was heavily impacted by 2017 Eagle Creek Fire; avoid crowds, weekdays are best; arrive early to park or use Columbia Gorge Express; privy available
GPS N45° 34.732' W122° 07.038'

ABOUT THE HIKE
SEASON Year-round
DIFFICULTY Moderate
ROUND-TRIP 2.4 miles out and back
HIGH POINT 900 feet
ELEVATION GAIN 700 feet

Multnomah Falls roars behind the historic Multnomah Falls Lodge.

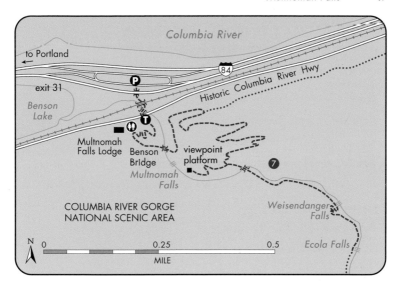

GETTING THERE

From Portland, take Interstate 84 east to exit 31 (Multnomah Falls) and park. Alternately, take exit 28 (or 35) and drive east (or west) on the Historic Columbia River Highway (US Highway 30), which passes right in front of the falls.

ON THE TRAIL

Most visitors to Oregon's most popular natural attraction don't wander any closer to 611-foot Multnomah Falls than the top of the stone steps above Multnomah Falls Lodge. Some take the asphalt path a short distance farther, to the Benson Bridge spanning Multnomah Creek below the falls. Fewer still follow that path to the overlook at the top of the falls—a 1.2-mile uphill trek. For children, the hike to the top provides a sense of accomplishment and even identification with a prominent landmark that most people know only through postcards. The trails around and above Multnomah Falls were heavily damaged by the 2017 Eagle Creek Fire. It may take until late 2018 or 2019 for all the pathways to reopen.

From the parking area off I-84, walk under the freeway, over Multnomah Creek, and across the historic highway to reach Multnomah Falls Lodge. The trailhead is really a tourist attraction with options for food and an interpretive station. Follow the crowd up the path to the right of the falls, cross Benson Bridge, and continue up the trail.

At 0.5 mile bear right at the trail junction and continue up, and up, and up as the trail switchbacks alongside the falls. At 1 mile a spur trail leads to an overlook platform, with a view not really of the falls but of the antlike people below. As long as your children aren't prone to unusually dare-devilish acts, it's quite safe. Return as you came, or continue up the (rockier, rougher) trail an extra 0.5 mile to beautiful Weisendanger and Ecola falls, for a 3.4-mile round-trip.

A WATERFALL VOCABULARY

The Columbia Gorge has more waterfalls per square mile than anywhere else in Oregon, but there are plenty elsewhere as well. They come in many shapes and sizes:

Block: A waterfall as wide, or nearly so, as it is tall.

Cascade: Water tumbling over a series of rocks rather than straight down.

Cataract: A very large waterfall.

Fan: A horsetail that spreads out as it descends.

Horsetail: When water falls in one or more streams down a cliff face.

Plunge: When the water free falls from the edge of a cliff.

Punchbowl: Where a narrow waterfall falls into a deep, wide pool.

8 HORSETAIL AND ONEONTA FALLS

BEFORE YOU GO
   MAP Download from scenic area website
   CONTACT Columbia River Gorge National Scenic Area
   NOTES Trail was heavily impacted by 2017 Eagle Creek Fire; to avoid crowds, weekdays are best; arrive early to park
   GPS N45° 35.426' W122° 04.114'
ABOUT THE HIKE
   SEASON Year-round
   DIFFICULTY Easy
   ROUND-TRIP 2.75-mile loop
   HIGH POINT 400 feet
   ELEVATION GAIN 500 feet

GETTING THERE
From Portland take Interstate 84 east to exit 35. Head west 1.5 miles on the Historic Columbia River Highway (US Highway 30). Park in the lot across from 176-foot-tall Horsetail Falls.

ON THE TRAIL
This trail starts at a narrow cataract and heads uphill, offering something you don't get on every hike: the chance to walk behind a waterfall. The trail also leads you above and below Oneonta Gorge. The trail was heavily damaged by the 2017 Eagle Creek Fire and may not reopen until 2019—check its status

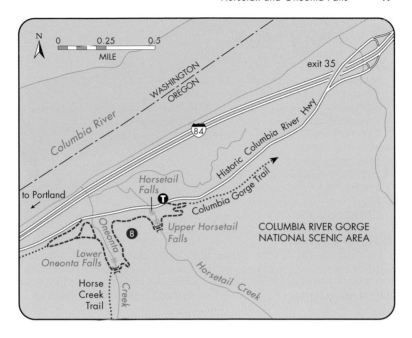

before visiting. Note that the loop hike ends with 0.5 mile along the road shoulder; take only children who will use appropriate caution here (or who are small enough for you to carry).

From the signed trailhead left of the falls, head uphill toward Upper Horsetail Falls (also called Ponytail Falls), passing through a garden of maidenhair and other ferns. At 0.25 mile turn west onto Columbia Gorge Trail and continue another 0.25 mile to the upper falls. (The hill drops away steeply here, but the trail is wide.) Here's where the trail leads behind the falls in a cavelike cleft in the basalt.

From the upper falls, the trail rolls along, offering views of the Columbia River and the Washington side of the Gorge. At about 0.8 mile the trail starts to drop and soon provides a view down into steep-walled Oneonta Gorge. Switchback down to a bridge crossing Oneonta Creek, listening for the roar of Lower Oneonta Falls below, then head back up briefly to a junction with Horse Creek Trail. Continue northwest then due west on Columbia Gorge Trail. Proceed another 0.75 mile or so to the last trail junction, making a sharp right to head down and east, following above the highway and dropping slowly to eventually meet it. Finish the hike with a 0.5-mile trek back up the old highway to your car. Caution: the road shoulder is narrow in places, but cars on the old highway tend to poke along slowly. Be sure to pause at the mouth of Oneonta Gorge for a different perspective on the chasm already seen from above.

9 ELOWAH FALLS

BEFORE YOU GO
  MAP Download from state parks website
  CONTACT John B. Yeon State Scenic Corridor
  NOTES Trail was heavily impacted by 2017 Eagle Creek Fire; to avoid crowds,
    weekdays are best; arrive early to park; privy available
  GPS N45 ° 36.752' W122 ° 00.326'
ABOUT THE HIKE
  SEASON Year-round
  DIFFICULTY Easy–moderate
  ROUND–TRIP 1.6 to 3 miles out and back
  HIGH POINT 333 feet
  ELEVATION GAIN 230 to 710 feet

GETTING THERE
From Portland take Interstate 84 east to exit 35 (Dodson). Turn left at the stop sign, then immediately turn right onto the frontage road paralleling the freeway. Drive east 2.1 miles and turn right into the trailhead parking lot (just before the road re-enters I-84) at signs for John B. Yeon State Scenic Corridor Trailhead.

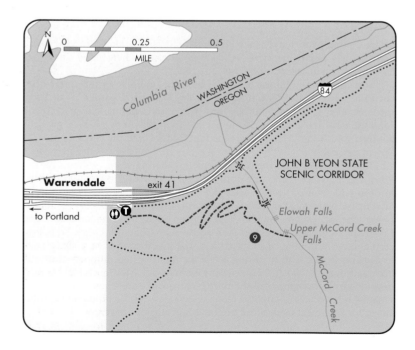

ON THE TRAIL

The hike is short, the waterfall immense, and crowd a bit smaller than at many of the Gorge's other iconic waterfalls. The primary goal of this trip is Elowah Falls, a 289-foot rope of a waterfall that plunges into an amphitheater of moss-covered basalt. Most of the hike is wide and kid-friendly. The trail was heavily damaged by the 2017 Eagle Creek Fire and may not reopen until 2019—check its status on the state park website before visiting.

The hike begins at John B. Yeon State Corridor trailhead, where parking is free and the handful of spots fill up quickly on weekends. The trail starts by following a former roadbed gradually uphill through second-growth forest with rich autumn colors. After just 0.4 mile, the trail reaches a junction. The uphill route climbs to Upper McCord Creek Falls—a fun option if you have extra energy after visiting Elowah. To see the main attraction, follow signs and eventually begin dropping down a series of fairly steep switchbacks. In winter this trail section can get

The long, thin rope of Elowah Falls is more impressive during the spring and winter after a solid rainstorm.

slippery and there's a bit of exposure; keep younger children close as you hike above fast-dropping McCord Creek.

At the bottom of the switchbacks, you'll begin to see Elowah: and at first, the waterfall can appear almost diagonal. As you hike closer, the amphitheater of stone rises overhead and the spray of the Gorge's second-tallest waterfall spreads mist across hiker's faces. A wooden footbridge crosses the creek near the waterfall's base amid gigantic mossy boulders.

The waterfall is most impressive to view in winter and to experience on a hot summer day. If you and the kids still have energy, head back to the trail junction to climb to Upper McCord Creek Falls. This section is steeper and adds an extra 1.4 miles to your day.

After a stretch in the forest, the trail breaks out with beautiful views of the Columbia River. It then tightropes (with guardrails) along the edge of a cliff. Look down at the right moment and you'll see Elowah Falls roaring below your feet. Upper McCord Creek Falls is just 65 feet tall and far less impressive than Elowah, but still beautiful. The trail continues a bit farther to a creekside glen before giving out. Hiking to trail's end makes for a moderate hike.

10 WAHCLELLA FALLS

BEFORE YOU GO
> **MAP** Download from scenic area website
> **CONTACT** Columbia River Gorge National Scenic Area
> **NOTES** Trail was heavily impacted by 2017 Eagle Creek Fire; USFS day-use fee at trailhead or Northwest Forest Pass; to avoid crowds, weekdays are best, arrive early to park; privy available
> **GPS** N45° 37.840' W121° 57.231'

ABOUT THE HIKE
> **SEASON** Year-round
> **DIFFICULTY** Easy–moderate
> **ROUND-TRIP** 2.2 miles out and back
> **HIGH POINT** 380 feet
> **ELEVATION GAIN** 380 feet

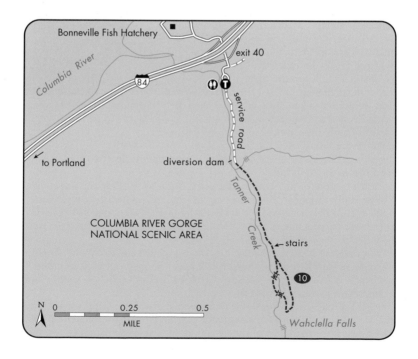

Two-tier Wahclella Falls roars in a deep canyon on the Oregon side of the Columbia River Gorge.

GETTING THERE

From Portland take Interstate 84 east to exit 40 (Bonneville). Turn right after the exit and follows signs to Wahclella Falls Trailhead.

ON THE TRAIL

Waterfalls small and large, a gaping creek canyon and boulder garden, and bridges of various sizes all contribute to the charm of this hike, which ends at two-tier Wahclella Falls. Start hiking on a service road 0.25 mile to a diversion dam, which directs water from Tanner Creek to a downstream fish hatchery. At this point the trail narrows to a footpath along the canyon wall. A wooden footbridge hugs the canyon wall at a waterfall-washed cliff face; notice the basalt columns rising next to the trail. From here the trail starts a steady climb to a wooden staircase at about 0.5 mile. Soon you'll reach a junction. The trail to the right leads to a bridge; cross it and follow the trail upstream across an old rockslide to reach the boisterous Wahclella Falls.

The trail was heavily damaged by the 2017 Eagle Creek Fire and may not reopen until 2019—check its status before visiting. The falls is a two-tier cataract, dropping perhaps 20 feet to a ledge then bursting through a rock niche to drop another 60 feet or so into a wide pool. Return as you came, or loop back on the upper side of the trail.

11 MEMALOOSE HILLS

BEFORE YOU GO
  MAP No official map available
  CONTACT Columbia River Gorge National Scenic Area
  NOTES Unofficial trailhead; no privy; easy-to-follow trail; beware of poison oak
  GPS N45° 41.606' W121° 21.046'
ABOUT THE HIKE
  SEASON Year-round, but best in spring
  DIFFICULTY Easy
  ROUND–TRIP 2.2 miles out and back
  HIGH POINT 815 feet
  ELEVATION GAIN 630 feet

GETTING THERE

From Portland, drive east on Interstate 84 past the town of Hood River to exit 69 (US Highway 30). Follow the Historic Columbia River Highway (Hwy. 30) southeast through the town of Mosier. About 3 miles past Mosier, stop at the

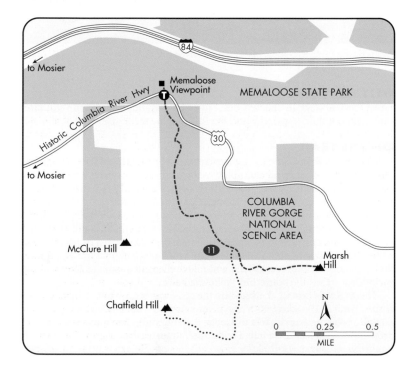

Balsamroot blooms in spring in the Memaloose Hills.

small parking area at Memaloose Viewpoint. The unsigned trailhead begins just across the road from the viewpoint.

ON THE TRAIL

Memaloose Hills started out as a well-guarded secret; but through social media and word-of-mouth, it has become well known in the hiking community of the Columbia River Gorge for its beautiful blooms of spring wildflowers.

This hike, although easy and great anytime, is best in April and early May, when blooms of yellow balsamroot and purple lupine blanket entire hillsides and highlight the edges of the trail. A major upside at Memaloose is that it's far less crowded than many of the other wildflower hot spots in the Gorge during spring. You'll need to be wary, however, of poison oak.

The hike is unsigned but easy to follow. From the Memaloose Viewpoint, simply cross over the road and follow the well-established trail that heads into oak savanna, which during peak blooms is speckled with wildflowers such as blue-eyed mary, gold star, and larkspur.

After 0.9 mile, you'll come to an unmarked junction at a swampy creek and have your choice of two Memaloose hills to visit. Stay straight (left) and you'll climb at a steady but not too steep pace toward an open hillside, where views of the Columbia River Gorge and Mount Hood open up. In another 0.3 mile, you'll reach the top of Marsh Hill, which is transformed into fields of gold and purple during peak blooms. Marsh Hill makes a good goal for kiddos.

However, if you and the kids still have energy, return to the junction and follow a trail to the right (south) for an optional hike addition. This steeper route navigates past some private land (so stay on the trail), climbing a steep-ish 0.5 mile to the top of Chatfield Hill. Even more impressive than Marsh Hill, there are wildflowers and views of Mounts Hood and Adams. Return the way you came.

12 ROWENA CREST

BEFORE YOU GO
MAP Download from Nature Conservancy website
CONTACT The Nature Conservancy in Portland
NOTES No privy; dogs prohibited
GPS N45° 40.963' W121° 17.992'

ABOUT THE HIKE
SEASON Year-round, best in spring
DIFFICULTY Easy
ROUND-TRIP 2.5 miles out and back
HIGH POINT 695 feet
ELEVATION GAIN Mostly level

GETTING THERE
From Portland, drive east on Interstate 84 past Hood River. Take exit 69 and drive through the small town of Mosier on the Historic Columbia River Highway (US Highway 30). After 6.6 miles, reach a large parking area at the Rowena

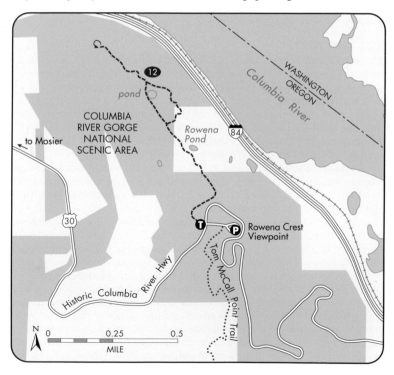

The hike out onto Rowena Plateau showcases beautiful views of the Columbia River.

Crest Viewpoint and park. Walk back west across the highway, following signs for Rowena Plateau Trail, for the featured hike.

ON THE TRAIL

Rowena Crest in the Tom McCall Nature Preserve is a wonderful place to visit for spring wildflowers, basalt cliffs, a fun drive to the trailhead and, of course, the great hiking. The only downside is that dogs are prohibited and there's almost no shade.

This preserve, named for Oregon's conservation-minded thirtieth governor and owned and managed by the Nature Conservancy, sits right on the edge of the transition zone between the lush west side and dry east side of the Columbia River Gorge. Rowena Crest gets 10 fewer inches of rain each year than the town of Hood River just 12 miles away. When it's raining in Portland, you may find sunny skies over the dry desert plains showcased on this jaunt.

Two hikes begin at the Rowena Crest Viewpoint. The easier one, highlighted here, follows the flat basalt tabletop of the Rowena Plateau Trail as it crests out above the Columbia River below. Created by lava flows, melt-water floods, and volcanic ash deposits, the plateau is a geological oddity that each spring hosts a breathtaking display of wildflowers. Best viewed from mid-April to early May—although wonderful any time of year—the hike is lighted by clusters of yellow balsamroot and purple lupine.

To get started, follow pointers just across the historic highway. The wide trail sets out across a plateau that offers almost nonstop panoramic views and, in spring, acres of wildflowers. Huge crevasses slice through the plateau, the result of ancient flooding. After a mile, the trail passes a small pond. Numerous side trails lead to a collection of viewpoints, making this easy hike as long or as short as you desire. The trail ends at a dramatic point on the cliff's edge overlooking the Columbia River. Head back the way you came.

For a tougher hike that's even more spectacular, follow pointers from the parking lot for the trail to the south to Tom McCall Point. This fairly challenging route is 3.2 miles round-trip with 1100 feet of climbing.

GREAT GETAWAY: HOOD RIVER

The tourist capital of the Columba River Gorge, Hood River is a small town packed with brew pubs, restaurants, outdoor retailers, and guide services. Summertime brings views of windsurfers skimming across the Columbia River with Mount Adams looming in the northern skyline. Hikers, bikers, and whitewater rafters all use Hood River as a basecamp during the year's hottest months. In winter, the town becomes a gathering place for skiers and snowboarders riding Mount Hood, just thirty minutes away. An active family could spend weeks here and not do everything. But here's a collection of the area's best assets.

Lodging. There is no shortage of hotels or bed and breakfasts in Hood River, as a quick web search will confirm.

Camping. The largest and best overall camping experience near Hood River is probably Memaloose State Park, located 17 miles east on Interstate 84. Although it's a bit close to I-84, the views of the river and cool breezes among maple, willow, and cottonwood trees are heavenly on hot summer days. There are sixty-five tent sites and forty-five full RV hookup sites.

Biking. A great family bike ride begins just outside downtown Hood River at the Mark O. Hatfield Trailhead. The route follows a section of the Historic Columbia River Highway that is blocked off to cars and features sweeping views of the Gorge, hillsides of wildflowers, and two historic tunnels. Ride 4.7 miles one-way to the Twin Tunnels Trailhead, or continue into the charming town of Mosier for refreshments.

Rafting. One of the best whitewater rafting trips on the West Coast sits just across the Columbia River on the Washington side of the Gorge. The White Salmon River's ice-blue water and nonstop Class III and IV rapids make this trip a thrill-ride popular with families. Multiple guide services offer full and half-day trips, starting around $50 per person.

Swimming. On hot days in the Gorge, a quick dip in the Columbia River hits the spot. In Hood River, there is easy river access at Hood River Waterfront Park, just south of downtown.

13 GIBBONS CREEK WILDLIFE ART TRAIL

BEFORE YOU GO
  MAP Download from refuge website
  CONTACT Steigerwald Lake National Wildlife Refuge
  NOTES Pets, biking, and jogging prohibited; privy at trailhead; northern section
    closed seasonally to protect wildlife
  GPS N45° 34.216' W122° 18.881'
ABOUT THE HIKE
  SEASON Year-round, with partial closure Oct.1 to April 30
  DIFFICULTY Easy
  ROUND-TRIP 3.2 miles out and back or 2.8-mile loop
  HIGH POINT 19 feet
  ELEVATION GAIN Almost entirely flat

GETTING THERE
From Portland, head north on Interstate 5 or I-205, crossing the Columbia River into Washington. Exit onto Washington Highway 14 (Washington's "Gorge Highway") and head east for 25 miles. Turn right at signs for Steigerwald Lake National Wildlife Refuge.

ON THE TRAIL
In June 2009 the Gibbons Creek Wildlife Art Trail opened, becoming one of just two art trails in the national wildlife refuge system. (The other is also in

Views of Mount Hood can be had on the hiking trails at Steigerwald Lake National Wildlife Refuge.

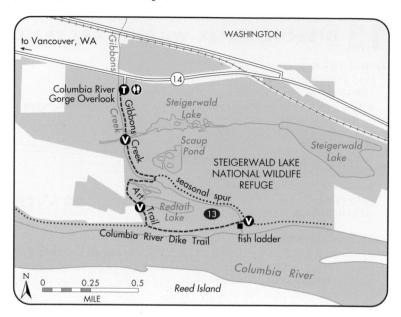

Washington, at Willapa National Wildlife Refuge.) The trail combines interpretive art—the bronze casting of a dragonfly, for example—with the natural experience of exploring this refuge along the Columbia River.

The trail is ideal for children, even small ones, because of its short distance, flat terrain, and bountiful wildlife. More than two hundred species of birds have been observed here, along with twenty species of mammals, fifteen species of reptiles and amphibians, and a wide variety of insects, fish, and plants.

The trail begins in a gravel parking lot and heads out along Gibbons Creek, winding through meadow, riparian forest, and oak savanna, all with views of Mount Hood on clear days.

At 0.6 mile, you'll reach a junction. The trail heading left (north) is called the seasonal spur. It allows for a 2.8-mile loop, but is closed October 1 to April 30 to protect wildlife during the winter nesting season. Instead of a gate, there's an actual door standing in the middle of the forest that either allows entry or closes passage to the spur.

When it's open, you'll return through this door to complete the loop. Either way, continue forward here on the art trail, open year-round, past marshy Redtail Lake. In another 0.5 mile, you'll reach the Columbia River; turn left to parallel the Columbia River Dike Trail. Hike another 0.5 mile to a junction with the seasonal spur and a nice view of the Columbia. If the spur is open, follow it along pretty Gibbons Creek for an additional 0.6 mile to complete the loop. If not, return the way you came.

14 BEACON ROCK

BEFORE YOU GO

   MAP Download from park website

   CONTACT Beacon Rock State Park

   NOTES Park day-use fee or Washington Discover Pass; privy available; trail often closes after windstorms; not recommended for children prone to climbing under safety rails; beware of poison oak

   GPS N45° 37.731' W122° 01.289'

ABOUT THE HIKE

   SEASON Year-round, but be wary of hiking in storms

   DIFFICULTY Moderate–challenging

   ROUND-TRIP 1.8 miles out and back

   HIGH POINT 841 feet

   ELEVATION GAIN 580 feet

GETTING THERE

From Portland, go north on Interstate 5 or I-205, across the Columbia River into Washington. Exit onto Washington Highway 14 (Washington's Gorge Highway)and head east for 34 miles. Beacon Rock Trailhead is at a large, well-signed parking lot on the right side of the highway.

The trail up Beacon Rock is composed almost entirely of steep switchbacks blasted into the side of the rock made safe for kids with rails.

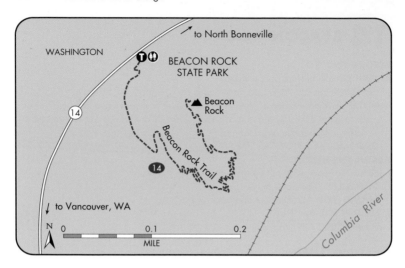

ON THE TRAIL

The trail up Beacon Rock, a volcanic plug rising above the Columbia River on the Washington side, is one of the Northwest's most unusual pathways. A mostly paved and railed trail zigzags and stair-steps up the hulking monolith, tight-roping past spectacular viewpoints to an 848-foot summit.

Perhaps the most amazing thing about this trail is that it was even built. Henry Biddle purchased the rock in 1915 for $1 and during the next three years blasted his way to the top, building handrails, bridges, and fifty-one switchbacks. Biddle's family donated the rock to Washington in 1935.

Today the trail is an iconic route in the Gorge and a great adventure for the youngest mountain climbers. Despite being constructed almost a century ago—and occasionally being closed by high winds and falling rocks—the trail is quite safe for older children willing to make a climb that goes up, up, up. Though steep and exposed, the entire route is hand-railed so it is relatively safe, providing your children aren't prone to climbing through fences and railings—that would not end well.

The hike starts at a large parking pullout on the side of Washington Highway 14. The trail heads through forest at the rock's base before beginning its ascent. Views of the Gorge begin almost immediately, taking in Angel's Rest across the Columbia and Cape Horn to the west. The only downside of this unique trail is that there's almost no shade and it can get very hot in summer. A cool breeze often helps.

The entire route is one switchback after another. Counting them makes a fun game for kids. The final stretch includes a passageway through the rock's forested top, an open set of stairs, before at last the summit. The top is less impressive than you'd imagine: a true panorama is blocked by trees. Even so, the vistas are excellent. A congratulatory sign at the top explains how ice age floods carved out the views now in sight.

The higher, upper section of the Arch Cape Loop at Catherine Creek features excellent views of Mount Hood.

15 CATHERINE CREEK

BEFORE YOU GO
   MAP Download from scenic area website
   CONTACT Columbia River Gorge National Scenic Area
   NOTES Privy available; dogs must be on leash
   GPS N45° 42.629' W121° 21.724'
ABOUT THE HIKE
   SEASON Year-round, but best from March to May
   DIFFICULTY Moderate
   LOOP 2.1-mile loop
   HIGH POINT 477 feet
   ELEVATION GAIN 480 feet

GETTING THERE
From Portland, drive east on Interstate 84 to Hood River. From I-84, take exit 64 and drive north across the Columbia River on the Hood River Bridge (a toll for passenger cars). After crossing the bridge, turn right onto Washington Highway 14 and drive east for 5.8 miles. Turn left at Rowland Lake onto County Road 1230 (Old Highway 8), which roughly follows the north side of the river. In 1.3 miles, find a large and well-marked parking area and trailhead on both sides of the road.

ON THE TRAIL
The Catherine Creek area is a geologically fascinating patch of oak savanna on the Washington side of the Columbia River Gorge that lights up with wildflowers in spring. Although the area is popular, there are multiple hiking options

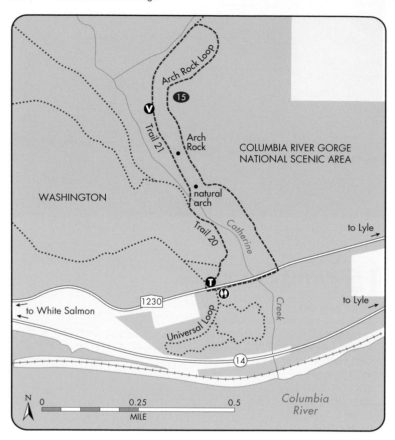

and lots of places to explore among the canyons and cliffs, giving this trek a feeling of greater adventure than other hikes in the Gorge.

The best overall option is known as the Arch Rock Loop, a trek that loops below and then atop a natural rock arch, a culturally significant landmark to Native Americans. This route features a bubbling creek, old homestead, grand views of Mount Hood, and more species of wildflowers than you can count during spring. The hike requires a bit of climbing and some route-finding, hence the "moderate" difficulty level despite the short distance. Many of the trails here are former dirt roads reverting to nature.

The hike begins by following the trail marked "020," which drops to the right along Catherine Creek. After about 0.4 mile of hiking upstream, the trail reaches a junction marked "021."

Follow Trail 21 across the creek on a wooden bridge to an enchanted forest of ponderosa pine in the shadow of cliffs of layered columnar basalt. Soon you'll pass an old homestead—marked only by an abandoned corral. Arch Rock rises above the corral and you can see it from a few viewpoints. In some areas, however, signs ask visitors to stay back from the base of the arch to prevent damage to sacred sites.

Beyond the corral and arch, the trail begins climbing up and to the right. Keep your eyes peeled for a trail junction. When you find it, stay right, climbing up toward the top of the arch rock cliffs. Though the trail is well established, it can still be a challenge to locate at times.

The trail atop the cliff is filled with wildflowers in spring, including camas lily, balsamroot, lupine, prairie stars, and many others. Views of the Columbia River and Mount Hood highlight this beautiful section of trail. You can also see your car at the trailhead. The trail slowly drops back downhill and actually ends on CR 1230 (it doesn't connect all the way back to the trailhead). Follow the highway a short distance back to the trailhead.

There are numerous other possible hiking routes from this trailhead, including a 1-mile paved pathway that drops down to the Columbia River.

16 COLUMBIA HILLS STATE PARK

BEFORE YOU GO

    MAP A map can be found at all three trailheads

    CONTACT Columbia Hills State Park

    NOTES Fee at trailhead or Washington Discover Pass required; privy available at all three trailheads; very little shade and can be extremely hot in summer

    GPS See directions below

ABOUT THE HIKE

    SEASON Year-round, but best in April and May

    DIFFICULTY Easy to moderately challenging

    ROUND-TRIP 0.2 to 4.1 miles

    HIGH POINT 1286 feet

    ELEVATION GAIN Flat to 650 feet

GETTING THERE

From Portland, follow Interstate 84 east to The Dalles. Take exit 87 and turn left onto US Highway 197 and cross the Columbia River. Drive 3.7 miles north and turn right (east) onto Washington Highway 14.

Petroglyphs: From the junction of US 197 and WA 14, drive east 1.6 miles on WA 14 and turn right at the main signs for the campground Columbia Hills State Park. Follow the entry road down past Horsethief Lake and follow signs for "Petroglyphs." Park in the large parking area besides the display. (When the parking gate is closed November to March, you'll have to hike an extra half mile from the gate). Coordinates: N45° 38.485' W121° 06.302'

Horsethief Butte: From the junction of US 197 and WA 14, drive east 2.8 miles to signs for Horsethief trailhead at a large parking area on the right side of the road. Coordinates: N45° 39.027' W121° 05.933'

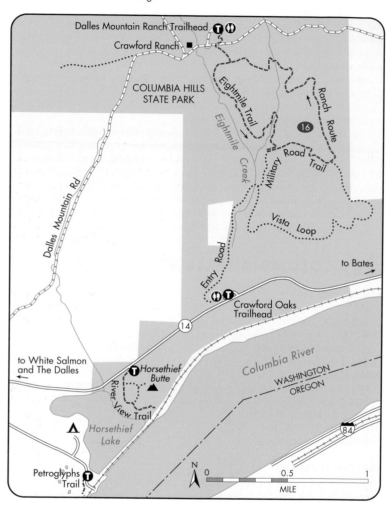

Dalles Mountain Ranch: From the junction of US 197 and WA 14, drive east 1 mile and turn left on Dalles Mountain Road at signs for Dalles Mountain Ranch. Follow this gravel road 3.6 miles to a collection of old ranch buildings. Just beyond the ranch, turn left at signs for "Dalles Mtn Ranch Trailhead" and follow into large parking area. Coordinates: N45° 40.808' W121° 05.307'

ON THE TRAIL

For centuries, this lovely park along the Columbia River was the site of a Native American village. The Lewis and Clark Expedition camped at the village and described its wooden houses in one of their journals. Today, the park is home to a reservoir, cliffs popular for rock climbing, and one of the best wildflower displays in the Pacific Northwest.

You can see everything—including a wonderful display of petroglyphs—on three hikes. Two are very easy; a third is more challenging but also one of the most rewarding in this book.

Petroglyphs Trail

Start a trip to this ancient area by viewing and paying respects to the ancient images created by the first people to inhabit the Columbia River Gorge. Originally located in Petroglyph Canyon two miles away, that sacred Native American site was flooded in 1959 by the inundation of John Day Reservoir, one of the seminal moments in Oregon history. Just before the floodwaters rose, the US Army Corps of Engineers cut out a handful of the numerous petroglyphs and relocated them first to Roosevelt, and now to this state park. A very short paved pathway takes in views of the petroglyphs and numerous signs tell you what you're looking at. Take a park tour to see more petroglyphs, offered Friday, Saturday, and Sunday, by calling (509) 439-9032.

Horsethief Butte Trail

One of the most popular rock climbing spots in the Columbia River Gorge is this ancient ring of basalt that rises above Celilo Lake on the Columbia River. A short, easy, and beautiful hike explores the edges of this ring on a 1.2-mile hike that's mostly flat and ends with a view of the river.

Petroglyphs can be viewed from a short paved walkway at Columbia Hills State Park in Washington.

Follow the River View Trail from the trailhead along the edges of the ring to the viewpoint. En route, you'll pass junctions to the Interior Trail, which climbs steeply into the rocks and is undertaken at your own risk.

Crawford Ranch

From mid-April to May—depending on conditions—yellow balsamroot and purple lupine cover entire hillsides on this enchanted route with stunning views of Mount Hood. Thirteen miles of often challenging trails surround the Crawford Ranch, the historic buildings passed on the way to the trailhead. Our featured route is a loop of 4.1 miles with 647 feet of climbing that's moderately challenging. There are multiple junctions, but trail posts keep you headed in the correct direction.

From the trailhead, you'll start by hiking downhill past views of the historic ranch and crossing over gravel Dalles Mountain Road. After 0.3 mile, you'll come to a junction. Turn right here to begin the loop (it's a more gradual climb back up on the return route) following a sign for "8 Mile Creek." You'll drop through meadows lit up by wildflowers in spring and along white oak forests along the creek. Keep your eyes peeled after crossing a small creek for a junction, at mile 1.6, of "Military Road Trail."

If you miss the junction, it's a steep drop all the way down to WA 14. Instead, turn a sharp left on this wide former road and follow it past stunning views of Mount Hood to mile 2.2 and a junction with "Ranch Route." Turn left and begin the gradual climb back toward the ranch and your car, visible in the distance. The final stretch is a challenging uphill trek, but like the rest of the route, it's so scenic you almost don't mind.

Opposite: A rock-lined path leads from Timberline Lodge to the Timberline Trail, Hike 23.

MOUNT HOOD

17 CASCADE STREAMWATCH AND WILDWOOD WETLAND TRAIL

BEFORE YOU GO
   MAP Download from BLM website
   CONTACT Bureau of Land Management, Northwest Oregon District
   NOTES BLM day-use pass; dogs must be on leash; privy available
   GPS N45° 21.019' W121° 59.800'
ABOUT THE HIKE
   SEASON Mid-March through Thanksgiving weekend
   DIFFICULTY Easy
   ROUND-TRIP 1.75-mile loop
   HIGH POINT 1230 feet
   ELEVATION GAIN 80 feet

GETTING THERE

From Sandy (about 28 miles east of Portland via Interstate 84 and US Highway 26), continue east on US 26 for about 16 miles. Just past milepost 39, turn right at the sign to Wildwood Recreation Site. Continue 0.5 mile to the trailhead parking area, on the left.

ON THE TRAIL

This hike takes in two interpretive trails at Wildwood Recreation Site, a forest park arrayed along the Salmon River. Wildwood Wetland Trail and Boardwalk takes you across the river and deep into a lush wetland, and Cascade Streamwatch Trail gives you a close-up of baby salmon inside a natural mountain stream. This is a managed experience—it's almost entirely on asphalt or wooden boardwalk— but the interpretive exhibits are exceptional, incorporating art and science. The

A wide bridge leads over the Salmon River to the Wildwood Wetlands Trail.

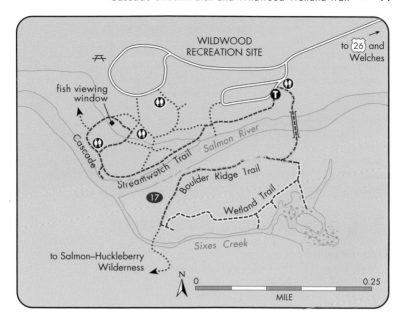

signage is aimed more at adults; let the kids experience the place with their own senses. You could walk just one of these two loop trails, but they're easy: might as well do both. For a wilder experience in this same environment, consider Old Salmon River Trail (see Hike 18), just 10 minutes away.

To begin with the 1-mile Wetland Trail loop, follow signs from the trailhead to an arching footbridge over the Salmon River and the beginning of a long wooden boardwalk with fingers that take you right into the marsh. Each viewpoint has what looks like a large naturalist's notebook with watercolor illustrations and engaging notes about flora and fauna. At the end of the long, curving boardwalk, turn right and follow Boulder Ridge Trail back to the footbridge and your starting point.

From here follow signs to Cascade Streamwatch Trail. It starts near the river, passing a variety of exhibits (including a large, touchable relief map of the surrounding forest). At about 0.25 mile look for signs to the underwater fish window, and follow them down a tunnel to a window cut into the side of a restored stream. Here you can watch juvenile salmon taking refuge in areas of slow water. Continue out the other end of the viewing tunnel, following more Cascade Streamwatch signs; they will lead you back along the river to your starting point.

The recreation site is gated in winter, but you can leave your car at the gate and walk in if you are so inclined.

WATER: KEEPING IT CLEAN

Tempting as that clear mountain stream may be, there is really no place in the wilderness where you can be sure the water is free from giardia. This protozoan, carried by human and animal feces, can cause severe diarrhea of a type that can be hard to diagnose (but easy to treat once diagnosed).

For short day hikes, drink only water out of water bottles filled at reliable sources—a home tap or a faucet at the trailhead. On longer outings, carry a portable water filter. Filters vary in cost and weight, but there are lightweight, reasonably priced models that can filter out giardia and other impurities and that kids can help use. Alternatives include boiling water vigorously for one minute (three minutes above an elevation of 6562 feet) or treating water with iodine or other chemicals from hiking stores.

18 OLD SALMON RIVER TRAIL

BEFORE YOU GO
    MAP Mount Hood National Forest, Zigzag Ranger District
    CONTACT Zigzag Ranger District
    NOTES USFS day-use fee; privy available
    GPS N45° 18.509' W121° 56.593'
ABOUT THE HIKE
    SEASON Most of the year
    DIFFICULTY Easy–moderate
    ROUND-TRIP 3 miles out and back
    HIGH POINT 1520 feet
    ELEVATION GAIN 280 feet

GETTING THERE

From Sandy (about 28 miles east of Portland via Interstate 84 and US Highway 26), continue east on US 26 for about 18 miles to the community of Zigzag, and turn right on Salmon River Road. Follow it south 2.7 miles to trailhead parking, on the right.

ON THE TRAIL

Though it threads a narrow corridor between the road and river and isn't exactly remote, Old Salmon River Trail has special charm for families with children. It's wide and virtually level and offers a lot of river views and occasional access. The huge

The shallow Salmon River rushes over mossy rocks.

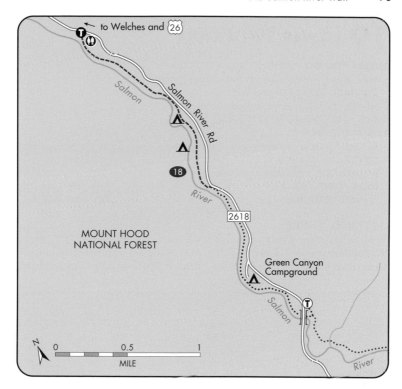

trees of the old-growth forest it traverses are a big part of the trail's appeal, as is the cold, rushing, boulder river (watch wading children carefully; the current is substantial). Official and unofficial spur trails lead directly from the road to several riverside camping sites, if you'd like a shortcut to haul in camping gear.

From the northernmost trailhead, the trail drops down to river level and leads upstream among tall western redcedars and hemlocks and a lush understory of ferns and oxalis. At about 0.5 mile a spur leads to a tiny sandy beach (the only one we saw) and, shortly, to the first of several campsites, this one at a boisterous, short drop in the river. Here the trail takes a sharp left turn to climb a set of stairs, then continues upstream on a narrow ledge above the river. Cross a footbridge and drop down to another riverside campsite. Just past a spur to another great campsite, cross a shallow creek by hopping from rock to rock (1.2 miles). The trail returns to the road at 1.5 miles. Return as you came.

To extend your walk, continue on the shoulder of the forest road for 0.1 mile until the trail resumes on the right. It continues between road and river for 1 mile, passing the Green Canyon Campground, then crosses the road just before the road crosses the river. From here the trail steepens and leads deep into Salmon-Huckleberry Wilderness.

19 LOWER TWIN LAKE

BEFORE YOU GO
  MAP Mount Hood National Forest, Zigzag Ranger District
  CONTACT Zigzag Ranger District
  NOTES USFS day-use fee; privy available
  GPS N45° 13.748' W121° 41.947'
ABOUT THE HIKE
  SEASON June–September
  DIFFICULTY Moderate
  ROUND-TRIP 4.2 miles out and back
  HIGH POINT 4400 feet
  ELEVATION GAIN 660 feet

GETTING THERE

From Government Camp (about 60 miles east of Portland on US Highway 26), continue east on US 26 for 3 miles. At the junction with State Highway 35, continue on US 26 south for 4.5 miles. Turn left into large Frog Lake Trailhead.

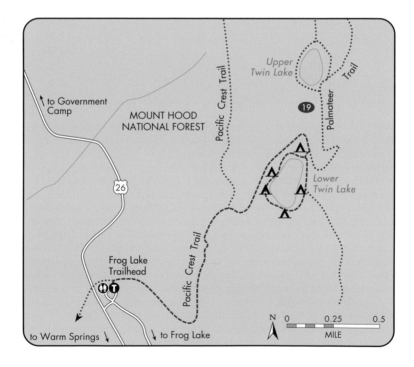

Lower Twin Lake is a great destination for a parent-child campout.

ON THE TRAIL

Lower Twin Lake is a good-sized lake encircled with a 0.8-mile trail. The distance, moderate ascent, accessible lake, and wealth of campsites make it just about perfect as a backpacking destination with young kids. No surprise that it tends to be crowded on summer weekends. So aim for a weekday, or go early in the season (when the rhododendrons are in bloom) or in early fall (bring warm sleeping bags). Or just make it a day hike.

From the trailhead, you go just a few steps before turning right to join the Pacific Crest Trail. The trail ascends steadily but not steeply to a switchback at 0.6 mile and continues up to a trail junction at 1.4 miles. Go right to leave the PCT and pick up Twin Lakes Trail. The trail tops out in another 0.1 mile and begins a descent. At the next junction, at 2 miles, go right to drop down to Lower Twin Lake. Follow the lakeside trail to find a campsite. Near the access trail the lakeshore is muddy; go to the far side of the lake to wade in on a gravelly beach. Return as you came.

If you're camping and have a layover day, consider a day hike to Upper Twin Lake, about 0.75 mile north. If you're really ambitious, continue all the way to Palmateer Viewpoint for an outstanding view of Mount Hood (for map and directions, search for Palmateer Trail on the Mount Hood National Forest website; see Resources).

20 VEDA LAKE

BEFORE YOU GO
   MAP Mount Hood National Forest, Zigzag Ranger District
   CONTACT Zigzag Ranger District
   NOTES Very rough access road; best suited to high-clearance vehicles; no privy
   GPS N45° 14.864' W121° 47.322'
ABOUT THE HIKE
   SEASON June–September
   DIFFICULTY Moderate
   ROUND-TRIP 2.4 miles out and back
   HIGH POINT 4800 feet
   ELEVATION GAIN 760 feet

GETTING THERE

From Government Camp (about 60 miles east of Portland on US 26), continue east on US 26. Pass the road to Timberline Lodge and, in 0.3 mile, turn right toward Still Creek Campground. At the end of the campground loop, continue straight on gravel E. Perry Vickers Road. In 0.4 mile, turn right on E. Chimney Rock Road. In 0.5 mile go straight through a four-way intersection and continue 3.6 miles on Sherar Burn Road (Forest Road 2613) to the trailhead. Those final 3.6 miles are on a very rough, rocky road; passenger cars must drive slowly.

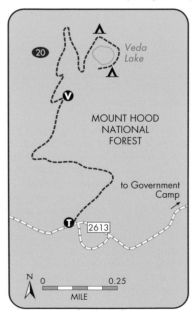

ON THE TRAIL

As you slowly drive up the rocky access road to the Veda Lake Trailhead, remember all the parked cars you saw at the Mirror Lake Trailhead just outside of Government Camp. No crowds here! Just a beautiful little lake nestled in a bowl below the mountain. There are several small campsites arrayed above the lake, making this a good choice for a backpack trip with kids. Be prepared to take it slow on the hike in (and out); it's not far, but the trail is steep in places. A June hike rewards you with blooming pink rhododendrons and white beargrass; in August the huckleberries will be getting ripe.

The trail starts out steep but moderates in about 0.2 mile and tops out at 0.5 mile. As you begin the descent, you'll be treated—in clear

weather—to a stunning view of Mount Hood and, far below, Veda Lake. That descent, too, is steep in places as the trail switchbacks down the hillside. Approaching the lake (which you'll glimpse through the trees), note the spur trail on the left leading to a fairly flat, roomy campsite. There's another campground spur just ahead, at 1.2 miles, near a couple of little creeks you step across. The trail continues 0.1 mile to a tiny rocky beach on the lake's edge. This seems to be the end of the trail, though you can continue a little farther on an informal trail. Return as you came.

Beargrass blooms trailside in June.

21 LITTLE ZIGZAG FALLS

BEFORE YOU GO
   MAP Mount Hood National Forest, Zigzag Ranger District
   CONTACT Zigzag Ranger District
   NOTES USFS day-use fee; privy available
   GPS N45° 18.843' W121° 47.763'
ABOUT THE HIKE
   SEASON April–November
   DIFFICULTY Easy
   ROUND-TRIP 0.8 mile out and back
   HIGH POINT 3250 feet
   ELEVATION GAIN 70 feet

GETTING THERE
From Sandy (about 28 miles east of Portland via Interstate 84 and US Highway 26), continue east on US 26 for about 24 miles. After passing milepost 48, turn left (north) on Kiwanis Camp Road (Forest Road 2639) and drive 2.3 miles to the trailhead parking area at the road's end.

ON THE TRAIL
This is a great hike for very young children on a visit to Mount Hood. It's just a few minutes' drive off US Highway 26, and other than a little scrambling up some roots and rocks, it's easy and short and ends at a lovely falls. Kids will enjoy wandering the easy path through the forest and playing by the pool at the base of the falls.

The trail follows alongside icy, clear, swift Little Zigzag Creek through a lush, narrow canyon. Listen closely to the sounds the creek makes as it tumbles

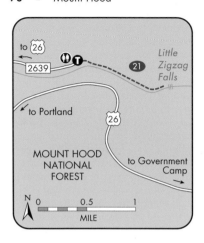

over rocks and logs and flows along sandy shallows; you can almost hear it converse with itself in different voices. Look for skunk cabbage in spring and blooming rhododendrons in early summer.

You'll reach the base of Little Zigzag Falls in a bit more than 0.3 mile. The falls tumbles about 75 feet in a series of short drops at the top then one long cascade down an angled, mossy, chiseled rock face. The trail continues, fairly rough and steep but short, up the left side of the falls to end at the top. Return as you came.

22 MIRROR LAKE

BEFORE YOU GO
   MAP Mount Hood National Forest, Zigzag Ranger District
   CONTACT Zigzag Ranger District
   NOTES USFS day-use fee
   GPS N45° 18.139' W121° 46.642' (as of 2018)
ABOUT THE HIKE
   SEASON May–October
   DIFFICULTY Moderate
   ROUND-TRIP 2.9-mile loop (or 4.4 miles; see On the Trail)
   HIGH POINT 4200 feet
   ELEVATION GAIN 649 feet

GETTING THERE
From Sandy (about 28 miles east of Portland via Interstate 84 and US Highway 26), continue east on US 26 for another 26 miles and look for the trailhead on the right, past milepost 52. Note: The US Forest Service plans to relocate the trailhead by the end of the 2018 hiking season (or sooner). The new trailhead will be 1 mile farther east, off US 26; at the sign to Mount Hood Skibowl, turn right, then immediately right again to reach the new trailhead parking area. When the new trailhead opens, the trail will no longer be accessible from the old trailhead.

ON THE TRAIL
One trip to Mirror Lake, and you'll understand why it's so popular. It is relatively close to Portland and just the right length for a moderately easy hike, and the reward is a classic view of Mount Hood towering above Mirror Lake. Even

YOU ARE WHAT YOU DRINK: WATER

Our bodies are made mostly of water—about 50 to 60 percent for most of us. The fitter you are, the more water in your body; adult athletes are close to 70 percent water. The more active you are, the more you sweat and the more water you need to drink to replace the water you're losing. Hiking in hot weather puts you at risk of heat exhaustion, but it's easy to prevent. You get it by not taking in as much liquid as you are eliminating, and you prevent it by drinking more water than you may think you need. Nearly everyone, no matter how young, should always carry his or her own water bottle. And everyone can do with a reminder to drink more.

The early symptoms of heat exhaustion are deceptively like those of the flu: muscle cramps, fatigue, weakness, sweating, sometimes nausea. Don't expect hot skin; people with heat exhaustion are more likely to have cool, clammy skin and a normal or slightly depressed temperature. If you suspect heat exhaustion in someone, get them to lie down in a cool, comfortable place and start sipping, then drinking, fluids—salty fluids are especially good, but anything will help. You should notice rapid improvement. If you do not, consult a medical professional.

on a weekday you probably won't be alone, so take particular care to have as little impact as possible by staying on the trail, keeping voices low at the lake, and scrupulously picking up after yourself.

Beginning at the traditional trailhead, hikers immediately cross rushing Camp Creek on a footbridge before beginning the ascent through a fir, cedar,

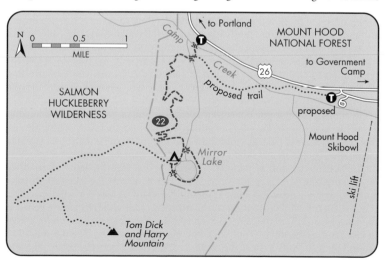

Photographers young and old appreciate the view of Mount Hood from Mirror Lake.

and pine forest and shortly crossing another footbridge across a side creek ravine. (Beginning at the new trailhead, the route will gradually ascend, cross Camp Creek, and rise some more before descending to connect up with the existing trail near the second footbridge at about 0.8 mile). About 0.3 mile farther the trail crosses a scree slope; listen for the high-pitched call of pikas—a small mammal that lives among the rocks. Back in the woods, the trail starts switch-backing up toward the lake. The far-off sound of eighteen-wheelers grinding up the highway accompanies hikers most of the way along the trail, until the trail drops into the lake basin.

In another 0.8 mile you'll meet the lake's gurgling outlet creek on the left and a trail junction: the start of a 0.5-mile loop trail around the lake. A sign indicates that campsites are to the right, and that's also the fastest route to the best lakeside picnic sites. Rough stairs lead down to the lake and up to campsites.

Toward the far end of the lake, the trail splits; take the left fork to circle around the lake. You'll cross a wooden boardwalk across the lake's boggy inlet and get postcard views of Mount Hood mirrored in the lake if weather permits. (Or, for a worthwhile extension of the hike for older children after a pause at the lake, bear right at the last junction to hike another 1.6 miles and 800 feet in elevation to the top of Tom Dick and Harry Mountain.) The 0.5-mile trail around the lake ends back at the outlet creek; cross it on a log footbridge and turn right to return to the trailhead.

23 ZIGZAG CANYON

BEFORE YOU GO
    MAP Mount Hood National Forest, Zigzag Ranger District
    CONTACT Zigzag Ranger District
    NOTES Privy available
    GPS N45° 19.833' W121° 42.545'
ABOUT THE HIKE
    SEASON July–October
    DIFFICULTY Moderate
    ROUND-TRIP 4.4 miles out and back
    HIGH POINT 6080 feet
    ELEVATION GAIN 500 feet

GETTING THERE

From Government Camp (about 55 miles east of Portland on US Highway 26), continue to the east end of the village and turn left at the sign to Timberline Lodge. Drive 6 miles to the large parking area at road's end.

ON THE TRAIL

A trip to grand Timberline Lodge, hand-built by artisans in the 1930s, is worthwhile any time of year. The round-the-mountain Timberline Trail (here part of the Pacific Crest Trail) passes right above the lodge, offering nonstop views and a taste of the alpine environment, bursting with wildflowers in

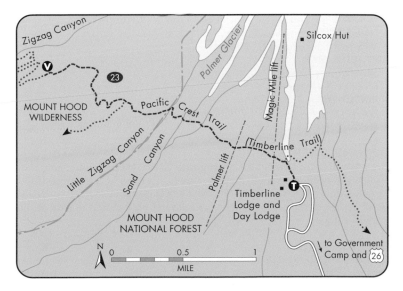

midsummer. We like walking the trail westward, ducking in and out of the tree line, to yawning Zigzag Canyon.

From the lodge, follow signs up the mountainside to join the Pacific Crest Trail; turn left to head west. The trail goes under a chairlift and into the high-elevation forest of gnarled fir trees. You'll pass through a succession of dazzling alpine meadows. At 1.1 mile after connecting with the main Timberline Trail, the route dives down into rocky Little Zigzag Canyon (a possible turnaround point), climbs back out, descends through forest and meadow, and passes a junction with Hidden Lake Trail at 1.5 miles, then at 2.2 miles reaches a grand view overlooking Zigzag Canyon and—on clear days—an array of peaks to the south. If you are backpacking, continue another mile to campsites at Paradise, a stunning high-mountain setting for overnighting. Return as you came.

Timberline's Magic Mile and Palmer chairlifts operate through Labor Day for visitors on foot as well as for skiers (fee charged). Consider riding up and hiking the 2 miles back down, possibly with a side trip to Silcox Hut, just east of the top of the Magic Mile lift. The old mountain chalet—first the terminus for the original Magic Mile chairlift, later a rustic hut for climbers—now offers lodging by reservation. Back at the bottom, be sure to wander through Timberline Lodge, perusing the historical exhibits on the first floor. Just below the main lodge is the day lodge with a cafeteria and other services.

24 UMBRELLA AND SAHALIE FALLS

BEFORE YOU GO
 MAP Download from USFS website
 CONTACT Mount Hood National Forest, Hood River Ranger District
 NOTES USFS parking fee; no privy
 GPS N45° 19.349' W121° 38.024'
ABOUT THE HIKE
 SEASON June–October
 DIFFICULTY Moderate
 ROUND-TRIP 4.1-mile loop
 HIGH POINT 5240 feet
 ELEVATION GAIN 800 feet

GETTING THERE

From Government Camp, take US Highway 26 east about 3 miles. Exit onto State Highway 35 and follow it about 7 miles. Turn left at the sign to Hood River Meadows (Forest Road 3545), about a mile east of the turnoff to Mount Hood Meadows Ski Area; continue 0.4 mile and park along the road at the signed trailhead.

ON THE TRAIL

Summer hikes don't get much better than this. Early in the season the trail is lined with pale-green huckleberry leaves and white beargrass plumes; later the

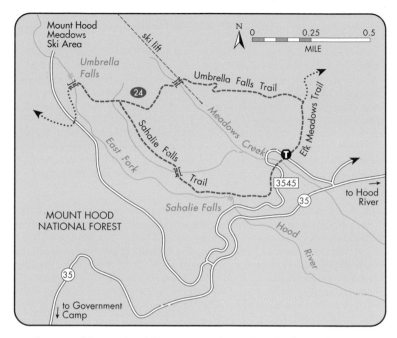

meadows are ablaze with wildflowers. Just about when the flower show starts to fade in late August and early September, the huckleberries ripen. Then there are the waterfalls and the views. The novelty of hiking across the ski runs at Mount Hood Meadows is fun for children who might ski or snowboard here in the winter. Although there are various ways to hike part or all of the trails around the ski area, this loop route makes a good, varied, moderate day hike for families.

For a clockwise loop, start hiking on the west side of the road, diving immediately into a cluster of huckleberries, which ripen in late August. The trail crosses a boggy area on a log, then leads to a creek that is crossed on rocks. Follow the creek up to a road, cross it, then continue up to a left-hand spur at 0.5 mile leading to Sahalie Falls (off a very steep, informal trail; take care exploring).

Back on the main trail, climb uphill steadily, following the East Fork Hood River's east

Young hikers poke around at the base of Umbrella Falls.

FERNS, FERNS EVERYWHERE

What's older than the trees in an old-growth forest? The fern family. As a family of plants, ferns are older than land animals and much older than the dinosaurs. They were thriving on earth 200 million years before the first flowering plants evolved. There may be more ferns per square foot in the forests of the Pacific Northwest than anywhere else on Earth—even the tropical rain forests. See how many different kinds you can identify on your next forest hike: sword ferns (the long leaves are shaped like the name), maidenhair (with black stems), deer ferns (slender and swordlike), licorice ferns (they often grow on tree trunks and die back in summer), and bracken fern, their triangle-shaped leaves abundant in more open spots with disturbed ground.

bank. At about 1 mile descend momentarily to cross a creek, then resume the climb, passing more little creeks and traversing some meadows. At 1.7 miles the trail reaches a T junction with Umbrella Falls Trail. Turn left and walk 0.3 mile to dramatic Umbrella Falls—impressive even in late summer—also on the East Fork Hood River. A bridge crosses the wide, sandy creek below the falls, which streams gently down a rounded rock face like rain down an umbrella. If you like, you could walk an extra 0.2 mile on an asphalt path to the top of the falls; if you continued a few more steps, you'd reach the parking area at Mount Hood Meadows Ski Area.

To continue the loop hike from Umbrella Falls, retrace your steps 0.3 mile to the junction and continue straight on Umbrella Falls Trail. About 0.2 mile from the junction the trail emerges from the forest and begins traversing a wide meadow (a ski run) with a great mountain view. The trail passes under a ski lift and continues in and out of forest and meadow for about a mile before reentering the forest. After about 0.2 mile in the woods, bear right at the three-way junction with Elk Meadows Trail. Continue another 0.4 mile back to the trailhead.

25 TAMANAWAS FALLS

BEFORE YOU GO
 MAP Download from USFS website
 CONTACT Mount Hood National Forest, Hood River Ranger District
 NOTES USFS day-use fee; privy available
 GPS N45° 23.832' W121° 34.307'
ABOUT THE HIKE
 SEASON May–October
 DIFFICULTY Moderate
 ROUND-TRIP 3.6 miles out and back
 HIGH POINT 3400 feet
 ELEVATION GAIN 630 feet

Cold Spring Creek plunges into a pool at Tamanawas Falls.

GETTING THERE

From Government Camp (about 50 miles east of Portland on US Highway 26), continue east on US 26 for 3 miles and exit onto State Highway 35. Follow it about 14 miles to the Tamanawas Falls Trailhead on the left, just past Sherwood Campground. (From Hood River, the trailhead is about 25 miles south on Hwy. 35.)

ON THE TRAIL

It's nearly 2 miles to the falls, but the elevation gain isn't bad. The route hops from one footbridge to the next, helping keep interest. The first third of the

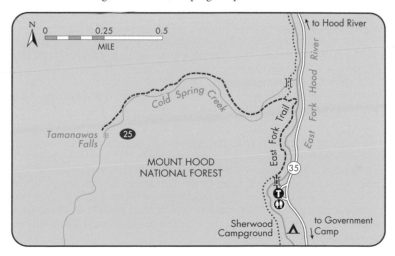

GREAT GETAWAY: GOVERNMENT CAMP

"Govy" has long been the hub of Mount Hood winter sports, and it has evolved into a great summer destination for families too. You can ski or snowboard until Labor Day at Timberline Ski Area, which stays busy with youth camps and teams from around the country and even abroad. Down the mountain, Mount Hood Skibowl is repurposed in summer as an adventure park, with zip lines, an alpine slide, disc golf, and much more. Dining options on the mountain range from fancy (Timberline) to taco take-out and a family-friendly brewpub. Contact Mount Hood National Forest (see Resources) for details on outdoor recreation options.

Lodging. Government Camp offers motel lodging in town and "chalet"-style rooms in the historic Timberline Lodge 6 miles up the mountain with bunk beds—perfect for a bunch of kids—along with more elegant, roomier guest rooms. Most visitors rent a condominium or cabin in or near town, available from various vacation rental agencies.

Camping. Dozens of Forest Service campgrounds are scattered around the mountain, several within minutes of Govy. Best bets are those alongside lakes, including quiet Frog Lake and larger Trillium Lake campgrounds: kids can fish for trout, swim, and paddle around (bring your own watercraft; no motors allowed). Timothy Lake, a little farther from town is a lot bigger; motorboats are allowed (10 mph limit), and shoreline campgrounds range from small and tent-only to big RV-friendly options. Reservations are available for these sites; smaller, more remote campsites are available on a first come, first served basis. See Resources.

Mountain biking. Mount Hood has become a popular mountain bike destination, with trails for every skill level. Right in town there's the Crosstown Trail, a good choice for beginners. Buses sport bike carriers: catch a bus up to Timberline and ride back down on the Timberline to Town Trail. This challenging single-track is doable for go-for-it kids with some experience. Down the mountain 17 miles, find the BLM's Sandy Ridge Trail System, with more than 15 miles of single-track. Trails here are rated for difficulty like ski runs; beginners might start with the easy, 0.75-mile Homestead Loop.

Swimming. Many of the hikes in this area offer cool dips in a lake, stream, or waterfall. Or drive to nearby Trillium or Timothy Lakes. Pick a hot day: these lake waters are cold!

route is just across the river from the highway; after that the trail begins its slow climb into the forest and toward the impressive falls.

From the trailhead parking area along the highway, walk south to a footbridge and cross the East Fork Hood River, then bear right on East Fork Trail. The trail roller-coasters alongside the highway to another junction at 0.5 mile; here you continue straight to join Tamanawas Falls Trail. The trail drops down into the cool canyon of Cold Spring Creek, crosses the creek on a planked log bridge, and heads up the boisterous creek's mossy south bank. Look at ground level for tiny bunchberry and twinflower blossoms or—later in the season—their inedible berries.

Continue upstream on the increasingly rocky trail, crossing a couple of scree slopes twice at about 1.5 miles. You'll then switchback up a steep field of boulders for about 0.3 mile to reach your reward: a grand view of the 100-foot tall, 40-foot wide waterfalls cascading down a depression worn into the middle of a natural columnar basalt amphitheater. Cliffs fan out like butterfly wings on either side of the stream of water. Return as you came.

26 LITTLE CRATER LAKE AND CRATER CREEK

BEFORE YOU GO
   MAP Mount Hood National Forest, Zigzag Ranger District
   CONTACT Zigzag Ranger District
   NOTES Stroller accessible; partially wheelchair accessible; privy available
   GPS N45° 08.867' W121° 44.863'
ABOUT THE HIKE
   SEASON May–October
   DIFFICULTY Easy
   ROUND-TRIP 1.4 miles out and back
   HIGH POINT 3300 feet
   ELEVATION GAIN 90 feet

GETTING THERE

From Government Camp (about 60 miles east of Portland on US Highway 26), continue east on US 26 for 3 miles. At the junction with State Highway 35, continue on US 26 south for 9 miles and turn right at the sign for Skyline Road and Timothy Lake. In 4.2 miles turn right at the sign to Little Crater Lake

A platform at the edge of Little Crater Lake invites hikers to pause for photos.

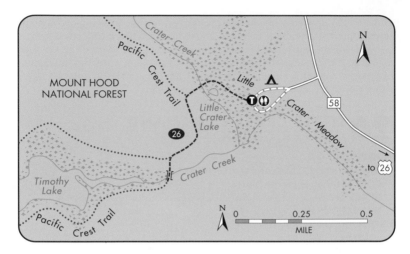

(Forest Road 58). In 2.3 miles turn left into Little Crater Campground. Trailhead parking is at the meadow's edge at the end of the campground loop.

ON THE TRAIL

The name is misleading: it's not in a crater, and it is tiny: no wider than the length of a basketball court. The color is what grabs you: as startlingly blue-green as Crater Lake is blue. An asphalt path leads to the lake, which has made it a favorite among the very youngest and oldest members of our family. But it's almost too short to be called a hike, so continue a bit farther to lovely Crater Creek.

From the trailhead, follow the paved path a scant 0.2 mile through the meadow, in and out of a grove of trees, and to the wooden viewing platform at the edge of Little Crater Lake. Signs explain how the lake formed: hundreds of years ago, water was forced up through a crack in a fault line, creating an artesian spring that washed away the sandstone under the meadow and created a small but deep (as much as 45 feet) lake.

Little Crater Lake isn't a swimming spot: to cool off, continue around the right side of the lake on the trail, walking on wooden planks laid to keep feet dry across the wet meadow brimming with tall stalks of hellebore blooms and other wildflowers in early summer. (The planks, and a narrow stile in a fence ahead, prohibit further access by wheelchair.) At 0.3 mile turn left at the trail junction with the Pacific Crest Trail. Continue to another junction at 0.6 mile; bear left onto a boardwalk and continue just 0.1 to a wooden bridge crossing shallow, 50-foot-wide Crater Creek. Its sandy bottom invites wading on hot days. Return as you came, or check a forest map to consider longer hike options, including a one-way hike with shuttle car to Oak Fork Campground (4.5 miles), the first of several campgrounds on the south shore of Timothy Lake.

Extend your outing with a visit to Clackamas Lake Historical Ranger Station. It's about 5 miles down Forest Road 42 from the turnoff to Little Crater

Lake. The 1930s ranger station alongside the Oak Grove Fork of the Clackamas River has been restored and is now period-furnished, from the potbelly stove to the photo of FDR over the desk. It now serves as a living museum and information center. Volunteer hosts are usually on hand in summer to share what they know about its history. It's a good spot for a picnic as well.

27 BAGBY HOT SPRINGS

BEFORE YOU GO
MAP Mount Hood National Forest, Clackamas River Ranger District
CONTACT Clackamas River Ranger District
NOTES Vendor fee for hot springs; privy available
GPS N44° 57.250' W122° 10.135'

ABOUT THE HIKE
SEASON Open year-round, but road often blocked by snow in winter. Spring and fall are most pleasant seasons.
DIFFICULTY Easy
ROUND-TRIP 3 miles out and back
HIGH POINT 2355
ELEVATION GAIN 200 feet

GETTING THERE
From Interstate 5 south of Portland, follow State Highways 212 and 224 to Estacada. Continue on Hwy. 224 south for 26 miles, past the Ripplebrook Guard Station. Continue straight onto Forest Road 46 for 4 miles and turn right on FR 63, following it 4 miles, before turning right onto FR 70. Continue on FR 70 for 6 miles to the large and well-established Bagby trailhead.

ON THE TRAIL
Once upon a time, Bagby Hot Springs was not a place you would consider taking children. Partying, nudity, and trash marred this grotto of cedar cabins and hot springs tubs until 2010, when the US Forest Service stepped in to clean up the area and install an on-site vendor to create a more family-friendly atmosphere. Nudity is no longer allowed in open areas.

Today, Bagby Hot Springs, while not perfect, has once again become one of the great hiking and hot springs trips in Oregon. The hot

Hot springs water rolls into one of the bathhouses at Bagby Hot Springs. Inside, there are group and individual tubs for soaking.

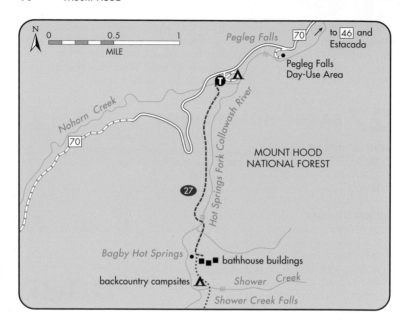

springs are best when the temperature is cooler in autumn and spring. A trip here in winter can be risky since a low-elevation snowstorm can block road access and the roads are not plowed. Call the ranger station in Estacada about conditions in advance. Weekend crowds can get large, so weekdays are best. To enjoy the hot springs, make sure to purchase a soaking pass before heading off on your hike, from the store on Hwy. 224 on the drive in where credit cards are accepted or at the trailhead for cash only.

The hike begins from a large and well-established trailhead and campground south of Estacada. The trail crosses a bridge and takes off through beautiful old-growth forest along the Hot Springs Fork of the Collawash River. The trail is wide and not too steep. Follow signs for the hot springs, and in 1.5 miles, you'll come across the large cedar bathhouses that make this area so special.

The collection of private rooms and large, community soaking tubs is popular, and if you come on a weekend, you may have to wait in line. The engineering of the soaking tubs is a model of simplicity. Hot spring water rolls into the bathhouse on a wooden chute, where uncorking a drain hole allows it to stream into the baths. A fountain of cold water is used to create the desired temperature.

A quarter mile downstream of the bathhouse is a collection of backcountry campsites and the 40-foot Shower Creek Falls. Camp here with the kids, or after your relaxing soak, return the way you came.

Opposite: *A stone stairway leads to the summit of Spencer Butte, Hike 31.*

WILLAMETTE VALLEY

28 BASKETT BUTTE

BEFORE YOU GO
   MAP Download from refuge website or pick up at trailhead
   CONTACT Willamette Valley National Wildlife Refuge Complex
   NOTES Privy at trailhead; horseback riding, pets, bikes, and jogging prohibited
   GPS N44° 57.716' W123° 15.444'
ABOUT THE HIKE
   SEASON Year-round
   DIFFICULTY Easy
   ROUND-TRIP 1.2-mile loop
   HIGH POINT 397 feet
   ELEVATION GAIN 200 feet

GETTING THERE
From Interstate 5 in Salem, follow State Highway 22 west through town, crossing a bridge over the Willamette and following signs for "ocean beaches." West of Salem, continue on Hwy. 22 west for 13 miles to exit 16, with signs for Monmouth and McMinnville. Here you'll turn left (north) onto US Highway 99W and follow it for 1.9 miles, then turn left on gravel Coville Road and follow it 1.5 miles to the trailhead parking lot on the right.

ON THE TRAIL
Baskett Slough National Wildlife Refuge is a rolling landscape of marshland and lakes west of Salem that many people mistake for farmland when they're heading toward the Oregon Coast on Highway 22. There's good reason for the confusion. Part of the mission of the Willamette Valley wildlife refuges is to lure migrating birds away from farmland to this more natural habitat. The refuges host more than two hundred species of birds throughout the seasons, including the dusky Canada goose, which spends winter at the refuges.

A long pathway leads through grassland and oak savanna at Baskett Slough National Wildlife Refuge.

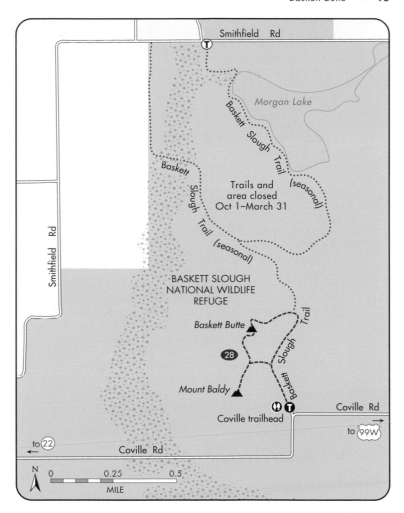

While the refuges are managed specifically for birds—and not people—there is one wonderful and easy hike worth taking at Baskett Slough. It includes a trek through oak forest to an open viewpoint with views into the Coast Range.

The hike begins from the Coville trailhead, following the trail through oak savanna for 0.2 mile to a trail junction. This is where you'll return to complete the loop. Turn right, and continue another 0.3 mile to another trail junction and turn left, heading up Baskett Butte. (The trail that continues straight, the Baskett Slough Trail, is only open April 1 to October 1, see Morgan Lake below for details). Heading up Baskett Butte, you'll be in a forestland of Oregon white

QUICK HIKES IN SALEM

Oregon's capital city doesn't have as many natural areas as its counterparts in Eugene, Portland, and Corvallis do, but there are some wonderful spots that mix history with nature and hiking opportunities.

Bush's Pasture Park. Historic buildings, forest, and multiple playgrounds make this park a favorite in Salem. Located just outside the city's downtown area, the park offers a peaceful place to hike among rose gardens, green fields, and creeks running through lush groves of trees.

Champoeg State Heritage Area. Oregon's pioneers voted to create the first provisional government—and take the first official step toward statehood—at this charming riverside spot in 1843. Now a state park, Champoeg offers an interpretative museum, hiking and biking trails, a campground, and many other fun reasons to visit. The park is located 24 miles north of Salem off Interstate 5.

Minto-Brown Island Park. Salem's largest city park features 7 miles of trail weaving through riparian forest and among ponds great for bird-watching. With kids, explore the blue and green loops beginning at the main trailhead (near the playground equipment).

Riverfront Park. Nestled between downtown Salem and the Willamette River, this park offers peace in the middle of the city. Paved pathways take families past playgrounds and statues and down to the river. On the north side, the Union Creek Railroad bridge crosses the river to Wallace Marine Park. On the south side, a pedestrian bridge completed in 2017 connects to Minto-Brown Island Park.

State Capitol State Park. Hike in the shadow of the Oregon Capitol, among cherry blossoms and around a wide green lawn, at this small state park in the heart of Salem. A sidewalk takes visitors among statues, flags, monuments, gardens, and giant trees. In summer, a splash pad offers a place for kids to cool down.

Willamette Mission State Park. Established in 1834 by Methodist missionaries, this state park along the Willamette River marks one of the earliest settlements in Oregon. History and a wonderful network of trails that wind among orchards, oxbow lakes, and river frontage make for good reasons to visit this park 11 miles north of Salem.

oak. The Fender's blue butterfly, an endangered species, is found here and the western meadowlark can often be heard singing. After 0.4 mile on the forested butte, cross onto an open grassy lump informally called Mount Baldy. A railed overlook on the butte's 397-foot summit offers views across the rolling Willamette Valley and into the Coast Range.

At the railed viewpoint, you'll find a plaque commemorating Rich Guadagno. The former refuge manager of Baskett Slough was a passenger on United Airlines Flight 93 on September 11, 2001. He died when the airplane crashed in rural Pennsylvania—those passengers are believed to have helped thwart an additional terrorist attack.

On the way down from the high point, take a gravel path that veers right, away from the trail you took on the way up, to complete the loop and return to the entry trail.

Morgan Lake option: If you're looking for a longer hike between April 1 and October 1, continue on a loop into the refuge's interior. From the seasonal boundary (posted), hike 0.4 mile to an overlook at an unmarked trail junction. Go right to drop down to Morgan Lake, an eerie body of water surrounded by cattails and often filled with waterfowl. Follow the trail to a parking area on Smithfield Road, turn left and pick up the return trail to bring you back to the overlook trail junction. From the Coville trailhead, the full route out and back from the trailhead to Morgan Lake is 4.6 miles.

29 RAIL TRAIL

BEFORE YOU GO
   MAP Download from refuge website
   CONTACT Willamette Valley National Wildlife Refuge Complex
   NOTES No privy; horseback riding, pets, bikes, and jogging prohibited
   GPS N44° 46.324' W123° 04.665'
ABOUT THE HIKE
   SEASON Year-round
   DIFFICULTY Easy
   ROUND-TRIP 1.5 miles out and back
   HIGH POINT 200 feet
   ELEVATION GAIN Mostly flat

GETTING THERE
From Salem, follow Interstate 5 south for 10 miles. Take exit 243 and follow Wintel Road south around a bend for a total of 2.5 miles. You'll pass a sign for Ankeny National Wildlife Refuge just before coming to well-marked trailhead for "Rail Trail" on the left.

ON THE TRAIL
A hike along Ankeny National Wildlife Refuge's Rail Trail feels a bit like entering a fairy tale. The boardwalk trail enters a forested swamp alive with bullfrogs and turtles, sparrows singing in the trees, and huge-winged hawks and herons soaring overhead. There's a sense of magic along the Rail Trail that's particularly effective with younger children. It helps that the trail is short, easy, and flat. After a short distance, the trail reaches an observation post that resembles the turret of a castle.

The hike begins from a simple gravel parking area in a quiet corner of the refuge. The trail first enters an open meadow surrounded by Oregon ash, cottonwood, and bigleaf maple before reaching a junction with the boardwalk—the official Rail Trail.

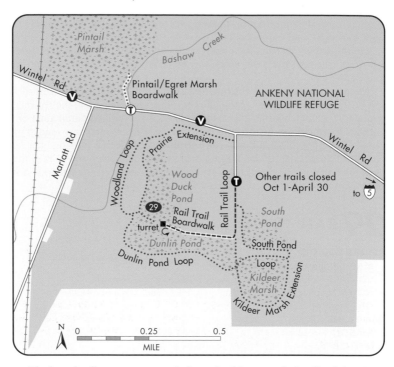

The boardwalk traverses a wooded marsh of Oregon ash that floods in winter and slowly dries out in summer. The entire trail is quite shady, which is nice for young children: shielding them from direct sun in summer and from cold rain in winter. In some ways, the boardwalk feels like a tunnel through the forest. Interpretive signs along the boardwalk help explain the sights, and the songs of meadowlarks, black-capped chickadees, and spotted towhee fill the trees.

An observation blind at mile 0.75, a wonderful stopping point, looks out onto Wood Duck Pond. Small slots in the circular blind allow you to watch and photograph larger birds such as great blue herons and hawks sweeping through the sky. This is the logical turnaround spot.

The boardwalk of the Rail Trail makes children feel as though they've entered a magic world.

From this point, the boardwalk travels another 0.25 mile to its end, where it joins the Prairie Extension of the trail. If this upland area is open (it's typically open between April 1 and October 1), you can hike a longer loop back to your car.

30 WOODPECKER LOOP

BEFORE YOU GO
  MAP Download map from refuge website
  CONTACT Willamette Valley National Wildlife Refuge Complex
  NOTES Privy at trailhead; horseback riding, pets, bikes and jogging prohibited; watch for poison oak
  GPS N44° 24.760' W123° 19.933'
ABOUT THE HIKE
  SEASON Year-round
  DIFFICULTY Easy
  ROUND-TRIP 1.2-mile loop
  HIGH POINT 420 feet
  ELEVATION GAIN 300 feet

GETTING THERE
From Corvallis, take US Highway 99W south 10 miles. Turn west at the sign to Finley Refuge and drive 1.3 miles. Turn south and drive another 2.3 miles (passing restrooms and an information kiosk at 0.8 mile). Park at the signed trailhead for Woodpecker Loop.

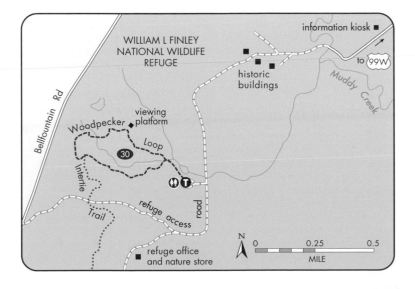

Some hikers may spot elk in the oak savanna habitat along Woodpecker Loop.
(Photo courtesy of Willamette Valley National Wildlife Refuge)

ON THE TRAIL

This loop trail winds through a variety of habitats typical of this transition zone between the Coast Range and the Willamette Valley. The largest of the refuges within the Willamette Valley system, William L. Finley National Wildlife Refuge offers a multitude of hiking options; but this is the only one open year-round.

Follow the trail past a signboard and a pond; look for frogs and newts. Just 0.1 mile from the trailhead, the trail splits to start the loop. Bear right to reach a huge oak encircled by a wooden viewing platform at 0.3 mile; it looks out over a dry, grassy hillside scattered with more native oaks. Interpretive signs offer in-

LOOKING AND LISTENING FOR WOODPECKERS

Woodpecker Loop boasts five different kinds of woodpeckers, but that's not unusual in the forests of Oregon. You might see them hopping up the trunk of a tree or flying between trees, or you might see the holes they've left where they bored into the wood looking for insects. Red-shafted northern flickers are the least flashy of the group; look for a pale spotted breast, a black striped back, and, on males, a red "mustache." If you see a white head on a woodpecker in Eastern Oregon's pine forests, it's—yes—a white-headed woodpecker! Most impressive is the pileated woodpecker, as big as a crow with a flaming red crest; it leaves rectangular cavities that are used as homes by many other creatures, from owls to bats.

formation about the area's ecology. From here, the nearly level trail winds mostly through a mixed forest of bigleaf maple, Douglas fir, and Oregon white oak, dipping also into Oregon ash swales and dense stands of second-growth Douglas fir.

Five different kinds of woodpeckers have been identified in these woods. Can you see or hear any? Also on this trail, make sure to tell the kids: watch out for poison oak.

31 SPENCER BUTTE

BEFORE YOU GO
   MAP Download Ridgeline Trail Map from City of Eugene website
   CONTACT City of Eugene
   NOTES Privy available; watch for poison oak
   GPS N43° 58.835' W123° 06.116'
ABOUT THE HIKE
   SEASON Year-round
   DIFFICULTY Moderate
   ROUND-TRIP 2.2 miles
   HIGH POINT 2050 feet
   ELEVATION GAIN 770 feet

GETTING THERE

From downtown Eugene, follow South Willamette Street south about 5 miles. Turn left at the sign to Spencer Butte Park, on the east side of the road. (If you reach the intersection with Fox Hollow Road, you've gone about 1 mile too far.)

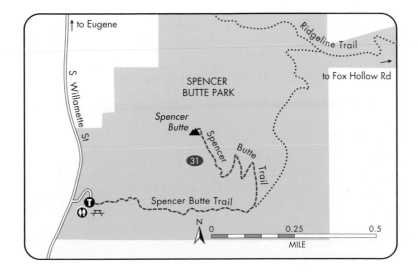

QUICK HIKES IN CORVALLIS

This college town in the Willamette Valley features plenty of spaces great for hiking with kids.

Avery Park. A rose garden, riverside trail, misplaced locomotive, and dinosaur bone playground make this 75-acre park a great stop for families. Follow a 1-mile trail through a collection of highlights, culminating with a stop at a full-sized locomotive you can climb aboard.

Bald Hill Natural Area. This network of trails on the outskirts of Corvallis includes a sweet 2.8-mile hike to benches atop Bald Hill with views of Cascade and Coast Range mountains all around.

Beazell Memorial Forest. A beautiful patch of temperate rainforest, located 15 miles northwest of Corvallis, offers a network of trails ranging from 2 to 5 miles.

Chip Ross Park. A family-friendly loop hike to views of Corvallis and the Cascade Mountains begins at a popular trailhead on the north edge of town. From a parking area, the looping trail swings 1.6 miles through forest to a hilltop meadow with views of the Willamette Valley and Cascades.

Peavy Arboretum. Gateway to the McDonald-Dunn Research Forest, owned by Oregon State University, the arboretum accesses multiple trail systems. More than eight different trails run through this life-sized petri dish where forestry experiments are conducted. The best route is the 4-mile Section 36 Loop, with old-growth forest and mountain views.

ON THE TRAIL

Forested Spencer Butte dominates Eugene's skyline, signaling the southern end of the Willamette Valley and the start of hilly southern Oregon. Like the hike up nearby Mount Pisgah (but shorter), it's a wonderful close-in summit hike for kids willing to do some trudging for a top-of-the-world view. Car vandalism can be a problem at the trailhead at less-busy times. Study the map, available from the City of Eugene, for more hiking options on and around the Ridgeline Trail.

From the top of the wide steps leading out of the Spencer Butte Park parking area, go straight rather than left (left leads to a shorter—0.8 mile—but much steeper summit route), following the wide path as it circles and ascends the butte. The trail can be muddy in the rainy season, though a boardwalk gets you across the worst spots. At 0.6 mile go straight where a spur trail on the right leads down to the Ridgeline Trail. Nearing the top of the forested part of the butte, the trail curves left and climbs a series of big stone steps, built in 2015 to make the route clear. Stick to the trail to avoid trampling the rare plant species that live up here. This final stretch is steep and tiring, but the view from the summit ridge (0.5 mile from the trail junction) makes it all worthwhile. Climb up the rocks to the flat concrete platform to reach the tiptop (but beware the poison oak growing in profusion on the east side of the summit rocks).

Return as you came. The tall steps and steep and gravelly path at the top can be challenging on the descent; take care.

32 MOUNT PISGAH WETLANDS LOOP

BEFORE YOU GO
   MAP Download from arboretum website
   CONTACT Mount Pisgah Arboretum
   NOTES Lane County day-use fee; dogs on leash; privy available
   GPS N44° 00.416' W122° 58.858'
ABOUT THE HIKE
   SEASON Year-round
   DIFFICULTY Easy
   LOOP 1.1-mile loop
   HIGH POINT 490 feet
   ELEVATION GAIN 25 feet

A bird blind made of woven sticks perches on the edge of a wetland at Mount Pisgah Arboretum.

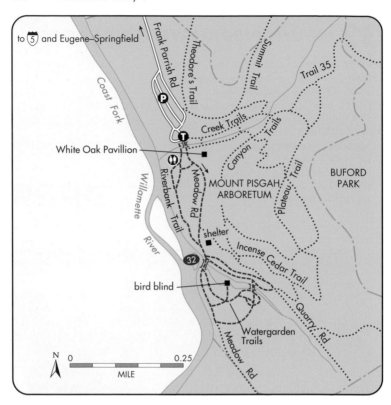

GETTING THERE

From Interstate 5 at Eugene–Springfield, take the 30th Avenue exit. Cross the freeway, turn left, then right (just past the service station), onto Franklin Boulevard East. In 0.4 mile, go left onto Seavey Loop Road. In 2.2 miles, after crossing a bridge over the Coast Fork Willamette River, bear right onto Frank Parrish Road and continue to the large parking area.

ON THE TRAIL

Buford Park and, within it, Mount Pisgah Arboretum offer 17 miles of hiking trails through forests of Douglas fir and oak savannahs. The most popular trek (among adults) is the 2.8-mile (or longer, depending on your route), 1050-foot-elevation-gain trail to the summit. You'll know when your kids are ready to tackle it (take your time and bring snacks.) Until then, this nearly flat trail is a great way to introduce young children to the arboretum; it leads to a large bird blind made of woven sticks. An out-and-back to the bird blind is just 1.1 miles; this loop route takes in a few more points of interest and is especially appealing during the spring wildflower bloom. (Note: None of the

QUICK HIKES IN EUGENE AND SPRINGFIELD

From historical orchards to wild wetlands, there are dozens of places to get outside with kids in and around Eugene–Springfield. Start with Hikes 34 (Spencer Butte) and 35 (Mount Pisgah Wetlands). Then check out the trails in these natural areas.

Alton Baker Park. Eugene's largest park, bordering the Willamette River in the middle of town, has miles of trails, some paved for bikes and some made of dirt or bark chip for walkers and runners. One of the running trails is 4-mile-long Pre's Trail, built in memory of Oregon long-distance runner Steve Prefontaine.

Dorris Ranch and Middle Fork Path. The first commercial filbert orchard in the country is now a large park with footpaths and a living history village. It is also the western trailhead for the Middle Fork Path, a 4-mile paved path (training wheels–friendly) that follows the north bank of the Middle Fork Willamette River and ends at Clearwater Park.

Hendricks Park. Eugene's oldest city park has huge Douglas fir trees more than 200 years old and thousands of understory rhododendrons that burst into bloom in April and May. A large network of short trails gives families lots of options for hikes.

Thurston Hills Natural Area. Acquisition of more than 300 acres of forestland at the eastern fringe of Springfield will preserve green views and wildlife habitat and soon offer a network of walking and mountain biking trails. Until then, explore the hillside meadows and woodlands on old roads.

West Eugene Wetlands. The vast conserved wetlands on Eugene's west side include Fern Ridge Bike Path; several short, developed footpaths; and raised dikes open to hikers.

Wild Iris Ridge. A natural area in Eugene's southeast hills is unfolding, with trails through grassy meadows blooming with native iris in April and May (and dense with poison oak in places; take care).

trails at the arboretum meet federal accessibility guidelines, but wheelchair users have successfully negotiated all the paths on this loop, as well as the Meadow Road and other flat trails.)

From the main parking area, head south over the footbridge and follow gravel Meadow Road trail past the White Oak Pavilion and restrooms. In 0.3 mile the road splits; bear right to continue on Meadow Road. Immediately pass Pond Lily Trail and take a left at the sign to Watergarden Trails. (If you were to continue on Meadow Road, you would quickly reach a popular swimming hole on the Coast Fork Willamette River). Follow this winding main path (passing spurs leading out to Meadow Road) to an intersection; go straight to reach a tunnel of woven branches and to the woven-branch bird blind at 0.5 mile.

Back at the intersection, go left. You will cross two low bridges on your way to a large, arched footbridge across a long pond. The pond dries down in summer but brims with water in winter and is lush with wetland vegetation year-round. To continue the loop, cross the footbridge, then turn left on Pond Lily Trail. It leads 0.1 mile back to the junction of Quarry and Meadow Roads. Start back on Meadow Road but quickly take a left on the footpath angling north toward the river. This trail follows the Coast Fork Willamette River past the Patricia Baker Wildflower Garden. Explore the spur trails leading into the garden, or stick with the main trail, which rejoins Meadow Road after crossing a footbridge. Cross one more footbridge to return to the parking area.

To extend your walk a little, from the junction of Quarry and Meadow Roads continue south on wide, gravel Meadow Road about 0.25 mile to enter the South Meadow. Immediately take the mowed path right toward the hand-built shelter on a short rise 0.1 mile ahead. It's just off a gravel path; follow that path to the right as it leads down into and out of a swale and to a stone-and-wood bench at a railed viewing area in another 0.1 mile. A railing keeps people out of brambles in summer and, in winter, high water. Return as you came for a 1.5-mile round-trip hike. Or wander some of the other trails branching off through the South Meadow before turning for home.

Opposite: *Hiking down a set of stairs at Silver Falls State Park, Hike 34.*
(Photo by Amy Rockwell)

CENTRAL CASCADES

33 BUTTE CREEK FALLS

BEFORE YOU GO
  MAP Download from state forest website or pick up at trailhead
  CONTACT Santiam State Forest
  NOTES Privy available; watch for drop-offs at lower falls viewpoint
  GPS N44° 55.257' W122° 30.671'
ABOUT THE HIKE
  SEASON Year-round
  DIFFICULTY Easy
  ROUND-TRIP 1-mile loop
  HIGH POINT 1940 feet
  ELEVATION GAIN 250 feet

GETTING THERE

From Silverton, take State Highway 213 north for 5 miles to Mt. Angel/Scotts Mills Road and turn right. Proceed into the hamlet of Scotts Mills and drive through town until you reach Crooked Finger Road, to turn right again. Continue 9.6 miles to the end of pavement then proceed another 2 miles over gravel. Turn left onto a wide road, County Road 400, traveling 2 miles and staying on the main route at all junctions. At one unmarked split in the road, stay left through an easy-to-spot orange gate, to Butte Creek Falls Trailhead on the left.

ON THE TRAIL

Lush forest and two unique waterfalls highlight this short, easy trail in the Cascade Foothills. An enjoyable trek year-round, Butte Creek is fun in winter,

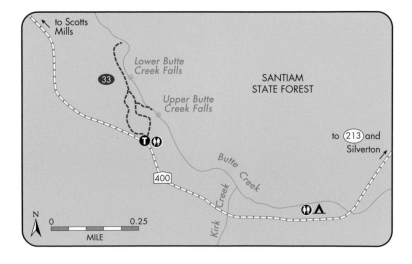

This stump on Butte Creek Falls Trail is shaped just like a chair.

when the waterfalls are roaring, and in summer, when the upper falls becomes a popular swimming hole. The only downside is the steep cliffs and narrow trail near the lower falls—if you have small, squirrelly children, make sure to hold their hand or pick them up. Do not attempt this hike if your children are prone to bolting.

From the trailhead go right to begin the loop trail. The pathway drops steeply through second-growth forest. After just 0.2 mile, the trail reaches a spur to

NEARBY FUN

Two other destinations in this area are worth a visit.

Camp Dakota. On the drive to Butte Creek Falls, you'll pass the excellent Camp Dakota (see Resources), open year-round. Camping options include yurt rentals, RV sites, tent sites, tepee rentals, cabin tents, and group camping sites. Activities available include zip lines, a high ropes challenge course and rock climbing wall, paintball, high adventure programs, team building programs, gold panning, treasure hunting, and an 18-hole disc golf course.

Scotts Mills County Park. This gem of a park is found in the town of Scotts Mills and is open May 1 to November 1. It offers a nice playground, lots of green space and another waterfall that makes a nice swimming hole in the summer. The park is located just after you turn right onto Crooked Finger Road.

Upper Butte Creek Falls, a wide 20-foot-high cascade. A muddy pathway leads into a cave behind the waterfall, which is probably the biggest highlight for kids and adults both on this hike. The behind-the-waterfall-cave is a smaller and more intimate version of the caverns found at Silver Falls State Park (Hike 34). In winter, you'll enjoy feeling the roar of 20-foot Upper Butte Creek Falls from the cave. In summer, it makes a good place to swim and cool down, out through the dripping falls.

To continue the hike, return to the main trail and follow it a short distance to another spur, this one to Lower Butte Creek Falls. This falls is much taller (70 feet) and more scenic, but requires following a trail that is dicey for small children. The trail is wide and perfectly fine for older kids who don't have issues staying on the trail; but for younger kids, any step off the main route could be dangerous.

The viewpoint for the lower falls travels out onto a steep point with cliffs dropping away on both sides; there are no guardrails. Enjoy the stunning view before returning to the main trail to complete the hike. On your way back, look for a tree stump that's been carved into a chair.

34 SILVER FALLS STATE PARK

BEFORE YOU GO

    MAP Download from state park website or pick up at entry kiosk

    CONTACT Silver Falls State Park

    NOTES Parking fee or state parks pass; no dogs on waterfall trails; can be icy in winter; privies available

    GPS N44° 52.766' W122° 39.252'

ABOUT THE HIKE

    SEASON Year-round

    DIFFICULTY Moderate

    ROUND-TRIP 2.6 to 3 miles (loops and out-and-back options)

    HIGH POINT 1490

    ELEVATION GAIN 380 to 440 feet

GETTING THERE

From Interstate 5 in Salem take exit 253, heading east on State Highway 22 to-ward Detroit Lake. After 5 miles, take exit 7, at signs for Silver Falls State Park, onto State Highway 214. Drive east 16.5 miles, following signs to Silver Falls. Once in the park, turn left into South Falls Day-Use Area. To reach trailheads for the other two hike options described here, continue east 1 or 2 more miles along Hwy 214.

ON THE TRAIL

One of Oregon's premier family parks, Silver Falls State Park has hiking trails, paved bicycle paths, a swimming area, a playground, a lodge to eat lunch in, and a great campground, all in a magnificent forested canyon. This popular park gets crowded on weekends. The park has ten major waterfalls, half of

A viewpoint of spectacular South Falls at Silver Falls State Park

which rise over 100 feet. Surprises wait around every corner, and hikes here never seem long; but there's no denying the long climb back from the canyon floor. The park is appealing in all seasons, even winter, when subfreezing temperatures nearly freeze the falls in place. But mist from the falls coats the trails with ice, too, so tour the frozen waterfalls with great care. Dogs are allowed only on the Rim Trail.

The configuration of trails offers numerous options, from short falls-viewing jaunts to longer loops. You can see all ten falls in an 8-mile loop starting at South Falls or the quieter North Falls area. Here are three kid-friendly, short loop options showcasing two, three, and five waterfalls, respectively.

South Falls to Maple Ridge Trail Loop

This loop closest to the park entry brings hikers past two waterfalls where you can hike behind curtains of falling water on a 2.6-mile route with 440 feet of climbing. To get to the start, from the South Falls parking lot follow the paved pathway past South Falls Lodge—where you can buy lunch or hot chocolate on the return trip—to signs for South Falls. From the viewpoint overlooking 177-foot South Falls, follow signs to the paved path leading to the base of the falls. Turn left at the junction to walk behind the falls, a truly magical experience.

For a shorter, 1-mile loop, follow the path down to the waterfall's base, crossing the footbridge to head back to the parking lot; otherwise, continue down the creek's west bank on the now unpaved trail. In 0.7 mile you'll see 93-foot Lower South Falls just before the trail plunges down 187 steps and

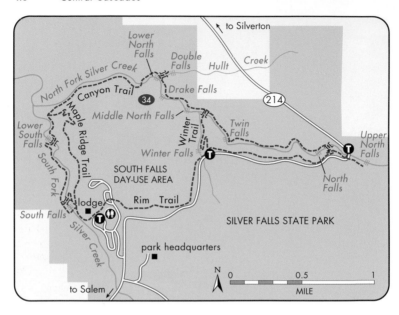

winds back behind the falls. Continue another 0.3 mile to a junction, and turn right to take the 1-mile Maple Ridge Trail up and out of the canyon and back to your car.

North Falls to Winter Falls Loop

This route beginning at North Falls trailhead runs a total of 3 miles with 380 feet of climbing. It features the very impressive North Falls and traverses a quieter section of the park. From the parking area above North Falls, cross the arching footbridge and bear left at signs pointing to North Falls. In a few minutes the trail reaches the top of North Falls. Continue along the railed, cliff-hugging trail, then down 78 steps and back behind the falls into a wide, deep, dry cave. The pounding of the falls on the rocks below reverberates in the cave, sounding like a jumbo jet at takeoff.

Walk with care; seeping water makes the trail slick in places. Continue downstream about 1 mile to Twin Falls, passing a huge, split boulder resting in the creek. Past Twin Falls, turn left across the north fork on a footbridge to Winter Trail and follow a side creek up to Winter Falls. At the top of the falls, the trail reaches a highway turnout; the trail resumes on the left, following close to the road 1 mile back to the arching footbridge at the hike's start. Return to your car, or walk under the footbridge (and road bridge) and take a side trail another 0.2 mile upstream to see Upper North Falls, then return as you came.

Five Falls Tour

This hike features five beautiful and lesser-visited waterfalls, but it's mainly worth hiking in spring, winter, and late autumn. That's because many of these waterfalls are fed by smaller tributary creeks that need rain to create their cascades. At 2.6 miles round-trip with 450 feet of climbing, the Five Falls Tour is the toughest hike of the three featured here. The good news is that with no dull moments, the miles fly by.

The hike starts at Winter Falls trailhead and passes a 134-foot waterfall of the same name. Winter Falls is mostly dry in summer and comes alive with the rains of winter. Just beyond the falls, you'll connect with the Trail of Ten Falls, also called Canyon Trail. Turn left, and you'll soon reach the very photogenic Middle North Falls (106 feet), the highlight of this hike since you can walk into a cave behind the falls.

Your route passes Drake Falls (30 feet) and Lower North Falls (30 feet), little more than steep drops in North Silver Creek, before arriving at the grand finale next, on the right side of the trail, at Double Falls. Fed by Hullt Creek, Double Falls is actually the tallest waterfall in the park, in two tiers dropping a total of 178 feet (beating out South Falls by 1 foot!). Turn around and hike back the way you came for another treat: you'll get to visit all these falls again in reverse.

35 OPAL CREEK

BEFORE YOU GO

MAP Willamette National Forest, Detroit Ranger District
CONTACT Detroit Ranger District or Opal Creek Ancient Forest Center
NOTES Parking fee or Northwest Forest Pass; privy available; very crowded on summer weekends
GPS N44° 51.592' W122° 15.869'

ABOUT THE HIKE

SEASON Year-round, except during low-elevation snowstorms
DIFFICULTY Moderate to challenging
ROUND-TRIP 6.6-mile loop
HIGH POINT 2200 feet
ELEVATION GAIN 280 feet

GETTING THERE

From Interstate 5 in Salem take exit 253, heading east on State Highway 22 toward Detroit Lake. Drive 23 miles to the small town of Mehama. At the second flashing yellow light, turn left onto Little North Fork Road. Follow this road for 21 miles of pavement and gravel as it becomes Forest Road 2209. Stay left at a junction with a sign for Three Pools Recreation Area, remaining on FR 2209, and park at a large trailhead and parking area at the road's end at a gate. Parking is at a premium on summer weekends; weekdays are best.

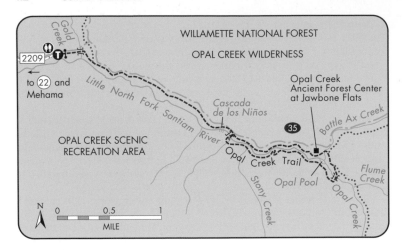

ON THE TRAIL

In 1981, the US Forest Service made plans to log the watershed of Opal Creek, one of the last primeval rainforests remaining in the Cascade Foothills. Clear-cut boundary markers were placed, and plans to cut 12.4 million board feet and build 7.3 miles of road moved forward. What happened next is the stuff of Oregon lore. Led by a charismatic miner-turned-environmentalist named George Atiyeh, an unlikely coalition of hikers, hippies, outlaws, celebrities, and lawyers managed to save the area's ancient forest during a high-profile fight that lasted almost two decades. In 1996, legislation that created the Opal Creek Wilderness and Scenic Area was signed into law.

The fruits of that effort can be enjoyed by visiting Opal Creek and Jawbone Flats, a former mining town. Today, Jawbone Flats is an environmental education center where you can take yoga-in-the-forest classes or rent one of the historic cabins (contact Opal Creek Ancient Forest Center; see Resources). This area's popularity has grown fast, especially in summer, so plan to visit midweek if possible. If you're backpacking—which isn't ideal but is possible—no campfires, only stoves, are allowed.

The hike is a bit long, but it's also mostly flat and full of enough interesting elements to keep most children interested. But for young ones, you might consider turning around early.

The hike begins on a gated road, but it's no ordinary road. Gigantic trees 700 years old rise overhead and spur trails lead to beautiful waterfalls and swimming holes. From the gate, the trail on old roadbed rolls gently through the forest, crossing high above Gold Creek on a 60-foot-tall bridge. At 2 miles, your route reaches the former Merton sawmill site, which operated for just two years a half century ago. Look for a spur trail on the right leading a short distance to a view of 30-foot Cascada de los Niños (Waterfall of the Children). Turning around here makes for a 4-mile hike.

A Gold Creek waterfall seen from the Opal Creek Trail

To continue, head another 0.2 mile to the start of a trail on your right leading to an old log bridge across the Little North Fork River. There's a little gravel river beach just downstream from the bridge—a good picnic spot and another possible turnaround.

Continuing onward, bear left after crossing the bridge to follow the river to dazzling Opal Pool (3.5 miles total from the gate). You'll hear it before you see it: a roar of water charging through a narrow rock chasm before landing in a deep, clear green pool. Now, cross another footbridge and follow signs to Jawbone Flats. Ruins of the area's mining days are everywhere; but today you'll see visitors, professors, and students studying the area's old-growth ecology. Atiyeh, godfather of the effort to protect this area, still has a cabin here and will sometimes greet people who come to Opal Creek.

Return via the road, when you are ready to head back. Another alternative for day hikers is simply an out-and-back hike from the gate to Jawbone Flats (6.2 miles total).

WHAT IS AN OLD-GROWTH FOREST?

It's as hard to define as it is to define an old person—everyone has a different opinion. It's not just about the age or size of the trees, scientists say. An old-growth forest has had time enough to develop into a diverse place with both living and dead wood that supports a wide variety of plants and animals. Typically such a forest in western Oregon is rare (most were cut over in the last century) and includes multiple layers of trees, many of them conifers 350 to 700 years old. Dead and fallen trees provide hiding places, nesting sites, and nutrients for wildlife. Large, fallen trees known as "nurse logs" harbor new plant life as they decompose; you may see huckleberries and vine maples and even young conifers growing out of them (see Hike 88).

36 HENLINE FALLS

BEFORE YOU GO

    MAP Opal Creek Wilderness, Detroit Ranger District, Willamette National Forest

    CONTACT Detroit Ranger District

    NOTES No privy; small parking area; can be closed by low-elevation winter
       storms

    GPS N44° 50.749' W122° 19.600'

ABOUT THE HIKE

    SEASON Year-round

    DIFFICULTY Easy

    ROUND-TRIP 2 miles out and back

    HIGH POINT 1763 feet

    ELEVATION GAIN 260 feet

GETTING THERE

From Interstate 5 in Salem take exit 253 and follow State Highway 22 east toward Detroit Lake. Drive 23 miles to the small town of Mehama. At the second flashing yellow light, turn left onto Little North Fork Road. Drive for 16.8
miles, as the road goes from pavement to gravel. At a junction, stay left to
remain on Forest Road 2209—avoiding FR 2207, which leads to Three Pools
Recreation Site. The Henline Falls Trailhead is on the left just 0.1 mile beyond
this intersection.

Henline Falls is a 126-foot roaring waterfall found in the Opal Creek Wilderness.

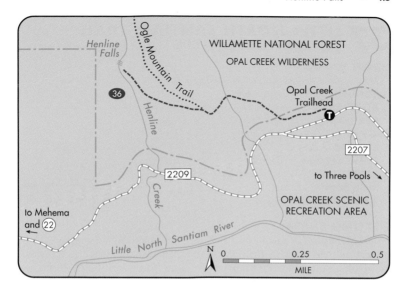

ON THE TRAIL

Less than an hour from Salem, and right in the heart of the Little North Santiam Canyon, Henline Falls is the definition of a quick, easy, and beautiful hike. The main highlight is the vertical curtain of 126-foot Henline Falls, which roars all season long but is best explored in spring or fall, when bright autumn colors liven up the hike.

From the small parking area, the trail begins on a mining road, originally built in the late 1800s, that's slowly being reclaimed by nature. Bigleaf maples highlight the opening stretch of trail, turning beautiful yellow and gold colors in fall. After a short distance, the trail enters the Opal Creek Wilderness, established in 1996 after a long and bitter political fight between environmental and logging interests.

The old road becomes a proper trail as you pass two trail junctions. The first is a wide trail that goes nowhere and the second is Ogle Mountain Trail, likewise not worth your time. Stay left at every junction and you'll soon come along the rushing water of Henline Creek as it drops down toward the Little North Santiam River. Soon thereafter, as the trail narrows, you'll arrive at impressive Henline Falls, a fanning cascade dropping into an emerald pool.

A large, flat, rocky ledge blasted out near the waterfall base makes a nice place to spend time in summer. The area was heavily impacted by the Silver King Mine, and if you look closely, you can still find the mineshaft burrowing down into the ground; the Forest Service has put bars across it to prevent entry. The whole family can enjoy the waterfall's spray before turning around and heading back the way you came.

37 LITTLE NORTH SANTIAM TRAIL TO ELKHORN FALLS

BEFORE YOU GO
  MAP Willamette National Forest, Detroit Ranger District
  CONTACT Detroit Ranger District
  NOTES Crowds heavy on summer weekends; no privy
  GPS N44° 49.270' W122° 21.321'
ABOUT THE HIKE
  SEASON Year-round
  DIFFICULTY Easy–moderate
  ROUND-TRIP 1.4 miles out and back
  HIGH POINT 1214 feet
  ELEVATION GAIN 160 feet

GETTING THERE
From Interstate 5 in Salem, take exit 253 and follow State Highway 22 east toward Detroit Lake. Drive 23 miles to the small town of Mehama. At the second flashing yellow light, turn left onto Little North Fork Road. Follow the paved road to just past mile marker 13 and turn right onto Elkhorn Drive (also marked on maps as Forest Road 201). Follow this paved and gravel road for half a mile, through the community of Elkhorn, a cluster of homes, to a small trailhead parking area on the left.

ON THE TRAIL
One of the most beloved streams in Oregon during the summertime, the Little North Santiam River has beautiful swimming holes. Deep and emerald green, and surrounded by waterfalls and old-growth forest, the swimming spots of the Santiam are tough to beat on hot days.

The problem is that everyone thinks so, and the Little North Santiam Canyon has gotten quite popular in recent years, especially at Three Pools Rec-

Rowdy and impressive in winter, Elkhorn Falls on the Little North Santiam River becomes an inviting swimming hole in summer.

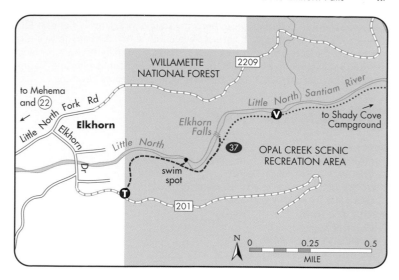

reation Area and upstream on Opal Creek Trail (Hike 35). The Little North Santiam (LNS) Trail, however, has remained a less crowded route to the area's many charms, and this hike features a nice taste of them.

If you choose to swim with children, we recommend you have them wear a life jacket. Although the pools mentioned here are typically calm by prime swimming seasons in July and August, unseasonably high water or recent rains can make them dangerous. There have been multiple fatal accidents—often involving children who are swept downstream—at swimming holes on this river. That's not a reason to avoid swimming, but keeping a cautious eye on children and conditions and wearing a life jacket will go a long way toward making this a fun day.

The LNS Trail is a total of 4.5 miles one-way from the Elkhorn trailhead to Shady Cove Campground but is a bit steep for most children. The hike featured here explores the gentler, western half of the trail, with the river, old-growth forest, and a recommended turnaround at Elkhorn Falls. Feel free to continue, of course.

From the small trailhead, the route heads immediately into lush green forest. You'll soon cross a small wooden footbridge. Many of the trees here are more than 100 years old and hung about with shaggy moss and lichen. The first stretch of trail stays away from the river, but at mile 0.4 you reach the river and are rewarded in summer with your first swimming hole. A well-worn user trail drops down to a beach on the river, where you can wade into the cool water.

The end of the recommended route is just a bit father. At mile 0.7, you'll reach another set of well-worn user trails, including a short side trip to Elkhorn Falls, a small waterfall that's rowdy and impressive in winter and calms down into a swimming hole in summer.

If you choose to continue from here, the trail stays relatively flat past Elkhorn Falls until, at mile 1.1, it starts a steep climb above the canyon to a nice viewpoint. The entire route is well worth hiking, especially if you have older children and can set up a shuttle at the eastern trailhead at Shady Cove Campground. The full route is 4.5 miles one-way with 1180 feet of climbing.

38 PAMELIA LAKE

BEFORE YOU GO
    MAP Willamette National Forest, Detroit Ranger District
    CONTACT Detroit Ranger District
    NOTES USFS fee and limited entry permit required; privy available
    GPS N44° 39.611' W121° 53.492'
ABOUT THE HIKE
    SEASON May–November
    DIFFICULTY Moderate–challenging
    ROUND-TRIP 4.4 miles
    HIGH POINT 3890 feet
    ELEVATION GAIN 800 feet

GETTING THERE
From Interstate 5 in Salem, take exit 253 and follow State Highway 22 east. Drive a total of 62 miles, passing Detroit Lake. Turn left on Pamelia Road (Forest Road 2246) and follow it about 3.5 miles to road's end and a large trailhead.

Pamelia Lake makes for a popular family backpacking destination in the Mount Jefferson Wilderness.

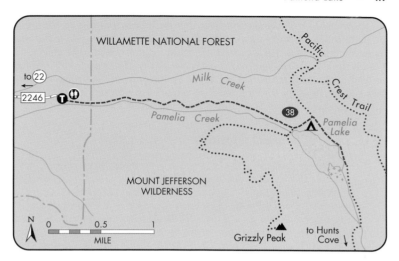

ON THE TRAIL

A generation of children from Salem have fallen in love with backpacking by traveling to this enchanted lake in the Mount Jefferson Wilderness. Mossy old-growth forest along a tumbling creek, wildflowers, and lakeside views of Oregon's second tallest mountain help explain why. The lake became so popular that in the mid-1990s the Forest Service instituted a limited entry system to keep visitors from destroying what makes the area so wonderful. So, to hike or backpack here in summer, you must get a permit first.

The hassle is more than worthwhile and the price is small. You can usually get a permit– although getting one well ahead of time is recommended for summer weekends—and there's good evidence the permit is helping maintain the area's natural beauty, as other lakes have been overrun in recent years. You must carry your Pamelia Limited Entry Area permit with you on your trip. Permits for the season go on sale May 1, on Recreation.gov (see Resources). The trailhead's low elevation means this route opens earlier than many in the Mount Jefferson Wilderness—but check ahead to ensure the trail is snowfree.

The trail begins in thick, mossy, old-growth forest bursting with wildflowers in spring. The low-elevation Cascadian forest is wonderful in late May and June. The trail can be challenging for kids because it climbs 800 feet at a steady clip. It never feels overly steep, however; and there are enough small waterfalls along the creek to keep kids interested.

At mile 2.2, you'll reach a trail junction right in front of the lake. Routes here branch off to the Pacific Crest Trail (left) and Grizzly Peak (right). Go straight ahead to the lake and, if you are backpacking, claim one of the fourteen campsites, each designated by a post. Once your camp is settled (or if you're here on a day hike), follow the Grizzly Peak Trail a short distance to the lake's southeastern side for a wonderful view of Mount Jefferson.

Many children will be tuckered out after the hike in, but inspect the area a bit more and you'll find a small waterfall on the upper western side of the lake, along the main trail. For a greater adventure open to older kids, follow the Grizzly Peak Trail to its summit. From Pamelia Lake, this trail climbs 2000 feet in 2.8 miles to the summit, making this an option only for the strongest hikers. Past Pamelia Lake, the trail continues into Hunt's Cove, an area usually traveled into by backpackers, which requires a different permit.

GREAT GETAWAY: DETROIT AREA

One of the most scenic and popular reservoirs in the state, Detroit Lake becomes a center for tourism and recreation during the summer in the central Cascade Mountains. Tourists arrive from Salem, Bend, and Portland to swim, fish, hike, and powerboat on this 9-mile-long impoundment of the North Santiam and Breitenbush rivers.

The small town of Detroit provides most of the essentials for a family, but there are several cool attractions not to be missed on a trip here.

Lodging. The town of Detroit features a handful of hotels and resorts; but if you're visiting during the height of summer—late June, July, and August—make sure to make reservations in advance. A famous lodging option is the Breitenbush Hot Springs Retreat and Conference Center, about 10 miles north of Detroit, which features overnight and day-use options, with thermally heated cabins and stone soaking pools in a lush old-growth forest setting.

Restaurants. There are a handful of family restaurants around Detroit, including the Korner Post, a local favorite.

Camping. Detroit Lake State Park features 350 campsites and a classic developed camping experience. There are modern restrooms with electricity and showers, along with boat ramps, boat moorage, and an accessible fishing dock. Horseshoe pits, volleyball and basketball courts, two playgrounds and five swim areas can be found here. The park's visitor center offers firewood, ice, souvenirs, and more.

For those interested in a less touristy experience, there are Forest Service campgrounds on the lake's quieter south side—Southshore Campground is probably the best—along with numerous campgrounds along State Highway 22 east of Detroit and Breitenbush Road (Forest Road 46) north of town.

Fishing and boating. Fishing platforms surround the lake, each providing a good chance to catch some of the lake's heavily stocked rainbow trout. To rent a boat, or get fishing gear and advice, visit Detroit's two marinas—Kane's and Detroit Lake Marina.

Swimming. There are multiple places to swim at Detroit Lake, including the state recreation site right off Hwy. 22. More enchanting places to swim are located at pullouts up FR 46, including Upper Arm Day-Use Area.

Rafting. Whitewater rafting is popular on the North Santiam River below Detroit Lake. The most popular stretches are between Packsaddle County Park and the town of Mehama. Outfitters in Mill City offer inflatable kayak rentals and guided rafting trips. North Santiam State Park makes a wonderful riverside place to boat in and camp for the night.

39 MCDOWELL CREEK FALLS PARK

BEFORE YOU GO
  MAP Download map from parks department website
  CONTACT Linn County Parks Department
  NOTES Dogs on leash; privy available
  GPS N44° 27.858' W122° 40.962'
ABOUT THE HIKE
  SEASON Year-round
  DIFFICULTY Easy
  ROUND-TRIP 1.8-mile loop
  HIGH POINT 774 feet
  ELEVATION GAIN 210 feet

GETTING THERE

From Interstate 5 near Albany, take exit 233 and follow State Highway 20 into Lebanon. About 4 miles past the city, between mileposts 18 and 19, turn left on Fairview Road at signs for the park. After 1 mile, veer left onto McDowell Creek Park Drive and follow it 7.7 miles to the park, on your right.

ON THE TRAIL

If it weren't for Silver Falls State Park (Hike 34), McDowell Creek Falls Park would be far better known for its dazzling waterfalls. This small county park and its cataract-filled canyon isn't nearly on the scale of the canyon at Silver Falls. But in less than 2 miles you can see three waterfalls, from 20 to 119 feet tall. Another bonus is being able to bring your dog, provided you have a leash—not an option at Silver Falls.

A boardwalk connects hikers to the waterfalls at McDowell Creek Falls Park.

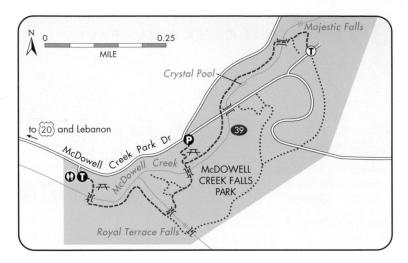

You can drive to within a few steps of two of the falls: 119-foot Royal Terrace Falls and 39-foot Majestic Falls. For an easy out-and-back hike, start at the lower parking area and follow the trail 0.2 mile to a junction and go left; from a footbridge you'll look up to Royal Terrace Falls. Follow the main trail another 0.3 mile to the road, cross it, and continue 0.3 mile more past Crystal Pool to the wooden stairs and viewing platform at Majestic Falls. Return as you came.

A right turn back at the first junction leads up steep stone steps to the top of Royal Terrace Falls—not much of a view—and through the forest, then down a narrow path (that splits, both forks leading to the road); you then have to follow the road back to hook up with the trail. You don't gain much in scenery—and with no road shoulder it's not a particularly safe option with young ones.

40 IRON MOUNTAIN

BEFORE YOU GO
    MAP Willamette National Forest, Sweet Home Ranger District
    CONTACT Sweet Home Ranger District
    NOTES Steep cliffs and loose rocks near trail's end; requires crossing highway on foot; USFS day-use fee; privy available
    GPS N44° 00.416' W122° 58.858'
ABOUT THE HIKE
    SEASON July–October
    DIFFICULTY Challenging
    ROUND-TRIP 3.6 miles out and back
    HIGH POINT 5455 feet
    ELEVATION GAIN 1350 feet

Walk through a garden of blooming wildflowers on your way up Iron Mountain.

GETTING THERE

From Sweet Home (southeast of Corvallis and Albany), drive about 34 miles east on US Highway 20 and turn right on Forest Road 15 to the trailhead just past milepost 63. From Eugene–Springfield, drive to the US 20/State Highway 126 junction and continue west on US 20 for about 9 miles to the trailhead turnoff at left on Forest Road 15. Follow it east 0.2 mile to the trailhead parking area.

ON THE TRAIL

The trail up Iron Mountain is a tough climb, but one tempered by grand views and the blaze of wildflowers that surrounds you at every step; about 300 species bloom in succession through the summer season. Except at the very end, the trail is never very steep, and you are rewarded with dazzling views of nearby Cascade peaks from a railed viewing platform. It's a favorite July wildflower trek among many Oregon hikers. Get an early start on hot days. No camping is allowed.

After starting up the trail, immediately turn right on Santiam Wagon Road Trail and, in about 100 yards, left to reach the highway. Cross with great care here (it's a bit of a blind corner for cars, and they're going fast) and start up the trail across the road. Here starts your gentle ascent through a deep, airy forest of old-growth Douglas fir. At about 0.9 mile the forest starts to open up, and at 1 mile the trail reaches a junction with Cone Peak Trail; bear right, then right again in just 0.1 mile to get on the trail leading to the summit.

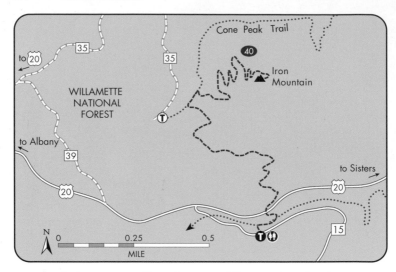

From the last junction, the trail is exposed (hot in summer) and quite steep. The consolation is the open fields of wildflowers blooming profusely in mid-summer. Take your time as the trail switchbacks toward the rocky summit knob, clearly visible above; enjoy the views and the profusion of flowers. At 1.8 miles you'll reach the railed summit platform (and a second platform steps away—helpful for handling the crowds on this popular trail). From here enjoy views of Mount Hood, Mount Jefferson, Mount Washington, the Three Sisters, and the tiptop of Three-Fingered Jack. Return as you came.

You can shorten this hike to 2 miles round-trip, and just 725 feet elevation gain, by starting at a higher trailhead accessible via a rough gravel road. You'll miss the old-growth forest but still get the best of the wildflower show. To reach that upper trailhead, turn north on Forest Road 35 from US 20 near milepost 62 (about a mile west of the turn-off to the lower trailhead), and follow it 2.8 miles to the road's end. Follow the trail 0.1 mile and turn left onto Cone Peak Trail to join the main route to the summit.

WHEN IS A FIR NOT A FIR?

Douglas fir, Oregon's official state tree, grows widely throughout western Oregon and Washington; you'll see it on many of the hikes in this book. The easiest way to identify it is by looking at the cones. They're 1.5 to 4.5 inches long, they hang down from the branches, and the bracts between the cone scales look like the hind legs and tail of a mouse trying to hide by scooting underneath. Douglas firs are firs in name only. The cones of true firs, like a noble fir, sit upright on the branch. They're bigger (4 to 6 inches long) too, with long, pointy bracts sticking upright out of the scales.

Large Douglas firs, with their deeply furrowed bark, line the Hackleman trail.

41 HACKLEMAN OLD GROWTH GROVE

BEFORE YOU GO
    MAP Posted at trailhead
    CONTACT Willamette National Forest, Sweet Home Ranger District
    NOTES USFS day-use fee; privy available
    GPS N44° 23.993' W122° 05.522'
ABOUT THE HIKE
    SEASON May–November
    DIFFICULTY Easy
    ROUND-TRIP 1.2-mile loop
    HIGH POINT 3520 feet
    ELEVATION GAIN 50 feet

GETTING THERE

From Sweet Home (southeast of Corvallis and Albany), drive about 37 miles east on US Highway 20. Turn right into the signed trailhead parking area between mileposts 66 and 67. (From Eugene–Springfield, drive to the

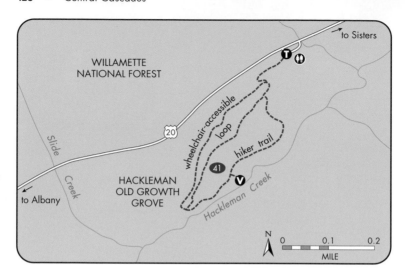

US 20/State Highway 126 junction and continue west on US 20 for about 6 miles to the trailhead turn-off at left.)

ON THE TRAIL

These interconnected loop trails take you into a high mountain forest with trees as much as 500 years old as well as young trees. It's just off the highway, making it a good stop on a drive between western and central Oregon. The hiker trail is narrower than the wheelchair loop, with a bit more up and down, but still easy. From the parking area go west, past the kiosk, to pick up the trail. The first junction is in not quite 0.2 mile; turn left here (unless you're going out and back via wheelchair; see below). Shortly you'll reach another junction; hikers go left, wheelchairs right.

Hikers follow the trail up and down through deep woods, approaching and hearing but not quite seeing Hackleman Creek, which hosts its own subspecies of cutthroat trout. (A couple of unmarked trail spurs get you to, or near, the creek.) How many different kinds of tree cones do you see on the trail? There are spruce, hemlock, and Douglas fir trees here, among others. At mile 0.7 you'll reach the end of a spur from the wheelchair loop. From here bear left at all junctions to join the main wheelchair loop and complete a loop hike.

Alternatively take the 1-mile (from the trailhead) wheelchair loop. At the far end of this loop is a spur that approaches the creek (in earshot, if not in view). Note that the grade of the wheelchair loop is a bit steeper than most accessible trails, and portions of the trail are deeply rutted or in soft sand; if you're uncertain, just go out and back on the wide, level northern leg of the loop.

42 TAMOLITCH POOL

BEFORE YOU GO
   MAP Willamette National Forest, McKenzie River Ranger District
   CONTACT McKenzie River Ranger District
   NOTES Weekdays are best to avoid crowds; swimming not advised; privy
     available
   GPS N44° 17.428' W122° 02.122'
ABOUT THE HIKE
   SEASON Most of the year
   DIFFICULTY Moderate–challenging
   ROUND-TRIP 4 miles out and back
   HIGH POINT 2450 feet
   ELEVATION GAIN 260 feet

GETTING THERE

From Eugene–Springfield, take State Highway 126 east to McKenzie Bridge and continue east and north on Hwy. 126 about 15 miles. Just past milepost 11, turn west onto Forest Road 730 at the sign to Trailbridge Reservoir. Cross the river and bear right up gravel FR 612 for 0.5 mile to a bend in the road. Park at the trailhead sign.

ON THE TRAIL

The 2-mile hike from Trailbridge Reservoir to Tamolitch Pool is a fairly uneventful (but not steep) ascent through the woods. Your reward is a view of deep, round, and impossibly turquoise Tamolitch Pool. This trail has been "discovered"

Admire deep-blue Tamolitch Pool from above, along the trail.

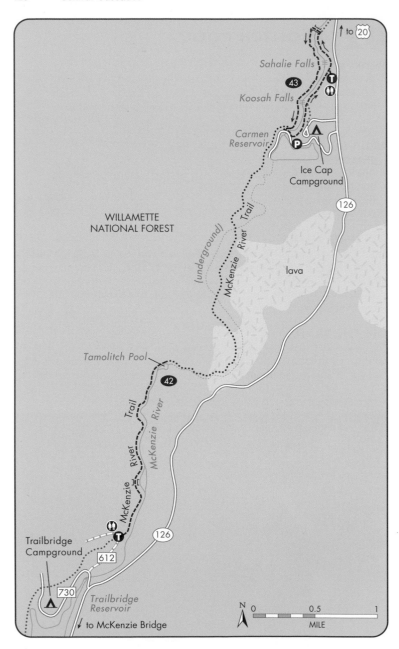

to 20

Sahalie Falls

43

Koosah Falls

Carmen
Reservoir

Ice Cap
Campground

126

WILLAMETTE
NATIONAL FOREST

McKenzie River Trail

(underground)

lava

Tamolitch Pool

42

McKenzie River

McKenzie River Trail

126

Trailbridge
Campground

612

730

Trailbridge
Reservoir

to McKenzie Bridge

N

0   0.5   1

MILE

in recent years and can be very crowded on hot days. Visitors have also worn unofficial (steep and dangerous) paths down to the pool from the main trail. We still love this hike, off-season, but strongly recommend you enjoy the view from the trail and don't yield to the temptation to descend to the pool.

The trail is mostly level for the first 1.5 miles or so, with the placid McKenzie River within view. Cross a footbridge over a side creek after about 1 mile. About halfway to Tamolitch Pool the river picks up steam, tumbling and churning, as the trail steepens. You'll know you're getting close to Tamolitch Pool when old lava rock appears on either side of the trail and underfoot. The trail stays above the river, granting occasional views down to the rushing water. Then, suddenly, the rushing stops, and you'll be looking down into clear Tamolitch Pool—alternately known as Blue Pool, or Tamolitch Falls—from atop a rock cliff.

It's easy to imagine the dramatic waterfall that tumbles down the sheer cliff at the far end of the pool when flows are high enough. Instead, most of the year the water seeps in invisibly. Above the pond, the river disappears into porous lava rock underground as far upstream as Carmen Reservoir. (Some flow would probably be seen on the surface if much of the river weren't also diverted from Carmen to Smith Reservoir, reentering the McKenzie below Tamolitch.) Explore, looking for molds of trees left in the rock years ago when flowing lava surrounded standing, live trees. Return as you came.

The McKenzie River Trail offers lots more opportunities for hikes, including one-way treks with a shuttle car. It runs 26.5 miles from McKenzie Bridge north to Fish Lake, with about ten access points along the way—and ten areas to choose from for day hikes. With a shuttle car, Tamolitch Pool could serve as a stop on a one-way, downhill hike 5.2 miles from Carmen Reservoir to Trailbridge Reservoir.

43 SAHALIE AND KOOSAH FALLS

BEFORE YOU GO
    MAP Willamette National Forest, McKenzie Ranger District
    CONTACT McKenzie Ranger District
    NOTES Top of trail (to falls viewpoint) wheelchair accessible; privy available
    GPS N44° 20.89' W121° 59.749'
ABOUT THE HIKE
    SEASON June–October, depending on snow conditions
    DIFFICULTY Moderate
    ROUND-TRIP 2.4-mile loop
    HIGH POINT 3000 feet
    ELEVATION GAIN 620 feet

GETTING THERE
From Eugene–Springfield, take State Highway 126 east to McKenzie Bridge. Continue east and north on Hwy. 126 about 22 miles to the parking area at Sahalie Falls, on the west side of the highway between mileposts 5 and 6.

Trails on both sides of the McKenzie River offer views of Sahalie Falls.

ON THE TRAIL

Koosah Falls and, especially, Sahalie Falls are popular stopping points along the McKenzie River Highway. Trails on either side of the rushing river enable hikers to make a 2.4-mile loop that takes in the falls from both sides. The forest is lush, with tall trees, and the terrain is gentle. Kids will enjoy getting to see the two dramatic falls twice, plus crossing the McKenzie River on a high, narrow, log footbridge. (Note that the privy at the trailhead seems to be chronically poorly maintained; avoid using it if possible.)

You can start the hike at several points; the simplest is the Sahalie Falls viewpoint. To hike counterclockwise, walk upriver (north), pausing to admire the falls from developed viewpoints along the way. Continue along the path 0.4 mile to its junction with the McKenzie River Trail. A right turn leads toward Hwy. 126 and Clear Lake; instead, turn left to cross a narrow footbridge over the river.

The trail rolls downstream through old-growth trees and past a small outcrop of lava, leading back past 68-foot Sahalie Falls, the foam at its base turning turquoise in sunlight. Continue down the trail, passing thundering 82-foot Koosah Falls about 0.5 mile past Sahalie. At about 1.6 miles bear left at a trail junction, leaving the McKenzie River Trail on a short spur leading to Carmen Reservoir.

The trail ends at the road around the reservoir. Follow the road to the left, across the McKenzie, then immediately look for a trail heading up the other side of the river. The trail up the east bank follows the river more closely. About 0.2 mile from the reservoir, pass a spur trail to Ice Cap Campground, then in another 0.2 mile arrive at a viewpoint overlooking Koosah Falls. Look for the springs gushing out of rocks at the base of the falls. The trail continues as a path and occasional stairs until it merges with the viewpoint trails at Sahalie Falls.

44 CLEAR LAKE

BEFORE YOU GO
   MAP Willamette National Forest, McKenzie River Ranger District
   CONTACT McKenzie River Ranger District
   NOTES USFS day-use fee; watch for mountain bikes; privy available
   GPS N44° 21.942' W121° 59.406'
ABOUT THE HIKE
   SEASON April–November, depending on snowpack
   DIFFICULTY Moderate–challenging
   ROUND-TRIP 5.2-mile loop
   HIGH POINT 3040 feet
   ELEVATION GAIN 250 feet

GETTING THERE

From Eugene–Springfield, take State Highway 126 east to McKenzie Bridge. Continue east and north on Hwy. 126 about 23 miles. Turn east at the sign to Coldwater Cove Campground (between mileposts 4 and 5). Follow the road to the boat ramp and trailhead at the end of the campground.

ON THE TRAIL

Clear Lake is an exquisite lake high in the mountains. The nearly level trail that encircles the lake is constantly changing; it passes through magnificent old-growth forest, winds along the sunny lakeshore, and crosses over an extensive lava flow. It's an easy and interesting hike; the distance is what makes it challenging for kids (and you can cut it short if you like). Wear sturdy sneakers or boots; ankle-twisting lava rocks are sharp through thin soles.

For a shorter out-and-back hike, start at the resort and hike clockwise 1.75 miles to the Great Spring. But starting a counterclockwise loop hike from Coldwater Cove, on the southeast shore, brings kids onto the intriguing lava flow quickly and gets the hottest part of the hike over with while they're fresh. Mountain bikes are allowed on McKenzie River Trail, but there aren't many here due to the rough lava. In summer, Clear Lake Resort rents rowboats and kayaks by the hour (no motorboats allowed).

Look for the McKenzie River Trail sign to the right of the boat ramp. The dirt-surface trail turns to asphalt when it reaches the lava flow. The vine maple here turns color sooner than in the forest, due to lots of sun and the stress of living with little water and among hot rocks. Continue across the lava for about 0.4 mile, pass through a cool forest, and get back onto lava for another 0.4 mile. At 1 mile you'll be back in forest for good and will see rustic Clear Lake Resort across the narrow lake. At 1.25 miles you'll reach a clear, blue-green cove—the

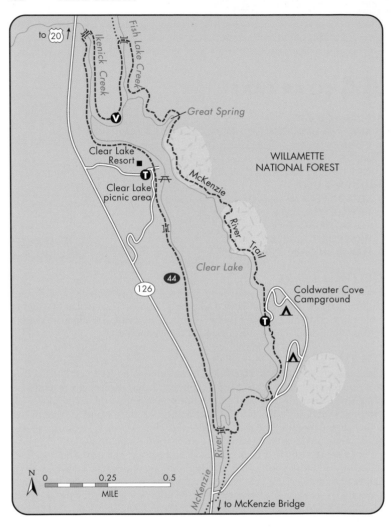

site of the Great Spring, one of the largest of several springs that feed Clear Lake.

After you cross a (possibly dry) streambed on a long footbridge, there's a trail junction; leave the McKenzie River Trail and turn left toward the resort. If the sky is clear, enjoy the view across the lake to the Three Sisters. The trail approaches the highway, then veers back toward the lake. Clear Lake Resort is at about 3 miles; the route through here isn't clear, but just follow trails or resort roads near the lake and jump back on the trail near the picnic area

Cross Fish Lake Creek on a long footbridge, part of the McKenzie River Trail.

and restrooms. Cross a small, musical creek, then cross the lake's outlet—the McKenzie River—on another long footbridge at 4 miles. In 0.1 mile turn left to rejoin McKenzie River Trail; follow it another 1.1 miles, crossing more lava outcrops, to return to where you started.

45 PROXY FALLS

BEFORE YOU GO
   MAP Willamette National Forest, McKenzie River Ranger District
   CONTACT McKenzie River Ranger District
   NOTES USFS day-use fee; privy available
   GPS N44° 10.082' W121° 55.638'
ABOUT THE HIKE
   SEASON July–October
   DIFFICULTY Easy
   ROUND-TRIP 1.3-mile loop
   HIGH POINT 3200 feet
   ELEVATION GAIN 420 feet

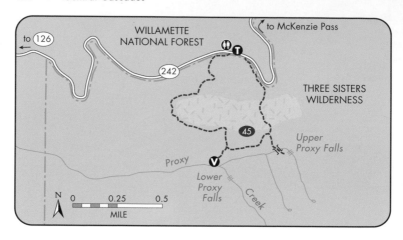

GETTING THERE

From Eugene–Springfield, take State Highway 126 east about 50 miles past the community of McKenzie Bridge and turn right on State Highway 242 (east of milepost 54). Drive 9 miles to trailhead parking, on the left side of the road.

ON THE TRAIL

For a short hike to two spectacular waterfalls, choose this trail. Shortly after the highway leading to this trailhead opens for the summer (usually late June), the rhododendrons and beargrass start blooming along the trail. A hike to Proxy Falls is a great way to break up a drive between Eugene and Sisters.

Cross the highway to the signed trailhead, which steers you on a counterclockwise loop. The trail immediately ascends, crossing an ancient lava flow and becoming rough and rocky. At 0.7 mile you reach a spur trail on the right leading to a rather distant view through the trees of Lower Proxy Falls, where Proxy Creek slides 200 feet down a curved cliff face. Head back to the trail junction and continue not quite 0.2 mile to a short spur trail leading to the base of Upper Proxy Falls. Here water from springs high above drops more than 100 feet over a stair-step cliff thick with velvety moss. The placid pool at the base is inviting for toe dipping. Back on the main trail, continue on the trail 0.5 mile back to the highway and the start of the loop.

Peek at Lower Proxy Falls through the trees.

46 LINTON LAKE

BEFORE YOU GO
  MAP Willamette National Forest, McKenzie River Ranger District
  CONTACT McKenzie River Ranger District
  NOTES USFS day-use fee; privy available
  GPS N44° 10.556' W121° 54.982'
ABOUT THE HIKE
  SEASON July–October
  DIFFICULTY Moderate
  ROUND-TRIP 3.4 miles out and back
  HIGH POINT 3566 feet
  ELEVATION GAIN 410 feet

GETTING THERE

From Eugene–Springfield, drive east on State Highway 126, past McKenzie Bridge, to milepost 54. Turn right onto McKenzie Pass Highway (State Highway 242). Drive 10.5 miles to Alder Springs Campground (just east of milepost 66); trailhead parking is on the left.

ON THE TRAIL

Trailhead parking for Linton Lake can be tight—for good reason. It's a very gentle descent to this stunning, deep green lake that feels more remote, and more distant from civilization, than it is in miles. Mosquitoes can be fierce here until late summer; in early fall, the reds and yellows of vine maple leaves along the trail are spectacular.

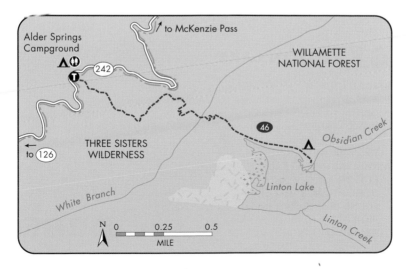

It's a short hike to Linton Lake, deep in Three Sisters Wilderness.

From the trailhead parking area, cross the road and start down the trail, quickly entering Three Sisters Wilderness. The trail rolls gently through the forest, making a sharp right at a trail junction and immediately crossing a scree slope at 0.7 mile. The more serious descent begins at 1 mile with a series of switchbacks. At 1.2 miles a spur trail leads steeply down to the creek's inlet, but bear left with the main trail as it continues the descent, ultimately granting glimpses of the lake through the trees. At 1.7 miles the trail enters a very large, flat camping area cut through by Obsidian Creek; look in the direction of the lake for a trail cut through the dense willowy underbrush and follow it out to the lake. Listen: what sounds like a waterfall is a creek tumbling over rocks to enter the lake far across the water. Return as you came.

47 BENSON LAKE

BEFORE YOU GO
   MAP Willamette National Forest, McKenzie River Ranger District
   CONTACT McKenzie River Ranger District
   NOTES USFS parking fee; privy available; thick summer mosquitoes taper off by
      mid- to late August
   GPS N44° 12.819' W121° 53.564'
ABOUT THE HIKE
   SEASON July–October
   DIFFICULTY Moderate
   ROUND-TRIP 3 miles out and back
   HIGH POINT 5190 feet
   ELEVATION GAIN 370 feet

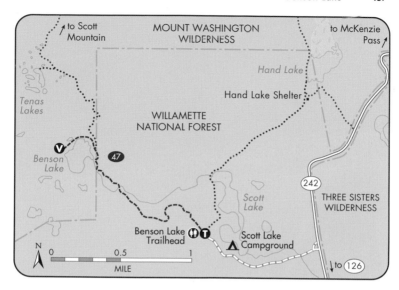

GETTING THERE

From Eugene–Springfield drive east on State Highway 126, past McKenzie Bridge, to milepost 54. Turn right onto McKenzie Pass Highway (State Highway 242). Drive 16 miles on winding Hwy. 242 and turn left at signs for Scott Lake Campground. Continue 1.5 miles on the gravel road along the lake, bearing left at the sign to Benson Lake trailhead. Park at road's end.

ON THE TRAIL

This hike offers some of the most scenic and rewarding hiking with children in the Cascade Crest. Clear, cold Benson Lake provides one of the best viewpoints in western Oregon. However, short hikes around Scott Lake and Tenas Lakes and to Hand Lake are also well worth considering. The nicest thing about this area are the options. The end of the road and start of the hike, Scott Lake, makes a wonderful family basecamp for outdoor adventure. Roadside and walk-in campsites are available with views of the Three Sisters.

Starting from the Benson Lake trailhead, you'll hike a trail that climbs gently through subalpine forest into the Mount Washington Wilderness. The trail climbs steadily, bordered by huckleberries and purple lousewort (a much prettier wildflower than the name implies) and shaded by mature alpine fir. There are no noteworthy landmarks until you catch a glimpse of Benson Lake at mile 1.3. The lake is surrounded by user trails with many options for exploration. At the first sight of the lake, on the southwest side, a trail leads past a muddy beach and left to a series of boulders that offer an excellent place for jumping into the lake's refreshing water.

The viewpoint above Benson Lake is one of Oregon's most dramatic, as it takes in the blue lake below and Three Sisters in the distance.

To savor the lake's secret charm, however, return to the main trail and follow it a short distance to a sign that says "user trail, not maintained." The way is rough but not long and if you follow it up the lake's northeastern cliffs, you'll be rewarded with one of the best views in Oregon. Atop the cliffs, the Three Sisters rise in dramatic splendor above the rich green and blue of the lake below. It's a memorable spot, and is a sacred spot for the Calapooia, the people native to this place. Officials ask that you not camp here. Turning around here makes the hike 3 miles round-trip.

It's tough to beat Benson Lake; but if you crave more mountain lakes, jump back on the trail and continue another 1.1 miles to Tenas Lakes. The setting of these pretty forested lakes is lush with huckleberries in good rainfall years. Turn back here and it's a 4.2-mile hike.

Scott and Hand Lakes

If you're camping at Scott Lake, be sure to hike the lakeside trail, which leads to walk-in campsites and pretty fishing spots.

To reach Hand Lake, which sits in a broad meadow and is not much more than a muddy handprint in late summer, bordered on the north by a lava flow, start at the same trailhead shared with Benson Lake. The trail follows the west side of Scott Lake, passing its walk-in campsites, before branching off to arrive in 1.5 miles at the Hand Lake Shelter. Bear left at the junction and continue another 0.25 mile to reach the lake.

48 LITTLE BELKNAP CRATER

BEFORE YOU GO
   MAP Three Sisters Wilderness Trail Map (Adventure Maps)
   CONTACT Willamette National Forest, McKenzie River Ranger District
   NOTES USFS day-use fee; don't take dogs (lava hard on their feet); avoid on hot
      days (no shade); privy at nearby Dee Wright Observatory
   GPS N44° 15.602' W121° 48.590'

ABOUT THE HIKE
   SEASON July–October
   DIFFICULTY Challenging
   ROUND-TRIP 4.8 miles out and back
   HIGH POINT 6188 feet
   ELEVATION GAIN 1030 feet

GETTING THERE

From Eugene–Springfield drive east on State Highway 126, past McKenzie Bridge, to milepost 54. Turn right onto McKenzie Pass Highway (State Highway 242). Drive about 22 miles nearly to McKenzie Pass, and turn left into the Pacific Crest Trail parking area, 0.4 mile before reaching rock-walled Dee Wright Observatory at the highway summit. (Westbound from Sisters, the trailhead is about 15 miles up Hwy. 242.)

ON THE TRAIL

Little Belknap is a hike like no other, crossing a huge lava flow most of the way. Wear boots; you'll shred your sneakers on the sharp rock. Is this a good kids'

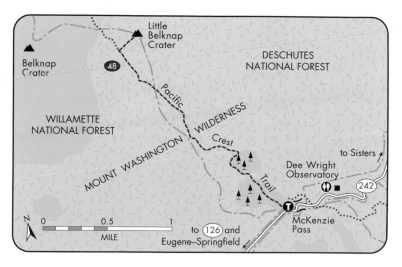

Backpackers hike through a moonscape of lava; behind them are the Three Sisters.

hike? I wasn't sure until I asked a couple of kids, ages eight and ten, halfway to the summit. Their response: all smiles, two thumbs up. "But not a first hike," they cautioned, and their parents nodded. Later, on the summit, I met three more children, ranging from six to twelve years old. The going may be tough, but not too tough for older motivated kids.

The route follows the Pacific Crest Trail north toward Mount Washington. It's not steep (except at the very end), but it's steadily up, with loose, rough lava stones underfoot most of the way. The trail begins in the forest, crosses a narrow band of lava, and returns to the trees for 0.3 mile more, following just inside the edge of a forested rise. (A lot of ripe huckleberries can be found here in late summer.) At 0.75 mile the trail makes a sharp left turn and the real hike begins, with nothing but lava from here to the summit. At 2.3 miles turn right on the spur trail to the summit. The final few footsteps to the top begin with a walk and end with a scramble. From the summit, survey the gray-black sea of lava that surrounds your perch, with red Belknap Crater rising smoothly to the west and snowcapped North and Middle Sisters to the south. Return as you came.

Extend your outing with a visit to Dee Wright Observatory, just 0.4 mile away, a rock parapet and viewpoint above the highway at McKenzie Pass. The paved Lava River Trail starts here and loops for 0.5 mile through the volcanic landscape.

THE PACIFIC CREST TRAIL: COULD YOU DO IT?

The Pacific Crest Trail is a 2650-mile hiking trail that starts at the border with Mexico, runs north through the deserts and high mountains of California and the Oregon and Washington Cascades and ends at the border with Canada. It is one of the world's longest continuous trails. Of the hundreds of people who attempt to hike it end-to-end—they're known as "thru-hikers"—each year, only about half finish it. Thousands more hikers follow stretches of it on day hikes or backpack trips. You may be one of them! Several hikes in this book are entirely or partially on the PCT or an alternative PCT route: Hikes 19, 23, 26, 48, and 57. To get to Canada before the autumn snowfall, thru-hikers have to walk at least 20 miles a day, carrying all their gear and several days' worth of food. Could you do it? Want to try someday?

49 FALL CREEK

BEFORE YOU GO
MAP Willamette National Forest, Middle Fork Ranger District
CONTACT Middle Fork Ranger District
NOTES Privy available; area impacted by 2017 Jones Fire
GPS N43° 57.813' W122° 37.142'
ABOUT THE HIKE
SEASON Year-round
DIFFICULTY Easy–moderate
ROUND-TRIP 6.5 miles out and back
HIGH POINT 1075 feet
ELEVATION GAIN 750 feet

GETTING THERE
From Eugene–Springfield, take Interstate 5 south to State Highway 58 and follow it 13 miles; approaching the long covered bridge, turn left toward the community of Lowell. Follow signs 3 miles north toward Fall Creek; turn right onto Fall Creek Road just before reaching the Unity Covered Bridge. Drive 10 miles (becomes Forest Road 18) to the trailhead on the right, across the road from Dolly Varden Campground.

ON THE TRAIL
Much of 14-mile Fall Creek Trail was devastated by massive forest fires in 2003 and 2017. Where tall trees once embraced the bouldery creek, now blackened snags line the sun-washed trail and pink fireweed blossoms reach high along the trailside. Fire spared the trail's lower stretch, however; it still has that deep forest magic. Hike the unburned stretch out and back—all the way or just a portion of the route.

From the lower trailhead, the trail rolls along Fall Creek, crossing a series of side creeks on footbridges. Most places it's a gentle up and down, but you'll get

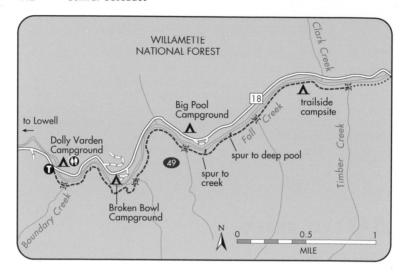

winded on some of the ascents. At 1.5 miles you'll spot Big Pool Campground, across the river—not quite the halfway point.

More footbridges follow, with occasional spur trails leading down to the creek for a picnic or a pause—and in one case at least, to a deep pool. At 3.25 miles the forest opens into the burn just 50 yards before the trail leads over a substantial footbridge crossing Timber Creek. This makes a good turnaround point. (There's road access just 0.5 mile ahead, allowing for a one-way hike with shuttle car, but there seems to be a lot of dispersed camping in this area, and we suggest avoiding it.)

With the tree canopy gone along much of the trail above this point, the

creekside boulders are bathed in sun all day, making the ice-cold swimming holes appealing. But some parts of Fall Creek are prone to pretty hard partying; use your judgment about where to settle in with the kids for a summer day of swimming in the ice-cold creek.

Fall Creek Trail offers a shady, shallow water-play spot.

50 GOODMAN CREEK

BEFORE YOU GO
   MAP Willamette National Forest, Middle Fork Ranger District
   CONTACT Middle Fork Ranger District
   NOTES USFS day-use fee; privy available
   GPS N43° 51.091' W122° 39.713'
ABOUT THE HIKE
   SEASON Year-round
   DIFFICULTY Moderate
   ROUND-TRIP 3.8 miles out and back
   HIGH POINT 1150 feet
   ELEVATION GAIN 400 feet

GETTING THERE

From Eugene–Springfield take Interstate 5 south and exit onto State Highway 58 toward Oakridge. Just west of milepost 21, pull off Hwy. 58 at signed Hardesty Trailhead parking area on the right.

ON THE TRAIL

A gentle walk through stunning old-growth forest, leading to a footbridge across a lovely, wide stream: the hike to Goodman Creek is appealing year-round. In late winter you may see newts crawling across the trail (though the trail can get pretty muddy); later look for flowering trillium at trailside.

Follow Hardesty Mountain Trail southeast out of the parking lot. It ascends 0.2 mile to a junction; turn right to pick up the Goodman Creek Trail. Here the route gentles to a moderate up and down leading toward and along an arm

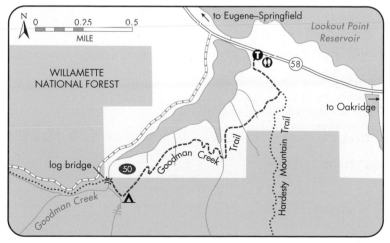

of Lookout Point Reservoir, occasionally crossing seasonal creeks. The forest is stunning, with moss and lichens draping the hemlocks and cedars. You'll reach a larger creek at 0.9 mile that's easy to cross on stones in summer but can be a bit challenging during winter high-water periods.

At 1.7 miles you'll reach the first of two level campsites; continue 0.1 mile to the second one at a good-size tributary of Goodman Creek. This is a great spot to picnic and wade on a hot day. The trail continues to the right, following the creek downstream 0.1 mile more to a log bridge crossing Goodman Creek itself. The trail continues on the other side, but the bridge makes a natural turnaround point. Return as you came.

A mossy log bridge spans Goodman Creek.

51 SPIRIT, MOON, AND PINARD FALLS

BEFORE YOU GO

  MAP Umpqua National Forest, Cottage Grove Ranger District

  CONTACT Cottage Grove Ranger District

  NOTES Pinard Falls Trail is very steep (avoid with very young children); privy available at junction of FR 17 and 1790

  GPS N43° 43.879' W122° 38.381' (Spirit Falls)

ABOUT THE HIKES

  SEASON Most of the year

  DIFFICULTY Easy–moderate

  ROUND-TRIP 0.8 to 1.4 miles out and back

  HIGH POINT 2050 to 3150 feet

  ELEVATION GAIN 250 to 290 feet

GETTING THERE

From Interstate 5 at Cottage Grove (20 miles south of Eugene–Springfield), head east on Row River Road for 12.3 miles (becomes Shorewood Drive for a few miles as it follows the south shore of Dorena Lake) to the junction of

Layng Creek Road and Brice Creek Road. Bear left onto Layng Creek Road (Forest Road 17) 8.8 miles to the junction with gravel FR 1790, on the right (vault toilet on left side of road). Turn right onto FR 1790 and follow directions indicated for each trail, below.

ON THE TRAIL

There are dozens of waterfalls in Umpqua National Forest; trailheads for these three, all on tributaries of Layng Creek, are just a few miles apart. Since it takes almost an hour to drive here from Eugene–Springfield, and since each hike is only about 1 mile round-trip, why not hike all three in a day? Each leads to a waterfall with its own particular character. The Layng Creek watershed serves as the source of drinking water for Cottage Grove, so stop and use the toilet on FR 17 before driving to any of the trailheads (to avoid making trailside pit stops).

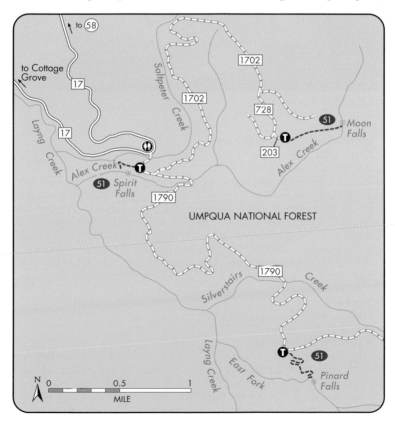

Moon Falls streams down through mossy boulders.

Spirit Falls
ROUND-TRIP 0.8 mile out and back
HIGH POINT 2050 feet
ELEVATION GAIN 270 feet

Getting there: Just after turning onto Forest Road 1790 look for trailhead parking on the right. **On the trail:** The trail drops gently, levels somewhat, and then begins to drop rather steeply down a dirt path that's rocky and slippery when wet. It ends at the base of 40-foot Spirit Falls, which gushes over domed cliffs. There's a picnic table at a viewpoint overlooking the falls, and the pool at the base of the umbrella-like falls is shallow and inviting for wading. Swimming is discouraged throughout the watershed, but it's mighty tempting to wade in for a shower on a hot day.

Moon Falls
ROUND-TRIP 1.4 miles out and back
HIGH POINT 3150 feet
ELEVATION GAIN 290 feet

Getting there: From Forest Road 17, follow FR 1790 for 0.2 mile and bear left onto FR 1702. Drive 2.8 miles and turn right onto FR 728. Follow it for 0.3 mile, bear left on FR 203, and continue 0.1 mile to a small parking area at road's end. The trail starts here. **On the trail:** Nearing the falls at 0.7 mile it steepens a bit, then drops down to a jumble of boulders at the base of the 100-foot falls. Moon Falls streams down a broad cliff in rivulets that run together before plunging into the pool below.

Pinard Falls
ROUND-TRIP 1.4 miles out and back
HIGH POINT 2850 feet
ELEVATION GAIN 250 feet

Getting there: From Forest Road 17, follow FR 1790 for 0.2 mile and bear right to continue on FR 1790. Continue on the main road for another 3.4 miles to the trailhead, on the right. **On the trail:** The trail starts with a gentle descent, then steepens; stone steps help you keep your footing. At the trail's last switchback, at about 0.6 mile, you get a great view of this 105-foot waterfall, which squeezes through a notch in the cliff, twisting as it drops. Descend the trail's short, near-vertical final stretch to reach the field of boulders surrounding the shallow pool at the base of the falls.

NEWTS: SAVED BY THEIR SKIN

The rough-skinned newt is a common sight on moist Cascades trails and at the edges of many lakes. But the newts can be hard to spot, given their coloring: muddy brown on top. It's the flash of orange belly that gives them away. There are many other salamander species in Oregon, but this one is most often out during the day because of the toxic skin secretions it has that protect it from predators. It's safe enough for humans to pick up and hold, but the poison it secretes is enough to sicken or kill a small animal that might eat it. But don't hold it long; newts need to stay close to the ground to be moist and healthy.

---

52 LOWER TRESTLE CREEK FALLS

BEFORE YOU GO
MAP Umpqua National Forest, Cottage Grove Ranger District
CONTACT Cottage Grove Ranger District
NOTES Privy available
GPS N43° 38.521'' W122° 39.509'

ABOUT THE HIKE
SEASON Most of the year
DIFFICULTY Easy
ROUND-TRIP 1.4 miles out and back
HIGH POINT 2160 feet
ELEVATION GAIN 160 feet

GETTING THERE

From Interstate 5 at Cottage Grove (20 miles south of Eugene–Springfield), head east on Row River Road for 12.3 miles (becomes Shorewood Drive for a few miles as it follows the south shore of Dorena Lake) to the junction of Layng Creek Road and Brice Creek Road. Continue straight on Brice Creek Road.

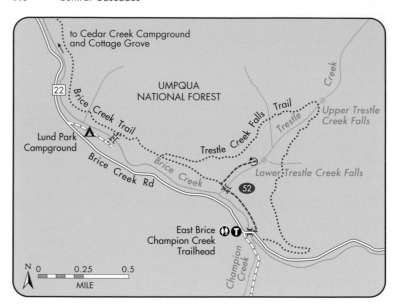

You will pass several other trailheads and campgrounds before, 8.2 miles from the last junction, reaching parking at East Brice Champion Creek Trailhead.

ON THE TRAIL

From the East Brice trailhead, cross Brice Creek on the road bridge walking up the road about 30 yards, to reach Brice Creek Trail on the left. Follow the trail northwest for 0.4 mile to a substantial footbridge over gushing Trestle Creek. Just past the footbridge, look for a trail on your right; it leads 0.3 mile up the creek to fan-shaped 60-foot Lower Trestle Creek Falls, nestled in a rocky grotto. Return as you came.

If your group is up for a challenge—one we would categorize as difficult for kids, but amazing—turn this hike into a 4.5-mile loop (with nearly 1000 feet total elevation gain) by turning right, not left, when you get back to Brice Creek Trail after your detour to Lower Trestle Creek Falls. Continue west on Brice Creek Trail for another 0.4 mile to its junction with Trestle Creek Falls Trail. Take a sharp right up this trail. From here the trail climbs steadily through a lush forest before topping out, turning a corner, and dropping into a natural amphitheater at about 1.2 miles from the last trail junction.

Here the creek streams over the lip of a cliff above you, falls onto rocks near your feet, and continues down the rock face to a tiny pool, 100 feet in all. The trail leads behind Upper Trestle Creek Falls; watch your step, as the misty atmosphere means it's always muddy and slippery here and the trail drops off steeply. Past the waterfall, continue on Trestle Creek Falls Trail about 0.4 mile to where it crosses a side creek; after that point, the trail starts a more serious

A threesome crosses the bridge over Trestle Creek on their way back from the falls.

1.5-mile descent, steep in places, to end on Brice Creek Road just east of the trailhead for Brice Creek Trail. Walk the road the short distance back across Brice Creek to the trailhead parking area.

Once you've explored the Trestle Creek area, consider exploring other sections of Brice Creek Trail, accessible from several trailheads; much of it is close to the creek, which has bedrock pools and short falls that are enticing on hot summer days. The canyon's low elevation makes these trails appealing for spring and fall hiking as well.

53 LARISON COVE

BEFORE YOU GO
   MAP Oakridge, Oregon, Trail Map (Adventure Maps)
   CONTACT Willamette National Forest, Middle Fork Ranger District
   NOTES Privy at canoe launch (0.2 mile away on FR 21); watch for poison oak
   GPS N43° 41.240' W122° 26.452'
ABOUT THE HIKE
   SEASON Spring–summer
   DIFFICULTY Easy–moderate
   ROUND-TRIP 1.6 miles out and back
   HIGH POINT 1600 feet
   ELEVATION GAIN 470 feet

GETTING THERE

From Eugene–Springfield, take Interstate 5 south and exit onto State Highway 58, following it to Oakridge (about 40 miles). About 1 mile east of Oakridge, turn right on Kitson Springs Road. In 0.5 mile, turn right on Forest Road 21, cross the Middle Fork Willamette River, and bear left with the main road. Follow it 3.4 miles to trailhead parking on the right.

ON THE TRAIL

Just outside of Oakridge, Hills Creek Reservoir stretches to the south, reaching its many arms into mountain creek valleys to create isolated coves. One particularly long cove, Larison, has an easy, quietly scenic trail following its north bank. The trail is snow-free most of the year; but it's not

A split-log footbridge crosses a side creek near campsites on Larison Cove.

very appealing in the winter, when the reservoir is drained down; the lake level starts rising in early spring and is drawn down again usually beginning in late August. No motorized boats are allowed on this cove; as you walk, you can spot little docks across the reservoir designed for canoes and kayaks. The head of the cove makes a good destination for an easy day hike or even overnight backpack. Watch for mountain bikes on the trail (though most users are hikers).

Just past the trailhead a couple of spurs lead to the water's edge; keep them in mind for cooling off on the return, though the muddy lake bottom and slight drop-off make these less-than-ideal swimming spots. At about 0.5 mile the trail turns up a cool canyon where you'll step across a side creek. The trail then returns to the shoreline, usually staying about 50 feet above the water. Watch for patches of poison oak on this more exposed portion of the trail before heading back into the hemlock and Douglas fir forest.

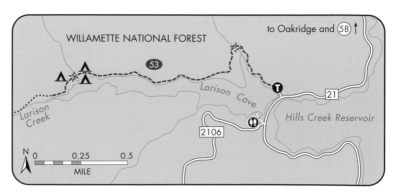

At 1.5 miles spur trails on the right and left lead to nearby campsites; the left spur also leads to the water's edge (no sandy beach, however). In another 0.1 mile you'll reach a log bridge crossing another side creek and, just across the creek, a third campsite on the right. The head of the cove (though not the end of the trail), where the reservoir ends and Larison Creek begins, is about 0.2 mile beyond the footbridge. Return as you came.

54 ERMA BELL LAKES

BEFORE YOU GO
    MAP Willamette National Forest, Middle Fork Ranger District
    CONTACT Middle Fork Ranger District
    NOTES Privy available; camp only at designated sites
    GPS N43° 51.679' W122° 02.721'
ABOUT THE HIKE
    SEASON Late June–October
    DIFFICULTY Moderate
    ROUND-TRIP 4.5 miles
    HIGH POINT 4618 feet
    ELEVATION GAIN 550 feet

GETTING THERE
From Interstate 5 just south of Eugene–Springfield, exit onto State Highway 58. Follow it southeast to just past milepost 33 and turn left at the sign to Westfir. Continue 3 miles to Westfir, and then continue onto Aufderheide Drive (Forest

There's a nice swimming and lunch spot at Middle Erma Bell Lake in the Three Sisters Wilderness.

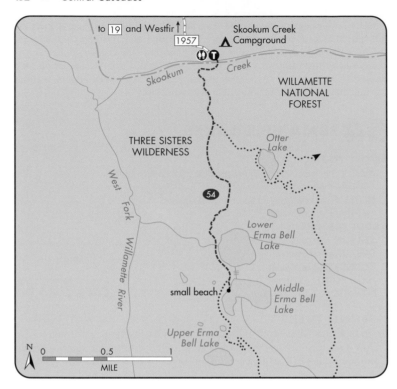

Road 19, also called West Cascades Scenic Bikeway). Follow it 37 miles along the North Fork Middle Fork Willamette River. Watch for signs for Skookum Creek Campground and turn right on gravel FR 1957. Follow it 4 miles to a large parking area for the campground and trailhead.

ON THE TRAIL

Located just inside the Three Sisters Wilderness, this shady trail to a trio of mountain lakes is heavenly on hot summer days. The trail works as a first-time backpacking experience for kids or as a day hike for those living in the Eugene area. Mosquitoes and weekend crowds are the only things that make this trek imperfect, so aim for midweek on the later edges of summer.

The hike begins in shaded forest on a wide, level, and well-maintained trail. Your route passes a junction to Otter Lake—worth exploring if you have extra energy—before arriving at Lower Erma Bell Lake at mile 1.7. This deep blue lake is surrounded by rocky terrain—there are no beaches here—and several nice campsites, each, as it should be, 200 feet or more away from the lakes.

Beyond Lower Erma, the trail climbs uphill, passing a pretty 30-foot water-fall, before arriving at a spur trail on the left. Take the spur and follow it to a pleasant spot in the forest with a small beach on Middle Erma Bell Lake. The beach isn't much, but it's a great place for lunch with the kids and a swim.

The beach marks the end of the recommended hike, but you can continue a half mile more to Upper Erma Bell Lake, which also doesn't have much in the way of lake access but does have more campsites.

GREAT GETAWAY: WILLAMETTE PASS

With three large lakes—Crescent, Odell, and Waldo—and a plethora of hiking and biking trails, the crest of the Cascades at Willamette Pass is a great base for a summer vacation in the mountains. Jet skis and waterskiing are allowed on Crescent and Odell lakes; but on Waldo, only electric motors are allowed and they may not exceed 10 miles per hour—making this lake the best choice for kayaking and canoeing (see below). Waldo is notorious for its mosquitoes in midsummer—at least on the lakeshore; once you're on the water, mosquitoes are no problem!

Lodging. Rustic resorts are located at either end of Odell Lake (Odell Lake Lodge & Resort; Shelter Cove Resort and Marina) and at Crescent Lake (Crescent Lake Lodge). You can rent cabins at any of these establishments (Odell and Shelter Cove also rent lodge rooms). All three rent boats (motorized and otherwise). Crescent Lake tends to draw the motorized watercraft crowd, and Odell Lake is popular with anglers (and famous for its kokanee fishing).

Camping. Forest Service campgrounds are located on all three lakes. Reservations are available through various private concessionaires; search online to find campgrounds and how to reserve them if you want to be sure of a spot on these popular lakes. RV camping is also offered at Shelter Cove Resort, and Odell Lake Resort offers both tent and RV camping near the lodge. For hiking families, Waldo is your best bet—preferably after mid-August, when the mosquitoes are mostly gone.

Boating. Bring your own kayak, canoe, paddleboard, or sailboat to Waldo Lake for day outings, or to paddle to and from your campsite. Kayaking is less appealing among the motorboats at Crescent and Odell lakes, but you can rent personal watercraft at the resorts on these lakes.

Mountain biking. Options for mountain biking abound. Do some research: bikes are not allowed on many of the trails in the national forest (for example, in wilderness areas); but many others are open to mountain biking, including the epic 20-mile trail circling Waldo Lake. Bikeable trails radiate out from all three lakeside resorts, and Crescent Lake offers mountain bike rentals. Willamette Mountain Mercantile in Oakridge, on your way up from Eugene, is a great source of information and advice, as well as adult bike rentals.

55 DIAMOND CREEK FALLS

BEFORE YOU GO
   MAP Oakridge, Oregon, Trail Map (Adventure Maps)
   CONTACT Willamette National Forest, Middle Fork Ranger District
   NOTES USFS day-use fee; watch kids carefully at steep drop-offs; privy available
   GPS N43° 36.712' W122° 07.674'
ABOUT THE HIKE
   SEASON June–October
   DIFFICULTY Moderate
   ROUND-TRIP 3.4-mile loop
   HIGH POINT 4350 feet
   ELEVATION GAIN 420 feet

GETTING THERE

From Oakridge (about 40 miles east of Eugene–Springfield on State Highway 58), continue on Hwy. 58 for about 22 miles. Drive through a tunnel and in 0.8 mile turn right (Forest Road 5893) at the sign to Salt Creek Falls. Continue 0.6 mile (bearing right at a junction) into the parking area.

ON THE TRAIL

This loop hike begins and ends at one of the Northwest's most impressive waterfalls: Salt Creek Falls, which at 286 feet is the third-tallest year-round plunge waterfall in Oregon. In the middle of the loop is Diamond Creek Falls, less than half that height but misty and boisterous and well worth the trip. Visit in

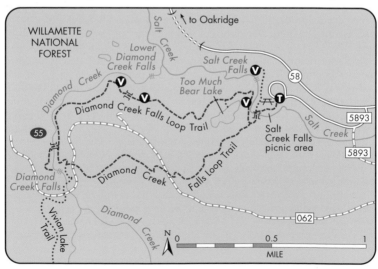

Lower Diamond Creek Falls streams down a wide cliff face.

June and you'll be hiking through a high forest understory of blooming pink rhododendrons.

You'll want to at least glimpse Salt Creek Falls before setting off on this hike; follow the paved paths behind the restrooms to viewpoints along the canyon rim. To start the loop hike from the canyon rim, head left into the shady picnic area to a footbridge crossing Salt Creek. Cross the bridge, bear right, cross another smaller bridge in about 50 yards, and you'll meet the start of Diamond Creek Falls Loop Trail. Go right (counterclockwise), passing a series of viewpoints overlooking Salt Creek Canyon (but none with good views of the falls). Watch children carefully at these viewpoints with their sharp drop-offs, especially at the cobblestone-like viewpoint atop a cliff of basalt columns 0.4 mile from the start of your hike. Continuing, you'll reach a short spur on the left to Too Much Bear Lake, reportedly named in the 1920s by a Forest Service horse packer who had stopped here to fish. (The brown, stagnant-looking lake is not appealing for swimming.)

At 0.8 mile you'll reach a viewpoint with a distant view through the trees of Lower Diamond Creek Falls across the canyon. Keep going, now walking alongside gurgling Diamond Creek. The trail steepens for about 0.2 mile just before, at mile 1.7, it reaches the spur trail to Diamond Creek Falls on the right. Follow it less than 0.2 mile down a notched-log staircase, along a muddy hillside, over a wide footbridge across the creek, and up the creek to the base of the dome-shaped, 120-foot falls.

Back on the main trail, continue 0.2 mile up to a junction with Vivian Lake Trail and bear left. (Or consider a short detour on the Vivian Lake Trail; in less than 0.2 mile it crosses wide, shallow Diamond Creek on a concrete bridge—an appealing spot for wading and a picnic.) Immediately cross a gravel road and continue ascending. The trail finally tops off at 2.3 miles and soon begins a gentle ascent through the forest of Douglas fir, hemlock, and rhododendrons, crossing the road once again. The loop ends at 3.2 miles; turn right to cross back over Salt Creek to return to the picnic area and parking lot.

Extend your outing with a 0.6-mile round-trip walk dropping 190 feet down to a viewpoint near the base of Salt Creek Falls. Follow the paved path along the canyon rim to the right, up a set of stairs, and onto a forest path that switchbacks through the forest to end at a viewpoint. (Some people scramble further down the scree slope, but it's very steep and not advisable.) Return as you came.

WHEN YOU'RE JUST TOO COLD

Hypothermia is a potentially life-threatening drop in core body temperature that most often occurs in cold, wet weather but can occur any time: on a windy spring day, for example, when you stop for lunch and don't bother donning a sweater over your sweat-cooled body. To help prevent hypothermia, wear clothing in layers, choose wool and polypropylene over cotton, and peel them off or pile them back on as your body temperature fluctuates. Always carry reliable raingear and keep it handy.

If someone in your party starts shivering; seems disoriented; has cold, clammy skin; or simply seems listless and whiny, get the person layered up, moving, and consuming with hot liquids. On cooler days it's helpful to carry a thermos of hot chocolate or cider—or have one waiting back in the car.

56 NORTH FORK TRAIL

BEFORE YOU GO
    MAP Oakridge, Oregon, Trail Map (Adventure Maps)
    CONTACT Willamette National Forest, Middle Fork Ranger District
    NOTES Privy available
    GPS N43° 45.551' W122° 29.752'
ABOUT THE HIKE
    SEASON Year-round
    DIFFICULTY Moderate
    ROUND-TRIP 4.8 miles out and back
    HIGH POINT 1200 feet
    ELEVATION GAIN 200 feet

GETTING THERE

From Interstate 5 just south of Eugene–Springfield, exit onto State Highway 58.
Follow it southeast to just past milepost 33 and turn left at the sign to Westfir.
Continue 3 miles to Westfir and turn left across the river through the long red
covered bridge to the trailhead parking area.

ON THE TRAIL

Barely 45 minutes from Eugene, this hike starts at a historic covered bridge and
follows the North Fork of the Middle Fork of the Willamette River. You could
make it a much longer hike—the trail continues upstream for several miles—but
river access sites between 2 and 2.5 miles from the trailhead make good destinations with kids. It's a great choice for springtime, when water is gushing; in
summer, when you're in need of shade or cold water to cool your feet; and in

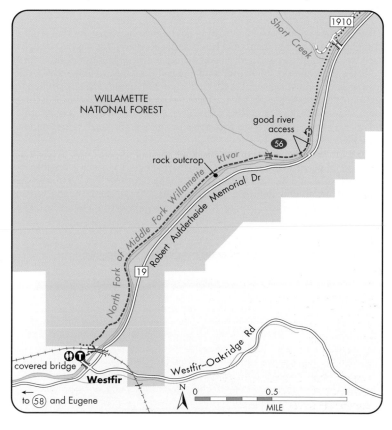

A black lab takes a bath at an outcrop in the North Fork.

fall, when the bigleaf maples are turning gold. (Even in winter this trail is good: it might be raining, but the trail is rarely snow-covered.) The covered bridge is itself worth a look; cars and pedestrians are separated, so kids can explore safely.

From the trailhead, follow signs up a gravel road toward and under a railroad bridge. As the road swings left, bear right onto a trail. The trail, rolling up and down but never steeply, passes briefly through a burned stretch of forest on its way into the lush forest that follows the river the rest of the way. At about 1.8 miles a rock outcrop invites you down to the river; it's shallow here and is a good place to wade with care.

In 0.2 mile farther you'll cross a footbridge; go another 0.2 mile to reach the first of three places barely 0.1 mile apart where the river is easily accessible, the bank not steep, and the shore a bit sandy. The last of these is at 2.4 miles—our suggested turnaround. Return as you came. Just 0.6 mile ahead the trail crosses a road next to a tall vehicle bridge over the river; there is room for a few cars to park at this alternate trailhead.

OREGON'S HISTORIC COVERED BRIDGES

Oregon has more covered bridges than any state in the West. Early settlers built roofs over their wooden bridge trusses to protect them from the damp weather. Most of Oregon's remaining four dozen covered bridges are in Linn and Lane Counties. The 180-foot-long Office Covered Bridge at the start of the North Fork Trail (Hike 56) is the longest in the state. It was built in 1944 by the Westfir Lumber Company to connect the company offices with the sawmill. You can see two more—Lowell and Unity Bridges—on the way from Eugene to Fall Creek (Hike 49) and another—Goodpasture Bridge—as you drive up the McKenzie River on US Highway 126 from Eugene–Springfield toward hikes near McKenzie and Santiam Passes. Interpretive signs at Lowell Covered Bridge, just off State Highway 58 on the way to Willamette Pass, make it a particularly good stop.

57 BOBBY LAKE

BEFORE YOU GO
    MAP Oakridge, Oregon, Trail Map (Adventure Maps)
    CONTACT Willamette National Forest, Middle Fork Ranger District
    NOTES Mosquitoes heavy until August; closest privy is at Shadow Bay
    GPS N43° 40.329' W122° 01.187'
ABOUT THE HIKE
    SEASON July–October
    DIFFICULTY Moderate
    ROUND-TRIP 4.6 miles out and back
    HIGH POINT 5600 feet
    ELEVATION GAIN 340 feet

GETTING THERE

From Eugene–Springfield, take Interstate 5 south to State Highway 58 and follow it 24 miles to Waldo Lake Road (Forest Road 5897), on the left at milepost 59 past Oakridge. Drive Waldo Lake Road 5.5 miles and park in the wide turnout on the left side of the road; trailhead is on right side.

ON THE TRAIL

Bobby Lake is one of dozens of lakes dotting the forest around Waldo Lake. The hike in is not very interesting but not difficult, and the good-size lake offers fine swimming and even decent fishing. Get an early start to soak up some sun on the big rock slab tilting into the lake's west end before the sun drops behind the trees at your back; or camp at the lake and catch the morning sun that way.

    The trail begins as a wide path through airy woods; it's flat or gently rolling the entire route. At 0.4 mile you will arrive at a junction with Gold Lake Trail,

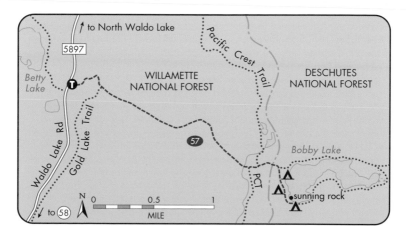

Dogs and *people appreciate the sun-warmed rock slab at Bobby Lake.*

on the right; go straight. The trail continues forward, without many distractions, to its junction with the long-distance Pacific Crest Trail at 1.9 miles. Turn left onto the PCT and then, in just 0.1 mile, turn right to reach the lake in another 0.3 mile. There's camping here, but there are more tent sites (and sunning on the lake's big rock) if you continue along the lakeshore to your right. Our favorite campsite is actually past the rock a short distance, but it's a little tricky climbing over the slab with full packs.

For more exploring, an informal trail continues along the shoreline to encircle the entire lake. Return as you came. Back at the trailhead, any hikers needing to work off more energy can cross the road to pick up the 0.4-mile trail to pretty Betty Lake.

SCRAM, MOSQUITOES!

Nothing can spoil a hike in the woods faster than a swarm of biting mosquitoes (especially given concerns about West Nile virus). The first best defense is to avoid boggy areas in spring and high mountain lakes early in summer. Wearing a hat, long-sleeves, and pants also helps; but it's challenging to completely cover up, especially on hot days.

The best defense many of us resort to is a chemical repellent of some kind. "Natural" repellents with ingredients such as citronella sometimes work, though they may require frequent reapplication. Otherwise, virtually all repellents use the chemical N, N-diethyl-m-toluamide, nicknamed DEET, as the active ingredient, in concentrations as high as 95 percent. Avoid the higher concentrations; they've been linked to serious health problems and are especially not advised for young children. (I've seen them melt paint and smear the color in vinyl car seats!) Anyway, the high concentrations are apparently not much more effective than low concentrations of about 6.5 percent, though you may have to reapply these formulas more frequently.

58 SOUTH WALDO SHELTER

BEFORE YOU GO
    MAP Oakridge, Oregon, Trail Map (Adventure Maps)
    CONTACT Willamette National Forest, Middle Fork Ranger District
    NOTES USFS day-use fee; privy available
    GPS N43° 41.550' W122° 02.646'
ABOUT THE HIKE
    SEASON July–October
    DIFFICULTY Moderate
    ROUND-TRIP 3.4 miles out and back
    HIGH POINT 5480 feet
    ELEVATION GAIN 250 feet

GETTING THERE

From Eugene–Springfield, take Interstate 5 south to State Highway 58. Follow Hwy. 58 about 66 miles to Waldo Lake Road (Forest Road 5897) on the left at milepost 59. Follow it 7 miles and turn left at the sign to Shadow Bay Campground (Road 5896). Follow signs to the boat ramp and trailhead.

In late August look for ripe huckleberries along the trail to South Waldo Shelter.

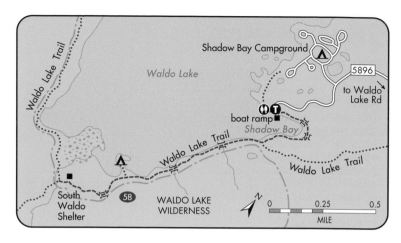

ON THE TRAIL

At 10 square miles, Waldo Lake is the second-largest lake in Oregon and is considered by scientists to be perhaps the purest large lake in the world. It's an especially grand place after mid-August, when the swarms of mosquitoes that plague campers earlier in the summer are gone. A 21.8-mile trail encircles this quiet lake (only electric motors are allowed). The short, level stretch described here offers excellent views of the lake and nice camping.

From the trailhead, pick up the shoreline trail heading south, following it around Shadow Bay and crossing a couple of small bridges. At 0.5 mile the trail joins the main Waldo Lake Trail, which comes in from the left. About this point, pause to see if anything seems different. It should: The trail is now beyond the protection of the bay, and even on a gentle day hikers should be feeling the wind across the lake and seeing waves lapping at the shore. Soon the trail crosses a substantial footbridge, then leads through a bog filled with skunk cabbage and, at 1 mile, crosses another beefy bridge. Here look for a particularly pretty beach; on hot summer days, its gentle surf is reminiscent of a tropical beach.

At about 1.3 miles look for a spur trail on the right leading to a peninsula with good swimming and a campsite; this may be the right turnaround spot for your group. Continuing on the main trail, you'll swing out of sight of the lake to skirt a marsh. Cross one more big footbridge before reaching shingle-roofed South Waldo Shelter at 1.7 miles. This three-sided shelter has a wood-burning stove and a couple of bunks, should you want to spend the night (or just get out of the rain on a day hike). We suggest this as your turnaround. But should you wish to continue hiking on Waldo Lake Trail, which continues around the lake, the lake comes back into view after about another 0.3 mile of hiking.

59 ISLET BEACH

BEFORE YOU GO

MAP Oakridge, Oregon, Trail Map (Adventure Maps)
CONTACT Willamette National Forest, Middle Fork Ranger District
NOTES USFS day-use fee; mosquitoes heavy until August; dogs prohibited on Islet
Beach; privy available
GPS N43° 44.88' W122° 00.604'

ABOUT THE HIKE

SEASON July–October
DIFFICULTY Easy–moderate
ROUND-TRIP 2.5 miles out and back
HIGH POINT 5450 feet
ELEVATION GAIN 170 feet

Waldo Lake was still this particular morning, but the wind picked up in the afternoon.

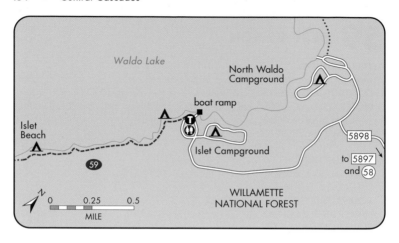

GETTING THERE

From Eugene–Springfield,, take Interstate 5 south to State Highway 58 and follow it to Waldo Lake Road (Forest Road 5897), on the left at milepost 59. Drive it 13 miles and turn left at the sign to Islet Campground. Follow signs 1.2 miles to the boat ramp and trailhead parking area.

ON THE TRAIL

Islet Beach is our name for the long white crescent of sandy lakeshore found 1.25 miles south by trail (or canoe) from Islet Campground. The beach is on the lake's east side, so it's bathed in sun all afternoon long, which warms the shallow water at the lake's edge.

Pick up the Shoreline Trail to the left of the boat launch and begin hiking south along the lake. (The main Waldo Lake Trail circling the lake is far from the lake at this point.) Immediately the trail passes a small gray-sand beach, then a small cove at 0.2 mile, then a peninsula with a fine campsite. Keep going to where the trail ends at a curve of beach about 75 sandy yards long. Look for a campsite on a promontory overlooking the lake just north of the beach. Return as you came.

Opposite: *There are lots of places to explore in Central Oregon, including Smith Rock State Park, Hike 64.* (Photo by Chad Altherr)

CENTRAL OREGON

60 BLACK BUTTE

BEFORE YOU GO
   MAP Green Trails 590 Sisters
   CONTACT Deschutes National Forest, Sisters Ranger District
   NOTES USFS day-use fee
   GPS N44° 23.702' W121° 38.867'
ABOUT THE HIKE
   SEASON June–October
   DIFFICULTY Challenging
   ROUND-TRIP 4 miles out and back
   HIGH POINT 6440 feet
   ELEVATION GAIN 1640 feet

GETTING THERE
From Sisters, head west on US Highway 20 for 5.7 miles and turn left on Indian Ford Road for 0.2 mile, then bear left onto Green Ridge Road (Forest Road 11), following it for 3.7 miles. Turn left on gravel FR 1110 and drive 5.3 miles to the trailhead parking area.

From the Willamette Valley, follow State Highway 126 (from Eugene), US Highway 20 (from Corvallis) or State Highway 22 (from Salem) to Santiam Junction. Then follow US 20 over Santiam Pass toward Sisters and turn right onto Indian Ford Road and follow above directions to trailhead.

ON THE TRAIL
Gaze at it from Black Butte Ranch resort, or drive by it on the highway, and the tall, black, symmetrical cinder cone of Black Butte invites you to climb. The road goes most of the way up; 2 miles of hiking finishes the ascent. On top you can

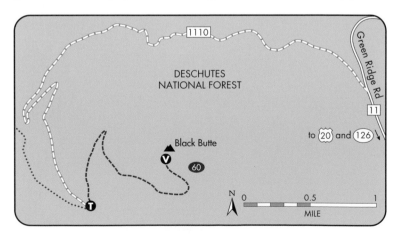

The lookout tower atop Black Butte allows for early warning of summer wildfires.

visit a couple of lookout towers, adding to the uniqueness of this hike. The steady ascent makes it a challenging hike but well worth doing for kids who are up for it.

The route starts northward around the butte, ascending steadily through a forest of ponderosa pines. Small signs identify manzanita, chinkapin, snow-brush, and other understory plants at trail side. At 0.6 mile the forest's char-acter changes suddenly and becomes cooler as you enter a grove dominated by grand fir. Round a switchback at 0.8 mile and soon the trail emerges from the trees, granting views of Mount Washington and the Three Sisters. Look for scarlet gilia, balsamroot, and other wildflowers on the open slopes here in midsummer.

The view just gets better and better—of nearby mountains as well as of the manicured fairways of the resort below. Just before climbing onto the sum-mit, the trail enters a grove of subalpine fir then passes through an old burn, evidence of the 1981 Black Butte fire. Look east to see Smith Rock (Hike 64) jutting from the high desert floor.

Once on top, you'll see a tall lookout tower and a yurt at its base; the lookout staffer cooks and sleeps there when he or she is not up in the tower watching for fires. Take a short walk to the north to see the historic 1924 cupola-style lookout tower. A sign describes the development of fire lookout facilities on Black Butte, starting with an open platform constructed between two fir trees in 1910. After you've relished the views, return as you came.

61 LITTLE THREE CREEK LAKE

BEFORE YOU GO
   MAP Bend Area Trail Map (Adventure Maps)
   CONTACT Deschutes National Forest, Sisters Ranger District
   NOTES Privy available nearby
   GPS N44° 06.104' W121° 37.346'
ABOUT THE HIKE
   SEASON July–October
   DIFFICULTY Moderate
   ROUND-TRIP 3.5-mile loop
   HIGH POINT 6710 feet
   ELEVATION GAIN 480 feet

GETTING THERE
From US Highway 20 (State Highway 126) at the north end of Sisters, turn south on Elm Street (becomes Forest Road 16, Three Creek Road). Drive 15.7

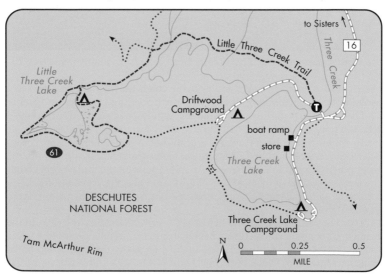

miles (the last 1.5 miles on very rough gravel road) to the sign for Driftwood Campground, and turn right; park at the trailhead just up this road. (See map for other trailheads at area campgrounds.)

ON THE TRAIL

A short drive from Sisters is Three Creek Lake, a good (and often busy) spot for primitive car camping, nonmotorized boating, and swimming in summer. A short hike from Three Creek Lake is Little Three Creek Lake, more remote and stunningly beautiful, with the rocky bluffs of Tam McArthur Rim as a backdrop. The hike is dusty and uninteresting at first; it gets better quickly. A privy is available at nearby campgrounds, though not at this trailhead.

Start up the hill, bearing left at the junction a couple of minutes up the trail. At 0.6 mile step across a tiny creek, then at

Backpacking through the piney woods near Three Creek Lake

0.8 mile cross another on a log footbridge, passing a boggy meadow on the left, one bursting with wildflowers even in late summer. At 0.9 mile, bear left at the four-way trail junction. You'll meet and follow a creek as the trail ascends to reach Little Three Creek Lake at 1.4 miles. A rough trail leads counterclockwise around the lake; to stay on this main lake loop trail, turn left here, crossing the lake's outlet on logs. (Or turn around here for a 2.8-mile out-and-back hike.)

For more hiking, after finishing your circuit of Little Three Creek Lake, at 2.3 miles you'll be back to Driftwood Campground road; go right to continue on the trail around Three Creek Lake. This larger lake is very appealing for swimming; and the sandy lakeshore is easily accessible from the trail. Big trees make this portion of the trail especially attractive on a hot day. The trail climbs well above the lake, crossing side creeks on log bridges. At 3 miles the trail ends at Three Creek Lake Campground; follow the gravel campground road 0.5 mile back to where you started. You'll pass a small store with canoe rentals near the lake's boat ramp; according to its sign, the store offers "Lotsa boats, few groceries, sum tackle, plenty bait."

62 METOLIUS RIVER

BEFORE YOU GO
MAP Pick up map in Camp Sherman store
CONTACT Deschutes National Forest, Sisters Ranger District
NOTES Privy available
GPS N44° 30.054' W121° 38.466'

ABOUT THE HIKE
SEASON April–October
DIFFICULTY Easy–moderate
ROUND-TRIP 5.4 miles out and back
HIGH POINT 2865 feet
ELEVATION GAIN Mostly flat

GETTING THERE

From Interstate 5 near Salem, exit onto State Highway 22 (US Highway 20) and follow it past Detroit Lake and over Santiam Pass a total of 98 miles. (From Sisters, drive US 20 west for 16 miles). At a sign for Camp Sherman and the Metolius River, turn onto Camp Sherman Road (Forest Road 1419) and proceed 5.6 miles, then continuing straight on FR 1420 for 3.3 miles. Turn right on FR 1420/400 toward Lower Canyon Creek Campground to a parking area and marked trailhead.

ON THE TRAIL

The magical Metolius River appears from the dry, dusty ground of Central Oregon via gushing springs that give birth to one of Oregon's most unusual streams.

The West Metolius River Trail heads through the burnt-orange ponderosa forest that characterizes this area.

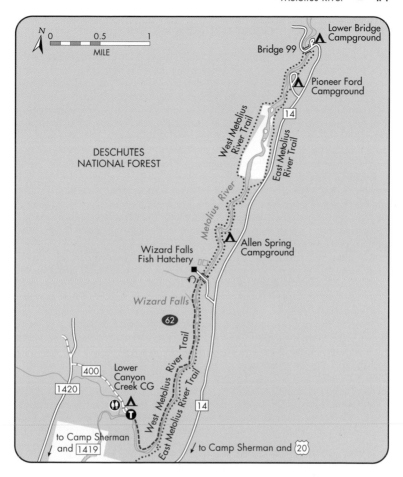

The ink-blue river rolls through burnt-orange ponderosa pine forest year-round, its flow changing little, fueled by a groundwater system below the Cascade Mountains. To witness the river's beginning, make sure to visit the head of the Metolius near Camp Sherman, a little river outpost town west of Sisters.

But for the best overall hike on a 15-mile trail system that covers both sides of the river, start at Lower Canyon Creek Campground, one of the many small campgrounds in this area. The Metolius is crowded with fly-fishermen during the summer, but this hike, best done in spring, explores a fairly quiet stretch of the river. The hike follows the West Metolius River Trail 2.7 miles to Wizard Falls Fish Hatchery and back for a tour of 5.4 miles (or shorter if you want to turn around sooner).

GREAT GETAWAY: SISTERS

A small town on the edge of the Cascade Range, Sisters could have declined with the timber industry and become like so many struggling rural towns across Oregon. Instead, Sisters rebuilt itself around tourism and recreation and has remained a thriving small town surrounded by dramatic Oregon scenery.

In 1978, the city passed an ordinance requiring 1880s-style storefronts—embracing its old West roots. While some could call it cheesy, the retrofitting gave the town an identity. Today, those old-time storefronts can be found on numerous brewpubs, family restaurants, gift shops, and novelty shops. An active family could spend a lot of time here eating, hiking, and biking.

Lodging. Plenty of hotels dot downtown Sisters, including a recently completed Best Western. Black Butte Ranch, an upscale resort with cabins, is just a short drive from town. Bed and breakfasts and vacation rentals are also numerous in Sisters on websites like Airbnb and VRBO (Vacation Rentals by Owner).

Restaurants. Downtown Sisters has most everything you could want, from upscale pub fare to locally made pizza pies.

Camping. Most people who stay in Sisters get a hotel; but there are also campgrounds on the outskirts of town. Sisters Creekside Campground is smack in the middle of town in a forested area and has a reputation for being clean and pleasant. Cold Spring and Indian Ford campgrounds are a short drive from town.

Hiking. Plenty of trails can be accessed in Sisters, including the Sisters Tie-In Trail, a forested pathway running 6 miles from Pine Street to Indian Ford Campground. The more spectacular routes are featured in this book, including Black Butte (Hike 60), Little Three Creek Lake (Hike 61) and Metolius River (Hike 62).

Fishing. Sisters is often home base for those fly-fishing the famed Metolius River. Get advice on making it happen at Fly Fisher's Palace in Sisters or at the general store in Camp Sherman.

Mountain biking. Originally created in 1989 from former Forest Service roads, the Peterson Ridge Trail system has grown to become one of the best close-to-town mountain biking experiences in Oregon. The bike trails begins in Sisters and feature 15 miles of excellent mountain biking with views of the Three Sisters, Jefferson, Black Butte, Broken Top, and Mount Bachelor. There are options for beginners to experts. Stop at one of the local bike shops to get started.

Rafting. Whitewater rafting is widely popular on the Deschutes River near Bend, and many outfitters offer trips, from one-day trips near Bend to multiday trips on the lower river.

From the small campground and trailhead, follow the trail downstream, past wildflowers in the spring and early summer, into a deep canyon. After just 0.4 mile the trail arrives at a cold spring, where water gushes into the Metolius direct from the hillside. A small beach on the side of the river invites those brave enough to dip a toe into the freezing cold water.

The river stays peaceful and pretty for the next mile or so, before the Metolius splits around a series of small islands. At mile 2.7, the trail stops at Wizard

Falls Fish Hatchery, a place where trout and salmon are born and then stocked in lakes and streams around Oregon. There are concrete display ponds where you can watch the process in action and even buy fish food to help fatten them up for a future angler.

From the hatchery, you can cross to the river's opposite side or continue downstream on the same trail. But if you're just here for a short and easy hike, turn around and head back to the car the way you came.

63 CANYON CREEK MEADOWS

BEFORE YOU GO
MAP Mount Jefferson Wilderness (Adventure Maps)
CONTACT Deschutes National Forest, Sisters Ranger District
NOTES Often crowded on summer weekends; no privy; little water
GPS N44° 29.515' W121° 47.661'

ABOUT THE HIKE
SEASON Late June–October
DIFFICULTY Moderate
ROUND-TRIP 4.5- to 5.8-mile loop
HIGH POINT 5726 feet
ELEVATION GAIN 660 feet

GETTING THERE
From Interstate 5 near Salem, exit onto State Highway 22 (US Highway 20) and follow it past Detroit Lake and over Santiam Pass a total of 95 miles. (From

Three Fingered Jack is one of the most distinctive peaks in the Cascade Range.

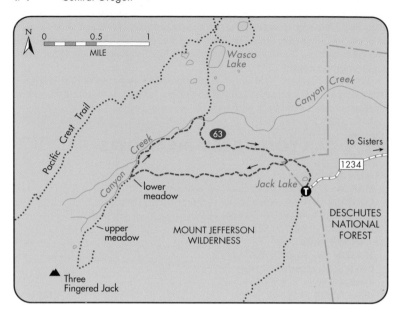

Sisters, follow US 20 west for 13.5 miles). Near milepost 88, turn north at a "wilderness trailheads" sign. Drive north 4.4 miles on paved Jack Lake Road 12, and then turn left on one-lane Forest Road 1230 for 1.6 miles to the end of pavement. Fork left onto FR 1234, for 6 miles of rough gravel to the trailhead at the primitive Jack Lake Campground.

ON THE TRAIL

There aren't many places in Oregon's Cascade Range where you can get postcard-worthy views without a difficult hike. Canyon Creek Meadows, which wanders into two alpine meadows just below Three Fingered Jack, is an exception to that rule.

This well-traveled loop features ponderosa forest, wildflowers in late July, and no shortage of spectacular mountain views. The beauty has brought major crowds, however, especially on summer weekends; a trip midweek is always the best option. Also, make sure not to step off the trail and onto the fragile meadows. The easier loop is 4.5 miles, while a slightly tougher but more rewarding trek is 5.8 miles.

The hike begins at Jack Lake, a not-particularly-amazing body of water but one with gorgeous views of Three Fingered Jack rising over it. It's your first view of a mountain that will take center stage on this trip. After an initial half mile, you'll enter the Mount Jefferson Wilderness and the trail reaches a junction that begins the loop. The Forest Service asks hikers to stay left here on the way in, making for a clockwise loop, to avoid running into other hikers head-on and forcing people to step off the trail. This gives you a good sense of how crowded the area can be.

The trail continues into forest burned by the 2003 B&B Complex Fire, but that's not such a bad thing. Fires opened views of Mount Jefferson, Mount Washington, and the Three Sisters. At the loop's upper junction, you'll arrive at the lower meadow along Canyon Creek to see Three Fingered Jack rising above like a wall of stone. In late July, the area lights up with red and purple wildflowers. Turn right and follow the loop back to your car for a 4.5-mile hike.

For the longer hiking option, and to reach the even more spectacular upper meadow, follow a wide, well-worn path toward Jack's imposing massif. In less than a mile, you'll reach even better views in the upper meadows. There are user trails all over the place, but be sure not to walk on or trample the wild meadows.

There are a couple of stories about the origin of the odd name for this 7844-foot shield volcano. The mountain was once known as Mount Marion and also Trident Peak in the 1800s, according to "Oregon Geographic Names," the authoritative source for Oregon nomenclature. At some point it was changed, perhaps in honor of a three-fingered trapper whose name was Jack.

Either way, Three Fingered Jack is one of Oregon's most striking mountains. Streaks of colored rock—red, yellow, and silver—waver across a crown of three distinct pinnacles. After you're done admiring the mountain, return to the trail's junction and turn left for the loop's return leg.

If you have energy on the way back, turn left at a junction to follow pointers to Wasco Lake. The hike to this deep blue lake is 0.7 mile (1.4 miles round-trip).

64 SMITH ROCK STATE PARK

BEFORE YOU GO
MAP Download map from park website
CONTACT Smith Rock State Park
NOTES State park day-use fee; privy available; avoid crowds by going midweek and early
GPS N44° 22.010' W121° 08.176'

ABOUT THE HIKE
SEASON Year-round
DIFFICULTY Easy or challenging
ROUND-TRIP 1.5 miles out and back or 3.6-mile loop
HIGH POINT 3320 feet
ELEVATION GAIN 180 to 840 feet

GETTING THERE
From Bend, follow US Highway 97 north 22 miles. At the sign to Smith Rock State Park, turn east and follow signs 3.2 miles to the main day-use area.

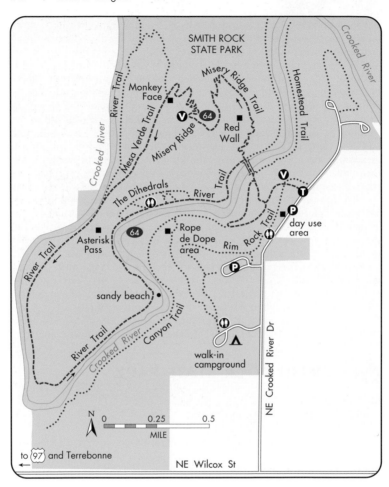

ON THE TRAIL

Smith Rock was once a destination that lured primarily rock climbers. This landscape of reddish-orange towers rising like skyscrapers from the central Oregon desert was one of the birthplaces of sport climbing, a form of climbing that relies on fixed anchors for protection. Hikers and families were in the minority, but just about everyone enjoyed the park's world-class beauty.

Dramatic changes have come to Smith Rock. The explosive growth of Bend combined with a tourism campaign labeling Smith Rock as one of Oregon's "Seven Wonders" have almost doubled the number of people visiting the park in just a few years. Oregon Parks and Recreation Department is planning changes, but as of this writing, the main issue is difficult weekend parking.

Hikers walk along the Crooked River and below the iconic rock towers at Smith Rock State Park.

If you want to hike Smith Rock, the best option is to go midweek and get an early start.

The crowds are not particularly bothersome once you're on the trail, so don't let the press of people stop you from visiting this amazing place. You can still hike along the spectacular Crooked River or plan a picnic lunch on its sandy beaches in relative solitude. With an extensive network of trails to choose from, here are two of the best options.

River Trail

This option offers an easy trek (2.2 miles and 180 feet elevation gain) with plenty of sights. Starting from the bluff at the day-use area, asphalt paths lead to a rock-walled viewpoint before descending 180 feet on either a gradual 0.3-mile trail or a steeper 0.2-mile path to a footbridge crossing the Crooked River. From here the hike is nearly level.

Look across the river for Rope de Dope Rock, a favorite spot for beginning climbers. Cross the footbridge and turn left onto the River Trail heading downstream. After another 0.4 mile, a spur route splits off uphill to the Dihedrals climbing area. A few minutes later, look up to the right to the round rock poised in Asterisk Pass. The trail narrows but continues; the sandy beach 0.9 mile from the footbridge makes a good turnaround spot. More energetic hikers could continue around to the base of the famous Monkey Face formation, or go even farther following a rough, steep path past Monkey Face to Misery Ridge.

Misery Ridge Loop

More spectacular views can be had on this route, but climbing up "Misery Ridge" is required on a loop of 3.6 miles with just under 1000 feet of challenging climbing. To start, from the bluff at the day-use area, follow asphalt paths to a rock-walled viewpoint, then hike down 180 feet in elevation to a footbridge crossing the Crooked River. From the footbridge, bear right, then immediately left away from the river and up onto Misery Ridge Trail. The trail steadily ascends the rock on a series of steps, a rickety wooden staircase, and a footpath.

Take it slow and you'll make it all the way to the aptly named ridge, just 0.5 mile but 660 feet from the river. Drop-offs are steep; keep a close eye on children. You could return as you came for a 1.5-mile hike, but since you've already done the work to get here, why not continue on? Follow the trail gradually downhill to views of Monkey Face—an iconic climbing spot that, you guessed it, looks a lot like a monkey's face. Turn left at a junction with Mesa Verde Trail and a half mile later stay left onto the River Trail. Follow this route back to the bridge and return to your car.

65 TUMALO FALLS

BEFORE YOU GO
    MAP Download map from USFS website
    CONTACT Deschutes National Forest, Bend/Fort Rock Ranger District
    NOTES USFS day-use fee; crowds are often large
    GPS N44° 01.915' W121° 33.971'
ABOUT THE HIKE
    SEASON June–October
    DIFFICULTY Ranges from easy to challenging, depending on your route
    ROUND-TRIP 0.4 to 2.0 miles out and back or 6.8-mile loop
    HIGH POINT 6040 feet
    ELEVATION GAIN 100 to 1000 feet

GETTING THERE

From the west side of Bend, head west on Galveston Avenue, which becomes Skyliners Road. Follow Skyliners Road 10 miles to gravel Forest Road 4601. Turn right and continue across Tumalo Creek on a single-lane bridge. Immediately bear left onto FR 4603. Drive 3.4 miles to Tumalo Falls picnic area.

ON THE TRAIL

Options abound at this popular recreation area home to Central Oregon's most impressive waterfall. An easy trek—good for young children—takes hikers to the top of the 80-foot Tumalo Falls on a 0.4-mile out-and-back walk with a bit of steepness. Those with more ambition can follow the trail upstream on a 2-mile hike to Double Falls, or continue on a 6.8-mile loop, passing more waterfalls and forest. This longer, steeper hike will tax most children but is a good choice for older children who like to hike and want to stretch themselves.

Tumalo Falls is one of Central Oregon's most impressive.

FUN UNDER THE SUN—SAFELY

Dermatologists now warn that sunburn on young children can be a precursor to skin cancer years later. So protecting children from sunburn in their early years does a lot to help them stay healthy as adults. Always carry and use sunscreen. Some children are allergic to PABA, the active ingredient in most sunscreens, so pediatricians suggest using a non-PABA lotion with a sun protection factor (SPF) of at least 15 to 30—particularly for skin that is very fair. Be sure to reapply sunscreen after a couple of hours.

Beyond PABA, watch out for other possibly problematic sunscreen ingredients. Vitamin A, or retinyl palmitate, has been linked to faster development of skin cancer, according to some scientists. And chemical ingredients, such as oxybenzone, have not been proven safe for frequent, repeated application to the skin. If you want to learn more, read the Environmental Working Group's analysis of sunscreen on their website. The safest approach is to cover up with hats, long sleeves, and sunglasses when your family plans to be outside for extended periods.

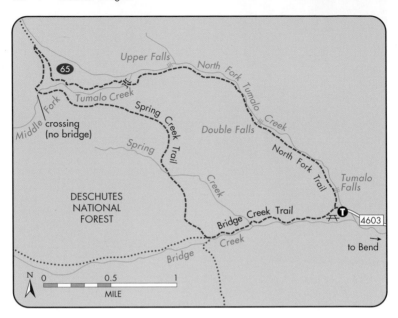

Close-in Tumalo Falls is a destination in itself: a wide cataract free falling onto a rock staircase. From the trailhead, follow signs up North Fork Trail and continue straight where Bridge Creek Trail comes in on the left. At 0.2 mile, the top of the falls, pause to take in the view from a platform cantilevered out from the cliffs.

To continue, follow North Fork Trail upstream. Tumalo Creek rushes below you as the trail gently ascends through the pines and firs. At 1 mile you'll see Double Falls, a series of two wide cascades spilling down basalt ledges into a green pool (steep drop-off; take care). Another 0.9 mile leads to Upper Falls, sliding over a steep dome of rock. Just 0.5 mile farther the trail crosses Tumalo Creek's Middle Fork on a narrow bridge—another possible turnaround or picnic spot. From here the trail steepens; and as it does, the waterfalls abound. At 3.4 miles you'll reach the junction with Spring Creek Trail; bear left to reach the Middle Fork of Tumalo Creek in another 0.3 mile.

To complete the loop, wade the creek or walk upstream a short distance to cross on a log. The Spring Creek Trail resumes across the creek, running level, then drops gently to reach a permit station (free at this writing) at the entrance to the City of Bend watershed, not quite a mile from the creek crossing. Continue dropping through forest, re-crossing Spring Creek and hiking 1 mile more to the junction with Bridge Creek Trail. At the junction, turn left and follow Bridge Creek Trail 1.3 miles alongside stair-stepping Bridge Creek back to its junction with the Tumalo Creek Trail just above the parking area.

GREAT GETAWAY: BEND AND CASCADE LAKES AREA

The outdoor tourism center of Oregon, Bend and the Cascade Lakes area overwhelm with beauty, recreation, and, increasingly, crowds. Bend is constantly listed by magazines and websites as one of those towns you simply must visit, and it's certainly true. With a beautiful downtown area highlighted by the Old Mill District and the grand Deschutes River, where people often float in inner tubes or cruise atop stand up paddleboards, Bend features more brew pubs and restaurants than you could ever want to visit.

For scenery and recreation, the Cascade Lakes Scenic Byway west of town offers a 66-mile tour of Oregon's most dramatic scenery. The highway provides access to Mount Bachelor Ski Area year-round; and in summer, it opens up a paradise of trails and lakes centered around South Sister, Broken Top, and the area's other mountains.

Lodging. There is no shortage of hotels, resorts, and vacation rentals in Bend. Just remember to make reservations well in advance for the peak of summer.

Restaurants. The culinary world has embraced Bend with a number of unique places to dine. A few favorites include The Village Baker (for breakfast), Spork, and 10 Barrel Brewing Co. (for lunch or dinner).

Around town. While in Bend, a great option with the kids is the High Desert Museum, home to indoor and outdoor activities and attractions for active kids.

Camping. Numerous campgrounds dot the Cascade Lakes Highway. Most are managed by the Deschutes National Forest and have affordable rates. A few favorites include Hosmer Lake, Soda Creek, and Cultus Lake campgrounds.

Hiking. Along with the hikes featured in this book, downtown Bend offers great options for family hiking. Nearby parks include easy and wonderful in-town treks such as South Canyon Reach, which begins at Riverbend Park or Farewell Bend Park and follows the Deschutes River Trail. Other great options just outside are Steelhead Falls, Todd Lake, and Tumalo Mountain.

Fishing. This area is probably best known for fly-fishing on the Crooked, Metolius, and Fall rivers. Inquire at local fishing shops. Many lakes are stocked with rainbow trout and offer good opportunities for family fishing.

Mountain biking. An endless number of mountain biking routes, from easy to more difficult, can be found around Bend, but the most famous and closest to the city is Phil's Trail Complex. Stop at one of the city's many bike shops for rentals, maps, and advice. Bend is a mountain biking mecca.

Rafting. The Deschutes River is the center of the watersports universe in Bend and home to everything from an artificial whitewater park to lazy and scenic float trips; contact one of the many outfitters in town for help choosing the right trip. Rentals and guided trips are not hard to find.

South Sister (left) and Broken Top loom above Sparks Lake.

66 RAY ATKESON MEMORIAL TRAIL

BEFORE YOU GO
  MAP Bend Area Trail Map (Adventure Maps)
  CONTACT Deschutes National Forest, Bend/Fort Rock Ranger District
  NOTES USFS day-use fee; wheelchair accessible for first 0.4 mile; privy available
  GPS N44° 00.78' W121° 44.210'
ABOUT THE HIKE
  SEASON Mid-June–October
  DIFFICULTY Easy–moderate
  ROUND-TRIP 1.4-mile loop
  HIGH POINT 5460
  ELEVATION GAIN 150 feet

GETTING THERE

From Bend, follow signs toward Mount Bachelor (Century Drive) and onto Cascade Lakes Scenic Byway. Drive about 26 miles into this land of volcanoes (past the turn-off to Mount Bachelor) and turn left at the sign to Sparks Lake (Forest Road 400). Stay left at a turn-off for Soda Spring Campground and continue a total of 1.6 miles to the trailhead parking area on the left, just above the boat ramp.

ON THE TRAIL

Ray Atkeson (1907–1990) was, in his day, the dean of Oregon landscape pho-tographers. He had a keen eye for the rugged beauty of places like Sparks Lake and the Three Sisters mountains. This trail is a fitting memorial to his vision and artistry and offers accessible hiking to people of all abilities.

Start up the paved trail and go only a short distance to the first junction; turn sharply right and continue on the paved trail which winds down to the edge of Sparks Lake, lined with rough lava rock and offering stunning moun-tain views of South Sister and Broken Top. Continue on the paved trail with the lake on your right (turns to dirt at 0.4 mile) to a junction at 0.7 mile; bear left to walk through a slot canyon in the basalt rock (quite narrow in places). It ends in just 0.15 mile at the "shortcut trail." Go left here to loop back through a pine forest growing out of the basalt to the start of the loop, taking the paved trail back to where you started.

If you're up for longer hike, add the Davis Canyon loop, turning right (in-stead of left) onto the shortcut trail after the slot canyon, then an immediate left

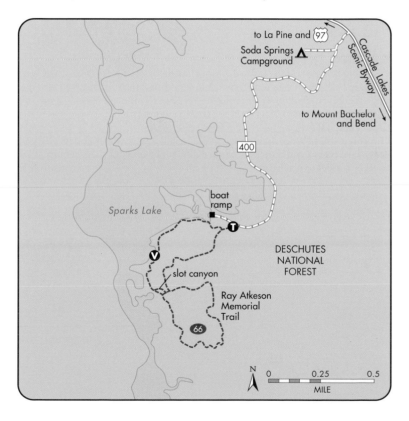

to loop back an extra 1.1 miles through Davis Canyon, ending up back at the main Ray Atkeson trail. There's a bit more up-and-down on this longer route, as it winds through basalt draws and over pine ridges, bringing your total hike distance to 2.5 miles and 350 feet elevation gain.

67 DORIS LAKE

BEFORE YOU GO
   MAP Bend Area Trail Map (Adventure Maps)
   CONTACT Deschutes National Forest, Bend/Fort Rock Ranger District
   NOTES No privy; mosquitoes abundant through July
   GPS N43° 57.205' W121° 48.162'
ABOUT THE HIKE
   SEASON July–September
   DIFFICULTY Easy–moderate
   ROUND-TRIP 4.8 miles out and back
   HIGH POINT 5320 feet
   ELEVATION GAIN 370 feet

GETTING THERE
From Bend, follow signs toward Mount Bachelor (Century Drive) and onto Cascade Lakes Scenic Byway. Drive about 33 miles, past Mount Bachelor and Elk Lake Resort, and turn right into the Six Lakes Trailhead parking area.

ON THE TRAIL
The Three Sisters Wilderness above Cascade Lakes Highway is dotted with gorgeous lake basins and hundreds of small lakes, but most of them require hikes of several miles to reach them. This hike gets you to one such lake in just 1 mile,

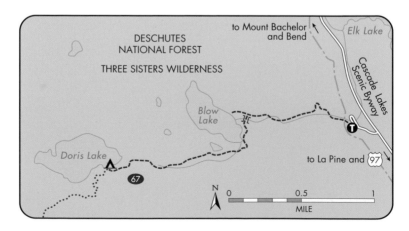

A family of backpackers pauses on the trail to Doris Lake. (Photo by Katy Siepert)

and a second—Doris Lake—in another 1.4 miles. Both lakes have small beaches that provide children the opportunity to wade or even dip into on hot days.

From the trailhead, the trail ascends very gradually through a forest of skinny lodgepole pines. After crossing Blow Lake's outlet (dry in summer) on a footbridge, watch for spur trails leading to the lake's small gravel beach.

Return to the main trail, which continues to ascend steadily but not steeply, until you see Doris Lake on your right. Follow spur trails to the lake's edge. Level spots around its perimeter offer opportunities to picnic or camp. The Pacific Crest Trail and Mink Lake Basin lie farther up the trail, but the next lake requires a few more miles of uphill hiking. Instead, return as you came.

68 LAVA RIVER CAVE

BEFORE YOU GO
   MAP Download brochure with map from monument website; map not included here
   CONTACT Newberry National Volcanic Monument, Lava Lands Visitor Center
   NOTES USFS admission fee; check website for open hours; dogs prohibited in the cave; privy available
   GPS N43° 53.733' W121° 22.179'
ABOUT THE HIKE
   SEASON May–September
   DIFFICULTY Easy–moderate
   ROUND-TRIP 2.2 miles out and back
   HIGH POINT 4500 feet
   ELEVATION GAIN 200 feet

GETTING THERE
From Bend take US Highway 97 south about 14 miles to exit 151 for Cottonwood Road. Turn left after the exit and drive through an underpass, following signs to Lava River Cave. The cave is 1 mile ahead on the left.

ON THE TRAIL
Hiking in a cave? Yes! Specifically, in a mile-long intact lava tube in Newberry National Volcanic Monument. The Forest Service opens the cave to visitors for five months each year, charging a small fee for admission (children under 12

TWO VERY DIFFERENT KINDS OF CAVES

Oregon hikers can explore two very different kinds of underground caves. The caves of Central Oregon, such as Lava River Cave (Hike 68) were formed quickly when a flow of hot lava, in this case from Newberry Volcano, began to cool and crust over. The lava inside the flow drained out, leaving an empty tube. The "river" refers to the river of lava; geologists believe no river of water ever flowed in the cave.

The caverns at Oregon Caves National Monument in southern Oregon (see Hike 114) have a completely different origin. They are marble caves formed over thousands of years by acidic water slowly seeping into an area of limestone rock, dissolving calcium carbonate (the main ingredient in limestone), and building calcite formations called stalagmites and stalagtites. If you visit the caves, notice the water present throughout them.

free) and another nominal fee for lantern rental. Take a flashlight or headlamp for a back-up light, but rent a lantern as well; you can see much more than with a flashlight, and responsible children can take turns holding the light. Be sure to wear warm clothes and closed-toe shoes; regardless of the temperature outside, the cave is always about 42 degrees Fahrenheit.

The cave is closed in winter to protect bat populations. To further protect them—in this case, from white-nose syndrome, a fungal disease that has devastated bat populations across the country—visitors are asked to not wear or bring into the cave any clothing or gear you have used in a cave or mine outside of Oregon or Washington.

Children will be awed by the whole experience: the darkness broken by the lanterns' light and the long shadows they cast, the eerie sounds of hissing lanterns and echoing voices, and just the knowledge that they're under the earth, out of touch with familiar landmarks. Some young children may find it too frightening. Adventurous types may need reminders not to wander too far from the light; it's easy to twist an ankle wandering alone in the dark. Rest assured there are no side chambers to mistakenly wander into.

A lantern helps illuminate the way through Lava River Cave. (Photo by Jeff Green)

You enter the lava tube at a point where the roof collapsed thousands of years ago, opening a path into the cave. Look back to see that the tube actually continues in the other direction (but is currently blocked off). Stairs lead down 55 steps into the cave; once on the cave floor, begin a slow descent on a rock and sand surface with a few stairs here and there. About 0.25 mile from the entrance, the lava tube crosses under the highway (don't bother listening for cars; they're a good 80 feet above you). Then at about 0.6 mile look for the Sand Garden, where dripping water has created a fantastical landscape in a field of sand that, over centuries, has slowly entered the cave. The hike through the tube ends after 1.1 miles, where sand blocks further progress.

Extend your outing with a stop at the High Desert Museum, about 5 miles north of Lava River Cave. Or stop at Lava Lands Visitor Center, 1 mile north of the exit for Lava River Cave. Learn about the area's volcanic history and get information about other points of interest in Newberry National Volcanic Monument.

69 BIG OBSIDIAN FLOW

BEFORE YOU GO
  MAP Bend Area Trail Map (Adventure Maps)
  CONTACT Newberry National Volcanic Monument, Lava Lands Visitor Center
  NOTES USFS day-use fee; requires stair-climbing; privy available
  GPS N43° 42.387' W121° 14.157'
ABOUT THE HIKE
  SEASON June–October
  DIFFICULTY Easy–moderate
  ROUND-TRIP 1.2-mile loop
  HIGH POINT 6600 feet
  ELEVATION GAIN 230 feet

BLACK GLASS AND ARROWHEADS: OBSIDIAN

Obsidian looks like what it is: black glass. It is formed when a type of volcanic lava comes in contact with water. What geologists call the Big Obsidian Flow came from the caldera between Paulina and East Lakes in Newberry Volcano about 1300 years ago, making it Central Oregon's most recent volcanic eruption. The rock under the caldera was rich in silica, the main ingredient in glass. When it melted from the heat of the earth, and later cooled, obsidian was formed. The First Peoples living in this area discovered how useful obsidian is for making cutting tools, from knives and scrapers to arrowheads. When it is fractured, the edges can be sharper than the finest steel blades. Tempting as it may be, don't pocket any obsidian souvenirs you find on a hike. It leaves less for others to enjoy (and it's against the law). Take only pictures!

GETTING THERE

About 24 miles south of Bend on US Highway 97, turn east on Forest Road 21 toward Newberry National Volcanic Monument. Follow it 15 miles, past the turn-off to Paulina Lake and the road to Little Crater Campground, to the sign to Big Obsidian Flow on your right.

ON THE TRAIL

Obsidian is a hard, dark, glassy volcanic rock. A mountain of obsidian (and pumice) is a rare thing to see. Being able to climb up onto one is even rarer, which makes this hike so compelling. At 1300 years old, Big Obsidian Flow is the youngest lava flow in Oregon. Interpretive signs provide lessons in geology for the readers in your group.

A mountain of obsidian juts above the forest near Paulina Lake.

Follow the asphalt path out of the parking area, past a picnic table, to the base of the obsidian flow. A metal staircase leads up onto the flow; from there, follow stairs cut into obsidian and, finally, a rocky path, which spits into a loop at about 0.2 mile. Either direction gets you to the trail summit, with its stellar view of Paulina Lake nestled in Newberry Crater. Loop back to the top of the stairs and return as you came.

The trailhead is a good hour's drive from Bend, so consider planning a day (or a full weekend) boating, camping, and hiking around or near Paulina and East lakes in the heart of Newberry National Volcanic Monument.

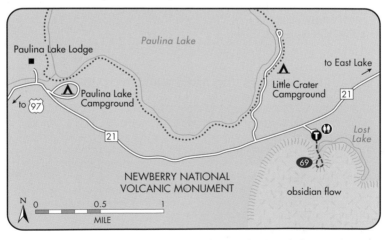

Opposite: *Hikers follow a boardwalk-style trail along Sweet Creek (Hike 73) in Oregon's Coast Range.*

COAST RANGE

Climb sevety-two steps into a replica fire lookout tower at Tillamook Forest Center.

70 TILLAMOOK FOREST CENTER

BEFORE YOU GO
    MAP Download map from center's website
    CONTACT Tillamook Forest Center
    NOTES Forest center is closed December to February, but trail remains accessible; privy at Forest Center
    GPS N45° 35.001' W123° 33.612'
ABOUT THE HIKE
    SEASON Year-round
    DIFFICULTY Easy–moderate
    ROUND-TRIP 2 miles out and back
    HIGH POINT 600 feet
    ELEVATION GAIN 250 feet

GETTING THERE
From Portland, take US Highway 26 northwest about 22 miles to the exit for State Highway 6. Follow Hwy. 6 southwest 20 miles to Tillamook Forest Center at milepost 22.

ON THE TRAIL
A series of massive forest fires devastated this part of the Coast Range in the 1930s and 1940s—hard to imagine when you drive through the lush (and well-logged) forest here today. Forest recovery and eventual resumption of logging

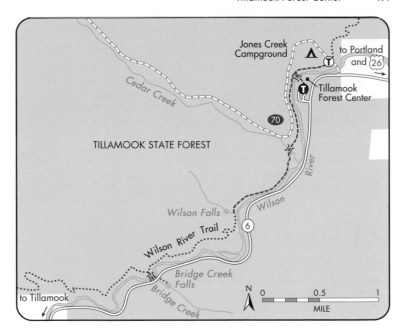

have been the management focus of Tillamook State Forest for most of the past half century; but a focus on recreation has resulted in a spreading network of trails—a boon to Portland families, who can get here in less than an hour. Coast Range winter rains are legendary, but the trails are snow-free most of the year. Look for delicate pink fawn lilies blooming in April.

Start this hike at the broad pedestrian footbridge crossing the Wilson River at the Tillamook Forest Center. Inside are lots of hands-on exhibits exploring the human and natural history of the surrounding forest. Outside are nature trails, an antique "steam donkey" once used for logging, and a replica of a 1950s-style fire lookout tower you can climb into. The bridge leads directly out from the exhibit area, crossing the river and intersecting the Wilson River Trail (which extends for several miles in both directions).

If the center is closed (see Resources for contact info and hours for the center), start your hike just upstream at the Jones Creek trailhead and walk west (downriver) about 0.5 mile to the footbridge.

From the interpretive center bridge, it's a gentle 1 mile of walking to reach the little log footbridge over Cedar Creek, a good turnaround or picturesque picnic spot. Continuing on, the trail stays close to the river, crossing a side creek with 40-foot Wilson Falls at mile 1.7. This is the suggested turnaround spot and highlight when hiking with children. There's a lot more to do: the Wilson River Trail spans 21 miles total, opening many other hiking options in this area.

FROM TILLAMOOK BURN TO TILLAMOOK FOREST

From 1933 to 1951 a series of devastating wildfires struck Oregon's northern Coast Range. The fires burned approximately every six years, taking out some 550 square miles of forest. With habitat lost, wildlife dwindled. Rivers became choked with sediment and debris. Then a huge replanting effort began. Using helicopters, professional tree planters, and hundreds of volunteers, including many schoolchildren, 72 million tree seedlings were planted. Those trees have now grown so tall that it's now hard to see evidence of the fires. What was called the Tillamook Burn for generations became, in 1973, Tillamook State Forest. Logging has resumed and, with it, debate over how best to balance the need for wood and jobs with the need to protect watersheds and forest habitat.

71 NIAGARA FALLS

BEFORE YOU GO
   MAP Siuslaw National Forest, Hebo Ranger District
   CONTACT Hebo Ranger District
   NOTES Confusing network of roads to trailhead; no privy
   GPS N45° 12.844' W123° 37.662'
ABOUT THE HIKE
   SEASON Year-round
   DIFFICULTY Moderate
   ROUND-TRIP 2.2 miles out and back
   HIGH POINT 1369 feet
   ELEVATION GAIN 450 feet

GETTING THERE

From Salem, head west on State Highway 22, toward the Oregon Coast, for 15.8 miles. Turn right on State Highway 18 and continue 1.8 miles into the town of Willamina. Turn left on Willamina Creek Road and follow it, passing Hampton Lumber Mills, a total of 6.2 miles. Turn left onto Coast Creek Road and follow it 1.3 miles. Veer right onto Gilbert Creek Road and follow it 4.1 miles, heading north. Turn left at Bible Creek Road (signed for Niagara Falls) and follow it 1.3 miles. At another Niagara Falls sign, turn left and then veer right onto gravel Forest Road 14 (the road also has a notation 4-7-21.3). Follow FR 14 a total of 3.5 miles. At a T junction, with signs for South Lake and Niagara Falls, turn right onto FR 8533 and follow it 0.6 mile. Finally, turn left onto Forest Road 131 and in 0.7 mile arrive at the trailhead and parking area on the left.

ON THE TRAIL

It would be difficult for this Niagara Falls to be any more different from its uber-famous counterpart. This version sits in a remote patch of the Coast

Niagara Falls roars in a remote patch of the Oregon Coast Range.

Range, is rarely visited, and certainly doesn't have any boat tours to its base. In fact, despite the famous name and two gorgeous waterfalls, few people in Salem visit this lush box canyon. Your family might have this trail to yourselves, which makes the pathway a real charmer.

The scenery is especially grand during the wet season when the rain has added some flow to the falls, which mostly dry up during the height of

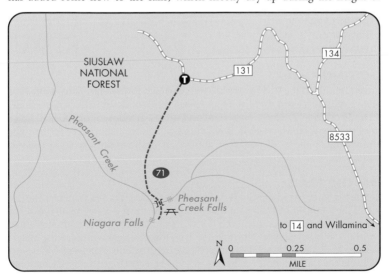

summer. You'll find trilliums here in spring and the occasional chanterelle mushroom in fall. The only downside is the drive to this remote location. From Salem, you must navigate a series of sometimes-confusing dirt and gravel roads.

From the trailhead, the trail drops gradually downhill through mossy, second-growth forest. The trail drops 450 feet, making the return hike fairly steep. You'll cross a few wooden footbridges before entering a tight box canyon where the two waterfalls reside. The first is Pheasant Creek Falls, which drops 122 feet down a thick slab of basalt. At high flows, the waterfall sprays a heavy mist onto a bridge that runs just below it and makes for a fun moment with kids who don't mind a little saturation. At low flows in midsummer this waterfall is little more than a trickle.

Around the bend is the just a little bit smaller, yet magnificent, 112-foot Niagara Falls. Niagara Falls runs year-round but, like its counterpart, gets pretty small in late summer. There's a picnic table at a small clearing that makes a pleasant spot for a picnic lunch.

72 MARYS PEAK

BEFORE YOU GO
   MAP Siuslaw National Forest, Waldport Ranger District
   CONTACT Waldport Ranger District
   NOTES Privy available
   GPS N44° 30.637' W123° 33.042'
ABOUT THE HIKE
   SEASON April–November
   DIFFICULTY Easy–moderate
   ROUND-TRIP 1.4 miles out and back; 1.6- to 3.5-mile loops
   HIGH POINT 4098 feet
   ELEVATION GAIN 340 to 660 feet

GETTING THERE
From Corvallis, take US Highway 20 west through Philomath. Turn south onto State Highway 34 and drive 10 miles to Marys Peak Road (which starts as FR 30 and becomes FR 3010). Turn right and drive 5.5 miles to the FR 3010 junction; stay right on Marys Peak Road, quickly passing a short spur to the right and staying on the main gated road another 3.5 miles to the gate at the summit parking lot.

ON THE TRAIL
As the highest peak in the Coast Range, 4097-foot Marys Peak can feel like the top of the world. For a young child new to hiking, the 0.7-mile trek to the top of the peak is a great adventure, even if it is on a gravel road. Older children may enjoy the longer, woodsier North Ridge Trail loop; all ages will enjoy the Meadowedge Trail loop. Other hikes are also possible, including one-way hikes with a shuttle car. Early summer is the best season here, with penstemon, Columbia

There's a nice viewpoint at the trailhead for Marys Peak.

lilies, lupine, and other wildflowers festooning the upper slopes. Think of visiting Marys Peak during shoulder seasons as well, when clouds sometimes swirl eerily among the noble firs and around the treeless summit.

Summit Hike

Walk the gravel road (closed to cars) leading up to the summit on a hike of 1.4 miles out-and-back with 337 feet of climbing. The route is mostly above tree line, though you'll pass through stands of Douglas fir and noble fir. Be prepared for wind on top. The communication towers on the summit are a bit ugly; but look outward and you won't feel so bad, as views on a clear day take in just about every major Cascade Peak in southern Washington and northern Oregon.

Meadowedge Trail Loop

This trail was constructed with young hikers in mind. It passes in and out of woods and meadows, keeping things interesting and varied on a hike totaling

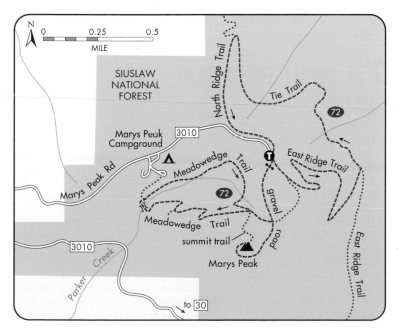

1.6 miles with 400 feet of climbing. From the gate at the main trailhead (end of the paved road), take the gravel summit road trail 0.2 mile to the signed start of Meadowedge Trail on the right. Walk the narrow path through the grassy meadow about 30 yards and enter a deep forest, where there is a trailhead sign and map.

To walk the 1.2-mile loop clockwise, go straight at the first trail junction. For the first few minutes you'll be walking just inside the forest's edge, until the trail enters a wildflower-strewn meadow. Your route loops back into the woods, which offer their own summer bouquet of bleeding hearts and oxalis. Wind down through the airy old-growth forest to a little bridge crossing Parker Creek, marking the loop's halfway point. Just beyond is the spur to Marys Peak Campground, on the left. Stay on the main trail as it climbs just inside the forest until it completes the loop, then bear left to return to the summit trail.

North Ridge Loop

The Tie Trail linking the East and North Ridge trails creates a meditative, moderately graded, woodsy loop on Marys Peak. The hike is 3.5 miles long with 660 feet of climbing. From the gate beyond the summit parking area, pick up the North Ridge Trail heading north, descending gently. After a couple of switchbacks, watch for a junction (easy to miss) with the Tie Trail, on the right at 0.7 mile. Follow it as it rolls along to the south to a more obvious junction with the East Ridge Trail at 1.8 miles. Bear right and climb the hillside switchbacks. At 3.1 miles the trail merges with a footpath leading down from the summit. Follow it back to the parking area.

73 SWEET CREEK TRAIL

BEFORE YOU GO
> **MAP** Siuslaw National Forest, Mapleton Ranger District
> **CONTACT** Mapleton Ranger District
> **NOTES** Privy available
> **GPS** N43° 57.483' W123° 54.142'

ABOUT THE HIKE
> **SEASON** Year-round
> **DIFFICULTY** Easy
> **ROUND-TRIP** 2.2 miles out and back
> **HIGH POINT** 600 feet
> **ELEVATION GAIN** 390 feet

GETTING THERE

From Florence on the Oregon Coast take Highway 126 east 14 miles to the Siuslaw River Bridge in Mapleton. At the east end of the bridge, turn south on Sweet Creek Road (County Road 48). Drive 11 miles. Park at the Homestead trailhead, on the right.

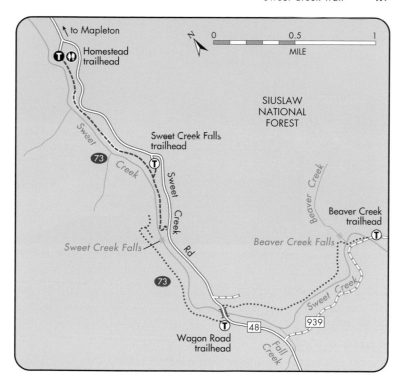

ON THE TRAIL

The wonderful thing about this sweet treat of a hike is that it works in both winter or summer. In the rainy season, the creek roars down bedrock ledges and forms eleven different waterfalls, including the main attraction, 70-foot-high Sweet Creek Falls. Even better is summer, when kids can wade into these pools and ledges and savor the sun and dappled shade of this lovable creek. Extensive boardwalks add to the fun. Sweet Creek is in the foothills of the Coast Range, about a half hour from US Highway 101.

You can access four trailheads from Sweet Creek Road (including one off gravel Forest Road 939); but most hikers start at the first one, the Homestead trailhead (the only one with a restroom). From here it's 1.1 mile up the gorge by trail to the main attraction at Sweet Creek Falls. The trail along this route from Homestead is especially appealing; where the creek gorge narrows, a railed catwalk hugs the cliff above the churning water. Spur trails on either side of the creek lead to views of water splashing down the basalt staircase. A trail climbs to an upper view of the falls as well.

If this 1.1-mile trek each way is more hike than you want, drive 0.5 mile farther up the road to the Sweet Creek Falls trailhead; the falls are just 0.5 trail

There are numerous places to stop and look around on Sweet Creek Trail in the Oregon Coast Range.

mile from here. Spur trails on either side of the creek lead to views of water splashing down the basalt staircase; and a trail climbs to an upper view of the falls as well.

OTHER HIKES

You can also start at the Wagon Road trailhead just down the road, hiking downstream on the west side of the creek for 0.8 mile one-way (1.6 miles round-trip) to Sweet Creek Falls. Wagon Road trailhead also lends access to Beaver Creek Trail, which runs 0.6 mile (1.2 miles round-trip) north to the semi-impressive Beaver Creek Falls, which is a nice, often-quiet spot to enjoy the roar of water.

74 KENTUCKY FALLS

BEFORE YOU GO
    MAP Siuslaw National Forest, Mapleton Ranger District
    CONTACT Mapleton Ranger District
    NOTES Privy available; complicated drive but well worth it
    GPS N43° 55.726' W123° 47.610'
ABOUT THE HIKE
    SEASON May–November
    DIFFICULTY Moderate–challenging
    ROUND-TRIP 4.4 miles out and back
    HIGH POINT 1560 feet
    ELEVATION GAIN 830 feet

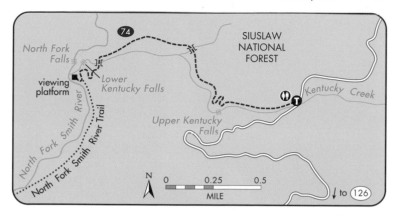

GETTING THERE

From Eugene–Springfield, take State Highway 126 west about 35 miles. Between mileposts 26 and 27, look for a sign marking the "Whitaker Creek Recreation Area" and turn left onto Siuslaw Road. Follow Siuslaw Road for 1.6 miles and turn right across a bridge over the Siuslaw River. Continue another 1.6 miles to where the road splits. Veer left at a sign for Dunn Ridge Road heading uphill, and follow it a total of 7.1 miles to where the pavement turns to gravel. Beware of logging trucks coming downhill.

At the gravel junction, turn left and follow the unmarked road 2.8 miles. You'll pass a large, open clear-cut with views across the Coast Range. Although many roads branch off, stay on the main route. At a sign for Forest Road 23, turn right and follow this rough, pothole-filled road 1.6 miles. At paved FR 919 (which is signed), turn right and follow it downhill 3.5 miles, passing a sign for Kentucky Falls Special Interest Area, to a trailhead with a parking area and privy on the right. The trail begins across the road at a trail sign.

ON THE TRAIL

Three spectacular waterfalls highlight what many consider the best short hike in Oregon's Coast Range. The problem is that the drive is long, rough, and confusing. And though the hike is open year-round, the drive from Eugene requires cresting a 2862-foot mountain, which may be blocked by snow in winter and spring, so make sure to call the Mapleton Ranger District for road conditions.

Despite the issues with reaching the trailhead, once you get there, the trip is heavenly. The hike in is easy—almost too easy—and the mostly downhill trail ends at a pair of side-by-side waterfalls at the confluence of two creeks. Winter rains swell the falls, adding to their drama.

From its start, follow the trail into gorgeous old-growth and second-growth forest, listening for bird songs and looking for wildflowers in spring. After about 0.6 mile of fairly level walking, you'll reach a viewpoint overlooking 88-foot Upper Kentucky Falls. The trail then drops quickly to the falls' base, at first following

Lower Kentucky Falls roars in the Oregon Coast Range.

Kentucky Creek then winding away from it a short distance to cross a side creek on a hand-railed log bridge at 1.4 miles. For the last 0.8 mile, the trail switchbacks steadily into the canyon, signaling to children that they're nearing the end (and that they'd better steel themselves for the return hike).

At the trail's end comes the real treat. From a wooden viewing platform covering a tangle of boulders, you can see both Lower Kentucky Falls (117 feet) and North Fork Falls (125 feet) roaring side by side. The best view is at a bench in the middle of the two creeks, but you'll need to scramble across wet rocks to reach it, so that might not be recommended with children.

It's likely you'll want to turn around here, especially given the steep hike back to the car. But families with an abundance of energy can follow the North Fork Smith River Trail downstream from the waterfalls' viewpoint through beautiful old-growth forest. It's 6.5 miles to the North Fork Trailhead, so hike as far as you please and turn around.

75 DRIFT CREEK FALLS

BEFORE YOU GO
   MAP Download from USFS website
   CONTACT Siuslaw National Forest, Hebo Ranger District
   NOTES USFS day-use fee; privy available
   GPS N44° 56.130' W123° 51.350'
ABOUT THE HIKE
   SEASON Year-round
   DIFFICULTY Moderate
   ROUND-TRIP 3.2 miles out and back
   HIGH POINT 910 feet
   ELEVATION GAIN 280 feet

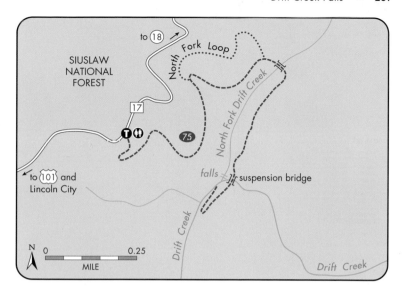

GETTING THERE

From US Highway 101 at the south end of Lincoln City, turn east just south of milepost 119 onto Drift Creek Road; follow it for 1.5 miles and bear right onto South Drift Creek Road. In 0.4 mile, veer left at the sign to Drift Creek Trail (Forest Road 17) and, in another 0.9 mile, left again. Continue following the main paved road another 9.5 miles to the trailhead parking area on the right.

From State Highway 18—usually coming from Salem or Portland—look for milepost 5 and a sign for Drift Creek Falls (near Rose Lodge). Turn south onto Bear Creek Road (which becomes FR 17). Follow the main road, bearing right at the fork at 4.6 miles and reaching the trailhead after 9 miles.

ON THE TRAIL

It's named for the dramatic waterfall that cascades 75 feet into a pool in Drift Creek. But it's the suspension bridge near the trail's end that catches the most attention on this hike. The bridge hangs between support towers 29 feet tall and is anchored to the bedrock on either side of Drift Creek. From the middle of the bridge you get a good look at the falls—if you dare; its gentle swaying motion can be a bit unnerving. It's a great hike for children with self-control and a well-developed sense of adventure—not for daredevils.

The hike to the falls descends gently, mainly through former clear-cuts now lush with second- or third-growth trees, plus a narrow band of old growth. You'll pass a wooden bench at 0.5 mile, then at 0.8 mile a junction with North Fork Loop Trail on the left. Continuing on the main trail, you'll pass the other end of North Fork Loop and, at 1 mile, cross a small footbridge over a creek. At 1.25 miles the trail reaches the suspension bridge overlooking the falls. To reach the

A suspension bridge offers a great view of Drift Creek Falls.

trail's end, cross the bridge and follow the trail's switchbacks down 0.25 mile, dropping 100 feet in elevation to the creek's edge.

Return as you came, or lengthen the hike a bit with a detour on the earlier mentioned North Fork Loop, which winds up through a magnificent stand of century-old trees. The loop ascends, steeply in places, before leveling off and dropping to meet the main trail. Follow the main trail back to where you started.

Opposite: *Geared up for a cool, rainy day on the beach at Sunset Bay State Park, Hike 94*

COAST

76 KWIS KWIS LOOP

BEFORE YOU GO
 MAP Download from park website
 CONTACT Lewis and Clark National Historical Park
 NOTES Dogs prohibited (on lower Fort to Sea Trail portion); no trailhead parking
   on Sunday mornings; privy along trail
 GPS N46° 7.155' W123° 55.377'
ABOUT THE HIKE
 SEASON Year-round
 DIFFICULTY Moderate–challenging
 ROUND-TRIP 4.6-mile loop
 HIGH POINT 370 feet
 ELEVATION GAIN 400 feet

GETTING THERE

From Astoria, drive south on US Highway 101 about 8 miles. Near milepost 12, turn west onto Patriot Way, toward Camp Rilea (Oregon National Guard), then immediately bear left toward Pioneer Presbyterian Church. Hikers are allowed to leave cars in the church parking lot except on Sunday mornings.

ON THE TRAIL

In 2006—just in time for its namesake expedition's bicentennial celebration— Lewis and Clark National Historical Park completed building the 6-mile Fort to Sea Trail. Since then there has been a flurry of additional trail building in the park, including the Kwis Kwis Trail, completed in 2014. Kwis Kwis Trail and Fort to Sea Trail meet in the middle, creating a figure-eight; the lower loop makes a fine loop hike easily accessible from US 101. Highlights include a long wooden boardwalk and a view of the ocean as Lewis and Clark's men might have seen it, on their way from their quarters at Fort Clatsop to the ocean beach.

Walk to the southeast corner of the lawn below the church to pick up the Fort to Sea Trail. Follow the asphalt path north and east, through a tunnel under US 101. In 0.4 mile you'll cross the upper Skipanon River (more of a stream here) and shortly reach a trail junction.

THE SWEET-SMELLING SKUNK CABBAGE?

You are sure to see bright yellow skunk cabbage blossoms whenever you hike past boggy areas in coastal Northwest forests in spring. They're known for their big leaves (up to five feet long!), their tall pokerlike flower stems, and, especially, their rank odor. But get down on your hands and knees to peer at the flower stem and you'll find hundreds of sweet-smelling little greenish flowers under a yellow hood. That skunk smell? It's from the leaves.

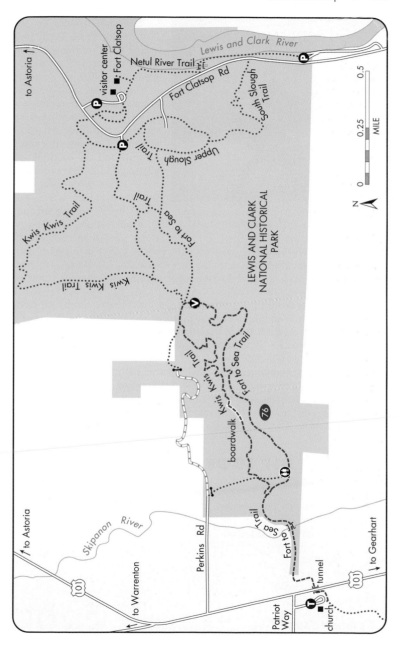

Listen for the kwis-kwis *call of the Douglas squirrel on coastal forest trails.* (Photo by Neal Maine)

Continue straight on the Fort to Sea Trail. You'll pass a vault toilet on the left. Soon the trail begins to ascend gradually, following contours of the ravines and granting glimpses of a wetland to your left, before switchbacking up a steep hillside to reach, at about 2.3 miles, the trail's summit and an overlook on Clatsop Ridge offering views to the ocean. From here continue on the Fort to Sea Trail briefly before veering left onto a continuation of Perkins Road (closed to cars). You'll pass the upper Kwis Kwis Trail on your right, shortly before turning left onto the lower Kwis Kwis Trail. (Listen for the *kwis-kwis* sound of a Douglas squirrel on a branch overhead; the trail is named after the Chinook people's name for this animal, which mimics its call.)

The trail winds down through the forest until it emerges into a lush creek valley brimming with skunk cabbage in early spring. Follow a long boardwalk through the valley. About 0.3 mile from the end of the boardwalk you'll reconnect with the Fort to Sea Trail; bear right and continue west, crossing the Skipanon River again and tunneling under US 101 to return to your starting point.

The park offers more hikes; study the park trail map. They range from the 0.9-mile (one-way) riverside walk from Netul Landing to Fort Clatsop to a one-way, 6-mile trek of the entire Fort to Sea Trail—something to keep in mind for older kids (and using a shuttle car). NPS day-use fee required for hikes starting at Fort Clatsop.

77 CLATSOP LOOP

BEFORE YOU GO
   MAP Download from park website
   CONTACT Ecola State Park
   NOTES State park day-use fee; privy available
   GPS N45° 55.867' W123° 58.707'
ABOUT THE HIKE
   SEASON Year-round
   DIFFICULTY Moderate
   ROUND-TRIP 2.7-mile loop
   HIGH POINT 800 feet
   ELEVATION GAIN 700 feet

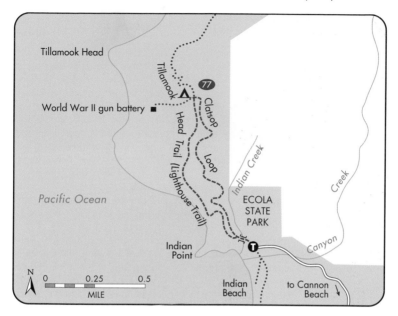

Tillamook Head

World War II gun battery ■

Tillamook Head Trail (Lighthouse Trail)

Clatsop Loop

77

Indian Creek

Pacific Ocean

ECOLA STATE PARK

Creek

Indian Point

Canyon

Indian Beach

to Cannon Beach

N

0   0.25   0.5

MILE

GETTING THERE

From the junction of US Highways 26 and 101, follow US 101 south 3 miles and take the first Cannon Beach exit. At the first stop sign, turn right, then right again in 0.2 mile onto Ecola Park Road. Follow it north 3.7 miles to the road's end at the Indian Beach parking area.

ON THE TRAIL

When you climb up Tillamook Head, in Ecola State Park, you're walking in the footsteps of the Lewis and Clark Expedition. In January 1806, during the winter they spent at Fort Clatsop (near present-day Warrenton), several members of the "Corps of Discovery" walked over Tillamook Head to the mouth of Ecola Creek (site of Cannon Beach) after hearing reports of a beached whale. They were hoping to get some blubber. What they got more of was what you'll get a lot of: amazing views. This loop hike gets you to the backpackers' camp on top of the headland

Wide and not too steep, Clatsop Loop is a good choice with very young hikers.

GREAT GETAWAY: ASTORIA

After some hard economic times, Astoria has bounced back as a hip rec-reation hub. The city is the oldest settlement of Euro-Americans west of the Rockies, and the area has been home to native people for millennia. So stop in at one of several engaging interpretive centers, then get outside for hiking, biking, and more. At mealtime, try one of Astoria's family-friendly brewpubs; you might spot a lounging sea lion through the viewing portal in the floor at riverfront Buoy Beer. Visiting journalists (beginning with Lewis and Clark) have often bad-mouthed the weather in Astoria; but summer and early fall tend to be sunny and mild, and winter and spring can surprise with dry days (and milder temperatures than in the valley).

Lodging. Every kind of lodging is available in Astoria and neighboring Warrenton. Splurge on a riverfront room, and you'll have huge ocean-going ships passing seemingly within inches (the shipping channel hugs the Columbia River's Oregon side).

Camping. Sprawling Fort Stevens State Park tucks its 470 campsites (plus yurts and deluxe cabins) in the deep forest so you don't feel crowded. Nine miles of paved bike paths wind through the forest here. Some kids will want to visit the military history area (the site was a military fort as far back as the Civil War); everyone will want to visit rusting remnants of the *Peter Iredale*, still resting where it wrecked more than a century ago. There is more camping across the river in Washington at Cape Disappointment State Park.

Bicycling. In addition to the paths at Fort Stevens, kids can bike Astoria's 5-mile Riverwalk Trail (a trolley runs on it too, if kids run out of gas) and, across the Columbia, 7-mile Ilwaco-Long Beach Discovery Trail. Both are incredibly scenic (and paved).

Historical sites. Top stops for families are the Columbia River Maritime Museum in Astoria and the replica of Fort Clatsop at Lewis and Clark National Historical Park in Warrenton. Climb to the top of the Astoria Column for the view and to launch balsawood airplanes (available at the gift shop).

There's more. For classic family fun, stop at the hardware store for a "clam gun" (a long tube for digging razor clams) to use, in season, on the long, wide ocean beach south of the Columbia. You can drive on much of this beach (a draw for some families, a safety concern for all). For a shot of adrenaline, clip in to any of the eight ziplines running through the tree canopy at High Life Adventures in Warrenton (not cheap, but fun).

and, on the return trail, offers good views of old Tillamook Rock Lighthouse in the ocean a mile off the headland.

From parking at Indian Beach, head north to the trailhead and cross Indian Creek. From here, the quickest and easiest way up is to continue straight up old Indian Creek Road. It rises at a gentle grade for 1.25 miles to a junction near a vault toilet. Make a right turn here and walk a few steps to the backpackers campsite, with its three-sided shelters and fire ring. (If you overnight here, be sure to hang your food to keep rodents from getting to it.) The Tillamook Head Trail continues north from here all the way to a trailhead at the south end of the town of Seaside (another 4.6 miles). Another trail leads west from the backpackers camp 0.2 mile to the ruins of a World War II Army radar station and gun battery, nearly obscured by vegetation.

To complete the hike, either return as you came or, back at the junction, pick up Tillamook Head Trail (also called "Lighthouse Trail" on this section) and follow it south to complete the Clatsop Loop back to Indian Beach. This trail footpath is narrower, muddier, and steeper in places than Indian Creek Road (and is a scant 0.2 mile longer) as it descends via switchbacks to the trailhead. It also has great views of the ocean and lighthouse, especially on the bottom 0.5 mile or so.

78 ECOLA CREEK FOREST RESERVE

BEFORE YOU GO
  MAP No others available
  CONTACT City of Cannon Beach
  NOTES Dogs on leash; bikes allowed on hard-surface road portions of route
  GPS N45° 53.244' W123° 56.983'
ABOUT THE HIKE
  SEASON Year-round
  DIFFICULTY Moderate
  ROUND-TRIP 3.2-mile loop
  HIGH POINT 100 feet
  ELEVATION GAIN 80 feet

GETTING THERE
From downtown Cannon Beach, take Hemlock Street south to "midtown" and turn east on Sunset Boulevard, crossing under US Highway 101. (Highway travelers exit at Sunset Boulevard south of milepost 29 and follow signs toward the RV park.) Drive Elk Creek Road east for 0.3 mile (turns to gravel) to a parking area and gate across the road.

ON THE TRAIL
Hardly anywhere on the Oregon Coast can you see huge cedars hundreds of years old—a tree of an age and size not uncommon on this coast until industrial-scale logging began

If you're lucky (and have good balance), you may be able to cross West Fork Ecola Creek on a fallen log. (Photo by Neal Maine)

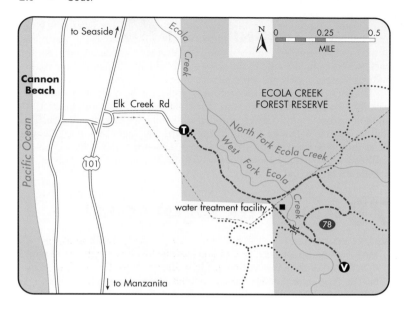

in earnest in the early twentieth century. Ecola Creek Forest Reserve, con-served by the citizens of Cannon Beach early in this century, hosts some giants. You don't need to know a lot about the importance of trees like this in a healthy coastal ecosystem to be impressed and humbled in their presence.

This route through the forested reserve follows a combination of gravel roads (used by public works employees accessing the city's water source) and dirt footpaths and requires you to wade across a shallow creek to complete the loop; if you're not up for getting your feet wet, you can do a shorter out-and-back hike to see the biggest trees. Or simply suit the family up in rubber boots!

Walk around the gate and down the road 0.6 mile through recovering forest (blown down in a December 2007 gale) and bear right at the first junction. Continue past the water treatment facility, across a bridge, and to another trail junction on the left at mile 0.9. From here the road steepens considerably and passes gorgeous ancient cedar trees, well worth the extra effort; turn around at the gravel road path's end at 1.2 miles and return to that trail junction. For an out-and-back hike, continue to retrace your steps back to the trailhead parking area from here.

Otherwise, at the ancient cedars junction, pick up the dirt footpath leading away from the road and follow it as it contours along the hillside, passing bogs filled with skunk cabbage that bloom in early spring. When this link trail ends at another old road, go left and follow it 0.5 mile, passing under a power line and alongside a cattail-filled marsh to West Fork Ecola Creek. Take off your shoes, roll up your pant legs, cross the creek, and follow the old road just 0.1 mile back to that first road junction; bear right to return to the parking area.

79 NEAHKAHNIE MOUNTAIN

BEFORE YOU GO
   MAP Download from park website
   CONTACT Oswald West State Park
   NOTES No privy; trail is narrow, rocky, and muddy in places
   GPS N45° 44.445' W123° 56.073'
ABOUT THE HIKE
   SEASON Year-round
   DIFFICULTY Moderate–challenging
   ROUND-TRIP 2.6 miles out and back
   HIGH POINT 1631 feet
   ELEVATION GAIN 890 feet

GETTING THERE

From Manzanita, drive north on US Highway 101 for 1.5 miles and turn right at the hiker sign on the east side of the road. Follow this rough gravel access road 0.5 mile to informal parking at the trailhead. From Cannon Beach, the turnoff to the trailhead access road is 13 miles south on US 101.

ON THE TRAIL

Legend has it that somewhere on Neahkahnie Mountain a treasure trove two hundred years old lies buried, waiting to be discovered. Whether or not it's true, it's a great source of speculation on a trek to the summit of this looming north coast landmark in Oswald West State Park. From the trailhead, the route ascends steadily, switchbacking up the hillside in and out of gloomy Sitka spruce stands and open hillsides thick with salal and salmonberry or, in spring, wildflowers such as the pink coast fawn lily. The fourth switchback (0.5 mile

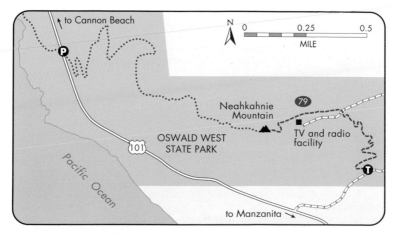

from the trailhead) offers the first of many great views. Kids may see land-marks they recognize, including US 101, the Nehalem River and Bay, and the towns of Nehalem and Wheeler.

Continue climbing the mountain's south side, up more than a dozen switchbacks, to the summit ridge at 0.9 mile, where the trail crosses a gravel road. Continue on the trail around the back of the summit ridge until, with a single switchback, it climbs over the ridge and leads to a scenic spot just below Neahkahnie's rocky crest. Scramble up to the tiptop if you like, but take care on the steep hillsides here. Return as you came.

The trail continues down the north side of Neahkahnie 2.2 miles to the trail's northern trailhead on US 101, but most hikers prefer a round-trip hike on the shorter, more scenic southern approach.

80 SHORT SAND BEACH

BEFORE YOU GO
   MAP Download from park website
   CONTACT Oswald West State Park
   NOTES Privy at trailhead and two more along beach trail
   GPS N45° 45.691′ W123° 57.472′
ABOUT THE HIKE
   SEASON Year-round
   DIFFICULTY Easy
   ROUND-TRIP 1 mile out and back
   HIGH POINT 150 feet
   ELEVATION GAIN 150 feet

Cape Falcon looms beyond Short Sand Beach.

GOOD TRAIL MANNERS

Follow these guidelines to preserve the environment and ensure a good experience for other hikers.

- Don't litter. Better yet, bring an extra plastic bag to bring out others' trash you might find.

- Don't pick anything or take shells. Leave the flowers—and for that matter, the colorful mushrooms and the hermit crabs—to live out their natural lives and to let others enjoy seeing them.

- Stay on the trail, rather than cutting across switchbacks, which leads to erosion.

- Don't camp on lakeshores or in other delicate environments.

- Keep dogs on leash if there are other hikers around—and *always* in state parks, wilderness areas, and on certain other signed trails.

GETTING THERE

From Cannon Beach, take US Highway 101 south about 10 miles. There are several trailhead parking areas along the highway; park in the second one (heading south), on the east side of the highway south of milepost 39.

ON THE TRAIL

Short Sand Beach is a favorite spot among Oregon surfers; if the waves are breaking favorably, you'll no doubt share the trail with plenty of surfers and their families. There are several routes to hike to this beach; the one described here is the most direct route.

Pick up the trail behind the restrooms. It leads through a tunnel under the highway and west down the hill following Short Sand Creek. Quickly you'll

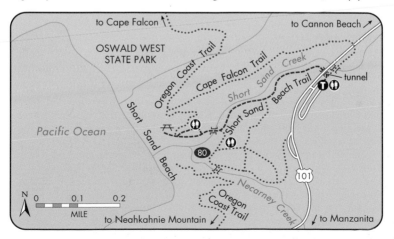

GREAT GETAWAY: THREE CAPES

A series of three prominent headlands—Cape Meares, Cape Lookout, and Cape Kiwanda—march down the shoreline west and south of Tillamook. Here you'll find a lighthouse, a wildlife refuge, long sand spits, and lots of trails. US Highway 101 swings away from the coast here; the towns are small, the views huge.

Lodging and camping. Lodging is available in the small towns that characterize this coast, but we recommend camping. Cape Lookout State Park is the big campground in this area. Most of its 205 campsites are tent sites with no RV hookups; it also offers yurts and deluxe cabins. The beach is just steps from your tent; head north to explore 5-mile-long Netarts Spit. Whalen Island County Campground, in the middle of Sand Island, is tiny, rustic, and perfect for families; walk from your campsite to Hike 82 around Whalen Island. Webb County Campground is less attractive but has great access to the action at Cape Kiwanda (more appealing for RVs than tents).

Bicycling. Bayocean Spit, enclosing Tillamook Bay, has a compressed gravel trail that's pleasant to walk and even more fun to bicycle—just a little ways, or all the way to the end.

On the water. Kayak Tillamook offers a wide variety of guided kayak trips in the rivers, sloughs, and bays of this region. Get out on the quiet Nestucca River in Pacific City on a rental paddleboard or kayak from kid-friendly Nestucca Adventures.

Cape by cape. Admire or even take a tour inside Cape Meares Lighthouse, and stand at the clifftop viewpoint here for amazing views of birds (even without binoculars). Even short legs can manage the short hikes to a huge Sitka spruce (possibly Oregon's largest) and the weird and wonderful Octopus Tree. The hike out Cape Lookout (Hike 81) is grand. A trail starting at the same trailhead leads down to the remote beach south of the cape.

Unlike the other two basalt headlands, Cape Kiwanda is made of golden sandstone that glows late in the day. You can hike up and over the sandy neck of the cape, but keep kids away from the cliffs above the ocean (it's fenced off for good reason). In summer watch the dory boats launch and return from the beach south of the cape—or find a charter boat outfit and arrange to go out with one yourself to fish for rock cod just offshore.

start encountering some really big trees: ancient cedars with wonderfully complex canopies, cedars of the kind that used to dominate this coastline. You will be walking in the temperate rainforest: that much will be obvious from the lush vegetation (if it's not actually raining).

The first trail junction is in 0.2 mile; bear right to stay on Short Sand Beach Trail. Bear right again at 0.4 mile, crossing over Short Sand Creek. Continue a short distance through a picnic area (with restrooms) under the trees and down to the beach. The ocean beyond this 0.5-mile stretch of sand is conserved as Cape Falcon Shoreside Protected Area and Marine Reserve, one of six such marine reserves off the Oregon Coast. These are areas where fishing and harvesting of shellfish or other marine resources is prohibited or strictly limited to ensure the health of the plants and animals that live in the near-shore ocean.

Return as you came, or take a detour on the network of paths between Short Sand and Necarney creeks to see more giant cedars, babbling streams, and wooden footbridges.

81 CAPE LOOKOUT

BEFORE YOU GO
    MAP Download map from park website
    CONTACT Cape Lookout State Park
    NOTES Privy available; trail drops off steeply in places
    GPS N45° 20.483' W123° 58.476'
ABOUT THE HIKE
    SEASON Year-round
    DIFFICULTY Moderate–challenging
    ROUND-TRIP 5 miles out and back
    HIGH POINT 850 feet
    ELEVATION GAIN 530 feet

GETTING THERE

From Tillamook, follow signs west and south 10 miles toward Three Capes Scenic Route and Cape Lookout State Park. Pass the park's campground entrance and continue 2.8 miles farther to the trailhead parking area, on your right. Alternately, from Pacific City follow Three Capes Scenic Route north 13 miles to the trailhead.

The Cape Lookout Trail frequently breaks out of the forest for sweeping ocean views.

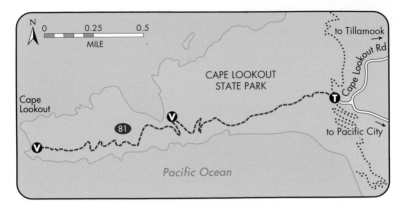

ON THE TRAIL

One appeal of a hike to the tip of Cape Lookout, in the state park named for it, is the chance to spot whales—motivation enough for some children. Cape Lookout is one of the best whale-watching sites on the Oregon Coast, and with more than two hundred gray whales now summering off Oregon, the chances of spotting a whale in midsummer aren't bad. Unfortunately, the best times are when the trail is at its muddiest: mid-March, during the northward migration, and December through early January, when the migrants are headed south to Baja for the winter. At those times, an average of fifteen to thirty whales may pass by in an hour. Bring binoculars if you have them, just in case.

Even if you don't spy whales, the hike itself is worthwhile for older kids who can go the distance and be counted on to behave where the trail drops off steeply. Take it slow and easy, enjoying the views and the forest along the way. After the hike, drive south to Pacific City and look north at the long headland sticking way out from the mainland to see what you have just accomplished.

Two trails start side by side at the west end of the parking area. The trail on the right leads north 2.5 miles to the park's campground. Instead, take the left-hand trail. In about 75 yards go straight where another trail comes in from the left (it leads 1.8 miles down to the beach).

The terrain that the trail follows to the cape tip is rolling, but mostly slowly descending. At 0.6 mile the forest opens up to grand views of the beach and headlands to the south. At 1.2 miles—about the halfway point—the trail reaches a fenced cliff on the north side of the cape, granting views of Oceanside and Three Arch Rocks. From here the trail's condition deteriorates for a while, with mud and tangled roots underfoot (it's scheduled to be improved in 2018). The route winds back to the cape's south side, teasing hikers on with occasional views. A single strand of wire cable strung along the cliff does little more than warn hikers to take care; it won't keep a child from falling, so take great care here. The trail ends at an opening at the tip of the cape. Perch on rocks to enjoy the view or picnic; plan to linger awhile if you want to spot any whales, as the whales travel on their own schedule. Return as you came.

FOR CLOTHES, CANOES, AND CURES: SITKA SPRUCE

Sitka spruce could be considered the signature tree of the Oregon Coast. Not because it is the tallest tree on the coast (though it nearly is), or the longest living (it's not). It is simply the most coastal of Oregon's trees, growing exclusively within a few miles of the ocean shore and the lower Columbia River. Identify it by its cones, scattered on the ground; they're 3 to 4 inches long, like Douglas fir cones, but lighter in color, with thin, papery scales and without bracts sticking out between the scales. Or identify it by touching the needles; they are quite stiff and prickly.

If you take a hike on an Oregon coastal headland, the forest you pass through will almost certainly include or be dominated by Sitka spruce. Coastal natives wove spruce's long, sinewy roots into baskets, rain hats, and ropes for whaling; used its pitch to caulk whaling canoes; and brewed its inner bark into a tea to soothe sore throats. Its strong, resilient, lightweight wood was used to build airplanes during World War I and has long been a favored wood for making guitars.

Currently the largest-known Sitka spruce in Oregon is at the end of the short Big Spruce Trail, just inside the entrance to Cape Meares State Scenic Viewpoint, west of Tillamook and north of Cape Lookout. But it won't be Number One for long; its core is deeply decayed, helping to ready it for its next role in the coastal forest's cycle of life.

82 WHALEN ISLAND

BEFORE YOU GO
   MAP See map posted at trailhead
   CONTACT Clay Myers State Natural Area at Whalen Island
   NOTES Short portion of path is wheelchair-accessible; privy available
   GPS N45° 16.402' W123° 57.009'
ABOUT THE HIKE
   SEASON Year-round
   DIFFICULTY Easy
   ROUND-TRIP 1.5-mile loop
   HIGH POINT 30 feet
   ELEVATION GAIN 100 feet

GETTING THERE

From the stoplight in the middle of Pacific City, turn west, following signs to Three Capes Loop. Cross the river and turn north (becomes Sandlake Road). Drive 5.5 miles total from Pacific City to the sign to Whalen Island. Turn left, cross the bridge over the estuary, and bear right into Clay Myers State Natural Area at Whalen Island (a left turn leads to the adjacent county park).

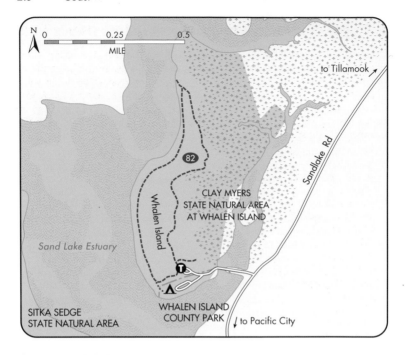

ON THE TRAIL

Sand Lake is really a shallow estuary—a place where freshwater and saltwater meet, nurturing a wide variety of marine plants and animals from clams to salmon. In the middle of it is mile-long Whalen Island, which is really an upland (isolated as an island only at high tide), densely forested in the middle and descending to tidal mudflats all around. The trail that circles the island just above the high tide line takes you through a variety of habitats, to glimpses of the estuary and to the sandy beach on the island's west side. Adjacent Whalen Island County Park is a small, rustic campground perfect for families (to reserve, see Resources: Tillamook County campground reservations).

A sandy spur off Whalen Island Trail leads to views of the estuary.

From the parking area, take the trail north, bearing left where a spur trail on the right leads to an overlook at the edge of the estuary. The main trail stays just inside the forest's edge most of the way, rolling up and down and rising toward the island's north end, where views open up of the water and hills to the north. The trail then curves south, following the island's ocean side and offering opportunities to detour onto the narrow sandy beach here, especially at the island's south end. Nearing the trailhead, the loop trail meets the gravel wheelchair-accessible path from the parking lot at a viewpoint overlooking Sand Lake. Follow it back to the parking lot, bearing left at the spur trail leading to the county park campground.

83 SITKA SEDGE

BEFORE YOU GO
    MAP Download from state parks website
    CONTACT Sitka Sedge State Natural Area
    NOTES Wheelchair accessible (compacted gravel) for at least 0.3 mile; privy available
    GPS N45° 15.782' W123° 57.234'

ABOUT THE HIKE
    SEASON Year-round
    DIFFICULTY Easy–moderate
    ROUND-TRIP 2.5-mile loop
    HIGH POINT 20 feet
    ELEVATION GAIN 120 feet

GETTING THERE

From the stoplight in the middle of Pacific City, turn west, following signs to Three Capes Loop. Cross the river and turn north (becomes Sandlake Road). Drive 4.8 miles total from Pacific City to the gravel parking area for Sitka Sedge State Natural Area, on the west side of the road.

Views of Sand Lake from the Sitka Sedge trails are lovely in any season.

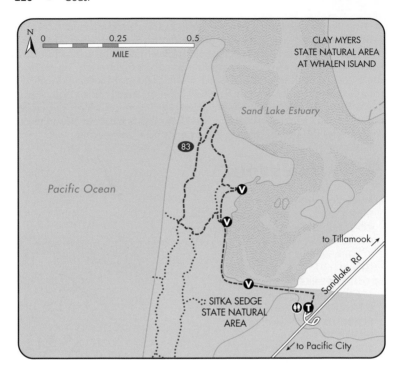

ON THE TRAIL

In 2015 Oregon State Parks acquired a large (357 acres) property on the southern edge of the Sand Lake estuary known as Beltz Farm, for the family that owned it. It had been a target for development into a golf course, but that plan was strongly opposed by locals in the nearby communities of Tierra Del Mar and Tillamook, and the gridlock eventually opened the door for it to become a state park.

One of the reasons it made an attractive state park was minimal development. Other than dikes built to keep out seawater and enable farming, the property was largely intact, allowing for a beautiful hike through wetlands and out to 1 mile of beachfront. The dikes are now the entry point to a trail system leading out to the beach and estuary, through sand dunes and coastal forests of Sitka spruce and shore pine. At certain times of year you're likely to see a variety of waterfowl in the estuary—even otters and elk, if you're very quiet (and lucky).

From the parking area, pick up the trail leading north briefly before turning left and following the dike west and north along the water's edge. Continue 0.9 mile to the first trail junction; bear right for 0.1 mile (including a sharp veer in the trail to the left) and then right again at the next junction. You'll leave the estuary and wind deep into the forest until, at about 1 mile, reaching another junction; turn right. The trail ends at a sandy beach near the mouth of the estuary just 0.2 mile ahead. From here you can follow the shore to the left to quickly reach the ocean beach.

To loop back, return to the main trail and walk south on the trail through the dunes 0.5 mile to a four-way junction; turn left here, then left again, winding through the forest and emerging at the salt marsh at the estuary's edge. Bear right at the next two trail junctions to get back on the compacted gravel path on the dike and return to the parking area.

84 CASCADE HEAD

BEFORE YOU GO
> **MAP** Download from Siuslaw National Forest website (Search: "Cascade Head")
> **CONTACT** The Nature Conservancy
> **NOTES** Dogs prohibited; privy available
> **GPS** N45° 02.518' W123° 59.537'

ABOUT THE HIKE
> **SEASON** Year-round
> **DIFFICULTY** Moderate–challenging
> **ROUND-TRIP** 2 or 4.6 miles out and back
> **HIGH POINT** 330 feet
> **ELEVATION GAIN** 100 to 270 feet

The viewpoint on Cascade Head Trail is often above the coastal fog.

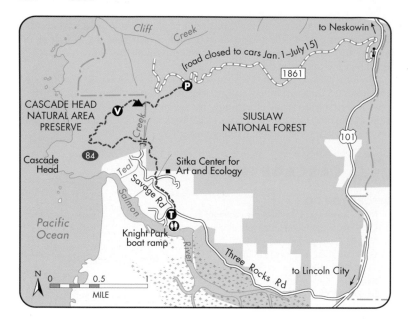

GETTING THERE

Lower trailhead: From the junction of State Highway 18 and US Highway 101, take US 101 north 1.3 miles and turn west onto Three Rocks Road. Follow it 2.5 miles; just past Savage Road on the right, turn left into the parking area for Knight Park boat landing.

Upper trailhead: From the junction of Hwy. 18 and US 101, take US 101 north 1.3 miles for 3.7 miles. Keep an eye out as you head uphill on US 101 for Forest Road 1861 on the left. Turn onto FR 1861 (closed Jan. 1 to July 15) and follow it 3.2 miles to the Nature Conservancy Trailhead on the left.

ON THE TRAIL

The hike to the grassy tip of Cascade Head traverses lovely woods and crosses boisterous creeks. But it's the view in a meadow at the end—of the Salmon River estuary and coastline to the south—that makes this hike so memorable. A visit late or early in the day may reward hikers with views of deer grazing on the headland's open slopes.

There are two possible ways to experience this area—from upper and lower trailheads. From the lower trailhead, the hike is beautiful and reaches a nice viewpoint but stops short of the summit (unless you want to climb a total of 1300 feet). From the upper trailhead off gravel FR 1861, which is open July 16 to December 31, it's a lot easier at just 2 miles out and back.

GREAT GETAWAY: NEWPORT

Base a nature-focused family vacation in Newport, on the north-central coast, and it will take more than a long weekend to fit in everything. Whatever your kids' ages, you'll find plenty to keep you busy, from a visit to one of the country's leading aquariums to whale-watching boat trips and trails galore.

Lodging. Options range from big hotels on the beachfront or bayfront to motels a short walk from the Oregon Coast Aquarium.

Camping. South Beach State Park sprawls in the dunes just south of Yaquina Bay Bridge. Its nearly 300 campsites and 27 yurts can be reserved. A tents-only area is open seasonally. State parks plans to build a campground at Brian Booth State Park, ten minutes to the south, but probably not before 2020.

On the water. Beaver Creek at Brian Booth State Park offers easy, flatwater kayaking and canoeing into a large freshwater marsh; bring your own boat, or join a guided kayak trip led by state park rangers (all equipment provided; check online for reservations). For an open-ocean adventure, watch for whales, dolphins, and seabirds on a nature-oriented charter boat trip; look online for outfitters operating out of Newport or Depoe Bay, a short drive to the north.

Interpretive centers. Newport has three. Best known (and most expensive) is the stellar Oregon Coast Aquarium, with its columns of otherworldly jellyfish, walk-through tank with sharks and rays, and outdoor exhibits featuring sea otters and other local marine life. Just down the street is Hatfield Marine Science Center; its public wing has exhibits about ocean research accessible to both kids and adults (no admission fee; donations accepted).

Drive north, across the Yaquina Bay Bridge to the north end of town, to reach Yaquina Head Outstanding Natural Area; the entrance fee includes admission to the small but worthwhile interpretive center tucked in an old gravel quarry. But don't stop there; head to the end of the road to see the lighthouse and the offshore rocks crowded with breeding seabirds in spring and summer. The view from the cliffs here is magnificent; follow trails up the headland for even grander views.

Bicycling. Make South Beach State Park your base, and you can easily bike (on paved paths) to the beach, the south jetty, and even (on side roads) to the aquarium and marine science center.

Year-Round Hike

The most popular trail on Cascade Head is the southern route from the lower trailhead to the headland's tip, which passes through a 300-acre preserve owned and managed by the Nature Conservancy since 1966. Though the preserve is open to the public, the conservancy is rightfully protective of this seaside gem. Be extra careful to leave no trace here. In addition to using ordinary trail etiquette (don't litter, don't pick any vegetation), leave your dog at home and walk only on the trail. Certainly don't camp or build a fire on the headland.

From Knight Park, walk back up Three Rocks Road to Savage Road, as you go watching for a boardwalk on the right signaling the start of a little access trail. Follow it 0.4 mile to the Sitka Center road and continue on Savage Road a short distance to resumption of the trail. It ascends a hillside steeply for 0.5 mile, then levels off, crossing several small creeks on wooden footbridges and boardwalks. Gently ascending, the trail follows the hillside's contours through the forest, emerging onto the open prairie a short walk from the south viewpoint at 2.3 miles.

Return as you came, unless you're in the mood for some anaerobic exercise in the form of a steep climb to the summit knoll, another 0.7 mile and 880 feet straight up. The trail continues another mile to the north trailhead (3.5 miles one way), accessible from Forest Road 1861 (closed to cars January through mid-July).

Upper Trailhead Route

The upper trailhead allows you to enjoy the spectacular summit point without all the bother of an uphill climb. From the trailhead on FR 1861, the trail traverses a shady forest before emerging after just 1 mile at an upper viewpoint in a meadow and epic summit view.

85 MIKE MILLER PARK

BEFORE YOU GO
　　MAP Download map from county website
　　CONTACT Lincoln County Parks
　　NOTES Kid-tailored interpretive trail; no privy
　　GPS N44° 36.137'' W124° 03.143'
ABOUT THE HIKE
　　SEASON Year-round
　　DIFFICULTY Easy
　　ROUND-TRIP 1-mile loop
　　HIGH POINT 150 feet
　　ELEVATION GAIN 120 feet

GETTING THERE

From Yaquina Bay Bridge at Newport, follow US Highway 101 south 1.2 miles and turn east on Southeast 50th Street at the sign to the trail, just north of the entrance to South Beach State Park. The trailhead is on the left 0.2 mile ahead, where the road curves to the right; there is room for several cars to park on the trailhead side of the road.

ON THE TRAIL

This short loop trail in Mike Miller Educational Park was specifically designed for kids—to introduce Lincoln County schoolchildren to a variety of coastal forest habitats, including some examples of mature trees, with huge stumps

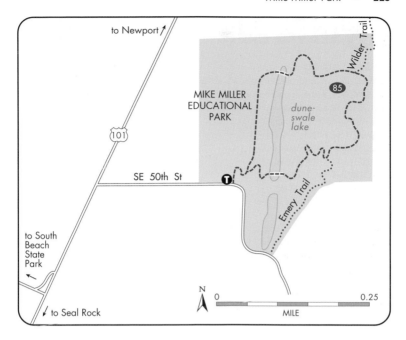

from long-ago logging and trees downed by the wind. It makes a pleasant, easy, forested loop hike close to the beach (and out of the wind, if it's a breezy day).

From the road, follow the trail uphill a short distance to where it splits into a loop; bearing left, the trail follows an old railroad bed for 0.2 mile, then veers right and descends to cross the end of a long, dune-swale lake on a wooden boardwalk. It climbs back up through a Sitka spruce forest, reaching a trail junction at 0.5 mile near where the trail crests. Bear right, wind down through the forest, passing another trail junction at 0.7 mile. Stay right on the main trail as it continues to descend, eventually recrossing the same long lake, but at its south end, on a long footbridge. Bear left at the next junction to return to the trailhead.

The Mike Miller Trail crosses this dune swale lake twice.

86 BEAVER CREEK

BEFORE YOU GO
　MAP Download from state parks website
　CONTACT Brian Booth State Park (Beaver Creek)
　NOTES Dogs on leash; privy available
　GPS N44° 30.136' W124° 02.515'
ABOUT THE HIKE
　SEASON Year-round
　DIFFICULTY Moderate
　ROUND-TRIP 2.7-mile loop
　HIGH POINT 280 feet
　ELEVATION GAIN 320 feet

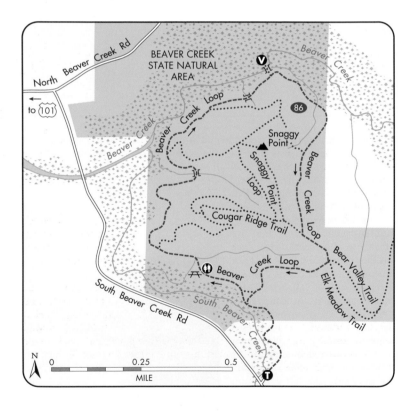

GETTING THERE

Watch for signs to Beaver Creek State Natural Area (part of Brian Booth State Park) between Waldport and Newport on US Highway 101; turn east on North Beaver Creek Road directly west of Ona Beach Day-Use Area. Follow North Beaver Creek Road 1 mile, turn right on South Beaver Creek Road, and continue 1 mile to a wide turnout on the right with room for about five cars across the road from a gated service road.

ON THE TRAIL

Beaver Creek meanders through a huge freshwater marsh before emptying into the ocean at Ona Beach, south of Newport; state park rangers offer guided kayak trips here in summer. Or hike the marsh! A forested hill rises in the middle of it. Old roads are linked with footpaths to create an elaborate trail network on this rise. Stick to the main trail for this simple loop hike, or branch off on connector trails for more exploring (and views).

A young tree takes root in an old snag along the Beaver Creek trail system.

Begin by walking around the gate and following the road 0.3 mile to where it splits and rises to meet Beaver Creek Loop. For a clockwise walk, bear left; you'll quickly reach an open barn that's been converted to a covered picnic shelter (with toilet). Continue along this perimeter trail as it circumnavigates Snaggy Point, bearing left at (nearly) all trail junctions.

At about 1.4 miles you'll pass a spur leading left to a planked footbridge over the main fork of Beaver Creek. Sticking to the main trail, you'll soon start to ascend more than 100 feet to a junction with Cougar Ridge Trail at 1.9 miles; bear left here (or bear right, and right again, for a 0.25-mile detour, there and back again, to a big view from the top of Snaggy Point). Back on the main trail, bear right at the next junction, with Elk Meadow and Bear Valley trails. In 0.4 mile more, bear left at the junction to return to the service road and your car.

87 YACHATS 804 TRAIL

BEFORE YOU GO
   MAP See map below; no others available
   CONTACT Smelt Sands State Recreation Site
   NOTES Don't walk on or climb offshore rocks; privy available
   GPS N44° 19.344' W124° 06.376'
ABOUT THE HIKE
   SEASON Year-round
   DIFFICULTY Easy
   ROUND-TRIP 1.6 miles out and back
   HIGH POINT 10 feet
   ELEVATION GAIN 25 feet

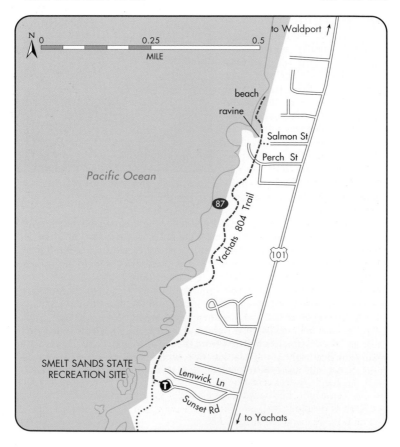

Yachats 804 Trail hugs the rocky shoreline north of Yachats.

GETTING THERE

From US Highway 101, at the north end of the town of Yachats between mileposts 163 and 164, turn west at the sign to Smelt Sands State Recreation Site.

ON THE TRAIL

This trail's rather odd name reflects the county right-of-way upon which it is built: it was set aside for a road that was never built, and thanks to community trail activists, it eventually became a public-access foot trail following the wave-sculpted sandstone bluff at Smelts Sands. It's a dramatic spot, with water crashing on the rocks and shooting up through blowholes at high tide. But stick to the trail; a recent tragedy memorialized in a sculpture at the site reminds us that the rocks and surf that pounds them are treacherous.

From the parking area, walk west and then north on the compacted-gravel trail. The route follows the bluff, then enters a stand of shore pines and skirts a narrow chasm at 0.4 mile. After crossing Perch Street it descends into a short, slippery ravine leading to the beach at 0.8 mile. Return as you came, or enjoy more of this very long beach stretching more than 4 miles north to Waldport.

Smelt Sands State Recreation Site is named for the little silvery fish that used to come ashore to spawn here every spring in huge numbers. However, the smelt population has diminished to the point that the fish are now protected under the Endangered Species Act.

88 GIANT SPRUCE

BEFORE YOU GO
MAP Download from scenic area website
CONTACT Cape Perpetua Visitor Center
NOTES USFS day-use fee; privy available
GPS N44° 16.852' W124° 06.499'

ABOUT THE HIKE
SEASON Year-round
DIFFICULTY Easy–moderate
ROUND-TRIP 2 miles out and back
HIGH POINT 290 feet
ELEVATION GAIN 140 feet

GETTING THERE
From Yachats, drive south about 3 miles on US Highway 101. Turn east at the sign to the Cape Perpetua Interpretive Center.

ON THE TRAIL
From a sweet cove beach with blowholes and tide pools at either end to the steep, forested headland towering above, Cape Perpetua Scenic Area offers plenty of options to hikers of all ages. The Giant Spruce Trail is a good one to

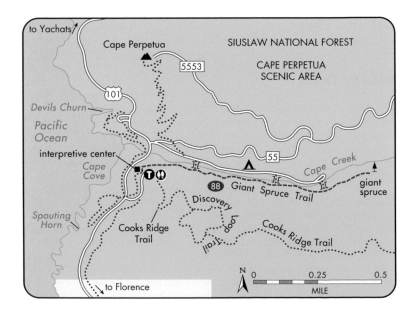

GREAT GETAWAY: CAPE PERPETUA AND HECETA HEAD

A whole bunch of hiking trails are clustered on dramatic, side-by-side headlands on the central coast, and you can hike right from your campsite at
either of two public campgrounds. Plus there's a lot to do besides hiking—like,
hanging out on the sandy beach or watching water explode through blowholes
where the coastline is rockier. Stop in at Cape Perpetua Interpretive Center for
more ideas, guidebooks, and—during spring and winter break—help spotting
gray whales during their annual migrations.

Lodging. Get a motel room in or near Yachats; there are plenty of options at
various price ranges, as well as family-friendly eateries. Florence is a little farther
away but offers more choices.

Camping. Carl G. Washburne Memorial State Park, tucked in the forest on
the east side of US 101, has one of the smaller state park campgrounds on the
coast. Most of its roughly fifty campsites offer full hookups but can't be reserved
in advance; two yurts can be. It also has seven walk-in tent sites, available May–
September. It's not right on the beach, but trails lead a short distance from campground to beach. It is open year-round.

Cape Perpetua Scenic Area also has a woodsy campground; it, too, is east of
the highway with trails leading to the (rockier) coastline. No showers (as in state
park campgrounds), but it has flush toilets. It is open mid-March through September, and campsites can be reserved in advance through reserveamerica.com.

Short hike highlights. In addition to the nearby hikes mentioned in this book,
there are loads of fun, short treks families can take here, including:

Hobbit Beach, a favorite among local families, is at the end of a 0.5-mile trail;
trailhead is shared with China Creek Trail (Hike 89).

Devils Churn is off the Restless Waters Trail at Cape Perpetua; time your visit to
high tide for maximum splash!

More high-tide attractions lie along Cape Perpetua's Captain Cook Trail, such
as Spouting Horn.

The 0.25-mile Whispering Spruce Overlook Trail at the top of Cape Perpetua
leads to a rock shelter built in 1933 and used as a Coast Guard lookout during
World War II.

Mountain biking. Most of the trails at Cape Perpetua are closed to mountain biking; Cummins Creek Trail is the exception. If you can arrange a shuttle,
drive to the top and enjoy an all-downhill single-track ride (doable for most kids
experienced with this kind of riding). Get driving directions at Cape Perpetua
Interpretive Center.

start with—easy and not too long. Stop in at the interpretive center for other
suggestions, ranging from quick-and-easy to all-day.

The destination at the end of this hike is a 500-year-old Sitka spruce that
kids can crawl under, thanks apparently to its having sprouted on a nurse log
that's long since decayed and disappeared, leaving it perched on roots that
look like legs. From the interpretive center, follow signs onto a paved path

heading downhill 0.2 mile to the north, toward a footbridge across Cape Creek. Rather than crossing the bridge, however, take a right and follow the trail east. It passes two more footbridges (leading into Cape Perpetua Campground) before reaching the giant spruce at the trail's end. The famed tree is about 15 feet in diameter and was 225 feet tall—until a 1962 windstorm snapped off its upper 35 feet. Return as you came.

Cape Perpetua Scenic Area is full of short hikes of all kinds. From the interpretive center, walk to the top of the parking loop and get on the Cooks Ridge Trail, then walk the Discovery Loop and return to the parking area for

One of the many giant Sitka spruces along the trail above Cape Creek

a 2-mile forest hike. Or follow trails down to the shoreline to walk to the Spouting Horn or Devils Churn, or both; these rock formations channel incoming waves into explosions of seawater, most dramatically at high tide. A round-trip walk taking in both amounts to 1.3 miles.

SHELL MIDDENS: CLUES TO OREGON'S FIRST PEOPLE

On some beaches, such as the beach at Cape Perpetua, you may come across eroding bluffs that seem to be made not of sand or rock but of shells. These are probably middens, or refuse heaps left by long-ago inhabitants. By studying middens, archaeologists glean clues about the lives of people who lived on the Oregon Coast in prehistoric times. Identification of the shells and bones in a midden reveals some of the foods people ate. Sometimes scientists find objects of daily living such as discarded tools made from stone, shell, and bone. By analyzing the size of middens, they gain clues to how long people occupied the site. The oldest known human settlement on the Oregon Coast, in Boardman State Scenic Corridor north of Brookings, is about 10,000 years old, but rising sea levels after the end of the last ice age would have wiped out the very earliest settlements on the coast of North America. Archaeologists are confident that people have been living on the Oregon Coast for at least 15,000 years—and maybe thousands of years longer.

89 CHINA CREEK

BEFORE YOU GO
  MAP Download from state parks website
  CONTACT Carl G. Washburne Memorial State Park
  NOTES Privies nearby in park campground and day-use area
  GPS N44° 08.603' W124° 07.060'
ABOUT THE HIKE
  SEASON Year-round
  DIFFICULTY Moderate
  ROUND-TRIP 3-mile loop
  HIGH POINT 140 feet
  ELEVATION GAIN 200 feet

GETTING THERE

From Florence, follow US Highway 101 north about 12 miles. Watch for the trailhead parking turn-out along the east side of the highway just south of milepost 177. The trailhead is 0.8 mile north of the entrance to Heceta Head Lighthouse State Scenic Viewpoint (Hike 90) and 1.2 miles south of the entrance to Carl G. Washburne Memorial State Park.

ON THE TRAIL

This trailhead is best known as the start of the Hobbit Trail, which leads west 0.5 mile, gently descending 200 feet to a great and somewhat remote beach. By all means walk it! But don't neglect this gem on the east side of the highway.

Combine China Creek Trail with a beach walk for a loop of 4 miles or more.

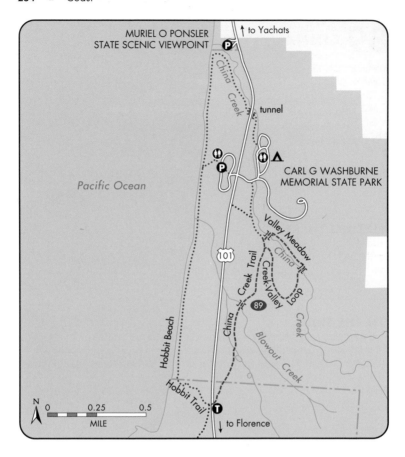

It leads into a lovely, mossy, forest and is a great choice when the weather is less inviting for lolling on the beach. Keep reading for the main China Creek 3-mile forest loop as well as two options for extending your hike into longer, forest-and-beach loops.

From the parking turnout on the highway's east side, the trail drops down briefly, then levels off, following the route of the old coast highway north along slow-moving Blowout Creek. At 0.5 mile the trail passes a couple of ponds; look for evidence of beavers. It crosses a creek and then continues north through the woods. At 1 mile you'll reach a trail junction; go right to pick up the Creek-Valley Loop. The trail crosses over a small creek then heads up briefly. It zigzags south and east across a carpet of moss, to the accompaniment of the ocean's roar. It then drops down and veers north, crossing a footbridge over babbling China Creek at mile 1.5, then follows the creek's east bank to a second footbridge at Valley Meadow at 1.8 miles, where the Creek-Valley Loop rejoins the main trail. Go left (south) here to complete the loop via China Creek Trail.

For a longer hike (4.1 miles) that folds beach time into your route, head north on China Creek Trail from Valley Meadow for 0.5 mile until you reach the road leading into Washburne State Park's campground. Follow it west a short distance to US Highway 101, cross the highway with care, and pick up the trail that cuts through the forest in the middle of the park's day-use parking area. Then follow a short trail out to the beach. Walk the beach south 1.1 miles and look for the west end of the Hobbit Trail about 0.25 mile north of the cliffs at the south end of the beach. Take the Hobbit Trail back to where you started (recrossing the highway at the trailhead).

For an even slightly longer hike (and one less scamper across the highway), rather than walking out the campground road to US 101, stay east of the highway to follow the campground road to the north end of the campground and pick up the paved path heading north. It leads along China Creek and under US 101, ending at the beach at Muriel O. Ponsler Memorial State Scenic Viewpoint. Turn south and walk 1.7 miles on the beach to the end of the Hobbit Trail, and follow it back to your car for a total hike length of 5.2 miles.

90 HECETA HEAD LIGHTHOUSE

BEFORE YOU GO
    MAP Download from state parks website
    CONTACT Heceta Head Lighthouse State Scenic Viewpoint
    NOTES State park day-use fee; privy available
    GPS N44° 08.096' W124° 07.373'
ABOUT THE HIKE
    SEASON Year-round
    DIFFICULTY Easy
    ROUND-TRIP 1 mile out and back
    HIGH POINT 400 feet
    ELEVATION GAIN 400 feet

GETTING THERE

About 12 miles north of Florence, south of milepost 178, turn off US Highway 101 at the sign to Heceta Head State Scenic Viewpoint and follow the access road down to parking along the shoreline.

ON THE TRAIL

The Oregon Coast has nine surviving lighthouses, most of them built in the nineteenth century. They are no longer used for navigation (except in a pinch); they've been replaced by modern technology. But some are still illuminated; Heceta Head's light can be seen as far as 21 miles out at sea. The 1884 lighthouse is sometimes open for tours; visit the state parks' website or call for schedule details.

A lighthouse stands at the tip of Heceta Head; east of it is the keepers' house.

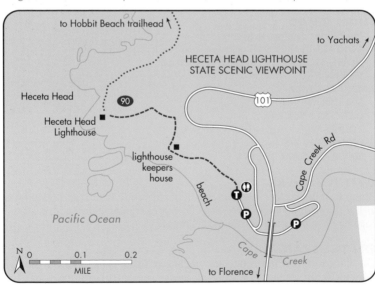

To tour, or just to see it up close, you need to walk 0.5 mile up from the parking area at Heceta Head Lighthouse State Scenic Viewpoint. Walk north, past the restroom, and head up the trail. At about 0.25 mile you'll pass the

GREAT GETAWAY: OREGON DUNES

Stretching for 40 miles, the Oregon Dunes between Florence and Coos Bay is the largest expanse of coastal sand dunes in North America, and much of it is conserved as part of Oregon Dunes National Recreation Area. You'll find large expanses of open sand as well as "tree islands," marshy wetlands, and wadeable (in summer) rivers. Parts of the Oregon Dunes are open to off-highway vehicles; the rest is for those who enjoy the wild on foot (such as the readers of this hiking guidebook, we bet).

Lodging and camping. There are motels in Florence and North Bend–Coos Bay and smaller towns between, but camping is what draws many families to this area. Jesse M. Honeyman Memorial State Park is the largest and most full-service campground, with more than 350 campsites and 10 yurts. Two miles of dunes separate the park from the ocean (with no trail access); instead enjoy swimming at Cleawox Lake and Woahink Lake or rent a pedal boat, kayak, canoe, or paddleboard at Cleawox.

Two more state parks in the area also offer lake access for fishing and swimming: Umpqua Lighthouse State Park and William M. Tugman State Park. Forest Service campgrounds in the area are smaller, quieter, and with fewer amenities. Some cater to OHV drivers; we recommend those that don't (Lagoon, Waxmyrtle, Carter Lake, Tahkenitch, and Bluebill campgrounds). All but Bluebill have trails (such as Hike 91) leading 1.5 miles or less across the dunes to the ocean.

Canoeing, kayaking, and swimming. Cleawox and Woahink lakes are just two of many lakes and rivers in the dunes that invite paddling; many restrict or prohibit motorboats. Bring your own canoe, kayak, or paddleboard or rent one in Florence. Families with some boating experience will enjoy following Siltcoos River Canoe Trail from Siltcoos Lake and through the forested dunes to the ocean and back.

The ocean off Oregon is fun to wade in but too cold to swim in; riptides and, in winter, sneaker waves add to the danger. But dune lakes (mentioned above) warm up in the summer sun and are ideal for a dip when the weather gets hot. Another less-well-known option: Hall Lake, west of Tugman State Park. Cross US Highway 101 and follow Wildwood Drive 0.5 mile to Hall-Schuttpelz Day-Use Area, where kids can slide down a tall dune into the lake.

hedge surrounding the 1893 lighthouse keeper's house, which is currently operated as a bed-and-breakfast inn. Continue up the trail, then up some steps, to reach the base of the lighthouse, which naturally has a spectacular view of the ocean and the coastline to the south. Come here Christmas week or during spring break and it's possible you'll see whales, or see them exhaling through their blowholes, as they migrate between birthing grounds off Mexico and summer feeding grounds off Alaska.

There's another way to hike to the lighthouse: from the north, via the Hobbit Beach trailhead (Hike 89). The route is a little longer (1.5 miles round-trip), but with a little less elevation gain, and there's no day-use fee at this trailhead.

91 WAXMYRTLE TRAIL

BEFORE YOU GO
> **MAP** Download from recreation area website
> **CONTACT** Oregon Dunes National Recreation Area
> **NOTES** USFS day-use fee; dogs and kites prohibited on trail's end beach
> Mar. 15–Sept. 15; privy in adjacent campgrounds
> **GPS** N43° 52.656' W124° 08.737'

ABOUT THE HIKE
> **SEASON** Year-round
> **DIFFICULTY** Moderate
> **ROUND-TRIP** 2.2 miles out and back
> **HIGH POINT** 40 feet
> **ELEVATION GAIN** 60 feet

GETTING THERE

From Florence take US Highway 101 south about 7 miles and turn west onto Siltcoos Beach Road. Drive 1 mile, passing the entrance to Waxmyrtle Campground on your left, and park in the Stagecoach Trailhead parking area, on the left side of the road.

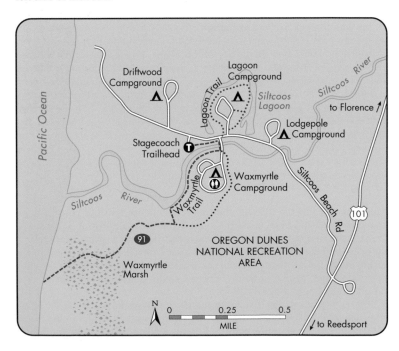

ON THE TRAIL

This trail follows the meandering Siltcoos River for its last 1.25 miles before reaching the ocean. It's short enough for almost any child to hike, and the ever-present opportunity to see wild birds on or near the river is a plus. The only minus is the (soft) sand road you follow for the second half of the hike to the beach. But the wild beach at the end makes it all worthwhile. If you hike with your dog, this is a good fall–spring destination (when snowy plovers are no longer nesting; dogs and kite-flying are prohibited on the beach at trail's end from March 15 to September 15).

Siltcoos River, seen from Waxmyrtle Trail, widens at its mouth; canoeists can paddle here from the lake.

From the parking area, follow a trail parallel to the road 0.1 mile back to the Waxmyrtle Campground road, cross the Siltcoos River, and turn west where the trail begins following the river's south bank. Climb stairs up a short hill forested with shore pines, continuing along the bluff. At 0.4 mile the trail veers south for 0.1 mile, then west again on a sand road past Waxmyrtle Marsh, on the left. The marsh is an old channel of the Siltcoos River that was cut off over time; water birds visit throughout the year, and beaver and nutria live here as well. Continue another 0.25 mile to the beach. At 1.1 miles you reach the beach; walk north on the beach about 0.4 mile to reach the mouth of the Siltcoos River, easily waded in summer (not in winter). Return as you came.

Extend your outing with a walk on the 1-mile Lagoon Trail, which follows an old arm of the Siltcoos River around Lagoon Campground on a combination of boardwalk and footpath. It starts just across Siltcoos Beach Road from the Stagecoach Trailhead.

HELP TO BRING BACK THE SNOWY PLOVER

If you visit the beach between mid-March and mid-September, especially near creek mouths on the central coast such as on Hike 91 or 92, you may see signs and fences blocking access to the dry sand and barring camping, kite-flying, and dogs (even on leash). It's all to protect the snowy plover. Unlike other shorebirds, this small bird nests on flat, open sandy beaches at the high-tide line. This makes it vulnerable to predators (and to disturbance by humans and their pets and by objects in the sky like kites that plovers might mistake for predator birds). Development of the shoreline has reduced the birds' habitat, and as a result its population, so that it is now considered a threatened species. You can help restore the plover population by observing the signs and avoiding prime nesting habitat spring through fall.

92 OREGON DUNES LOOP

BEFORE YOU GO
 MAP Download from recreation area website
 CONTACT Oregon Dunes National Recreation Area
 NOTES USFS day-use fee; dogs, kites, and camping prohibited on beach
  March 15–Sept. 15; privy available
 GPS N43° 50.005' W124° 09.112'
ABOUT THE HIKE
 SEASON Year-round
 DIFFICULTY Moderate–challenging
 ROUND-TRIP 4.5-mile loop
 HIGH POINT 80 feet
 ELEVATION GAIN 300 feet

GETTING THERE
From Florence, follow US Highway 101 south about 10 miles (or, northbound, about 10 miles north of Reedsport) and turn west at the sign to Oregon Dunes Day-Use Area.

ON THE TRAIL
The overlook at Oregon Dunes Day-Use Area gives motorists on US 101 a taste of the dunes on a quick detour off the highway. It's also the trailhead for a wonderfully varied loop hike that takes in open dunes, the ocean beach, tree islands, and coastal forest. Though there's not much elevation gain, the going is more difficult than on forest hikes of comparable distance because much of the walking is on soft sand. Post-to-post routefinding across the shifting dunes adds an element of adventure. If you're not up for a 4.5-mile hike, consider a 2-mile round-trip hike over the dunes to the beach and back.

Start off from the parking area either of two ways:

The post in this dune marks the beach end of the trail from Oregon Dunes Day-Use Area.

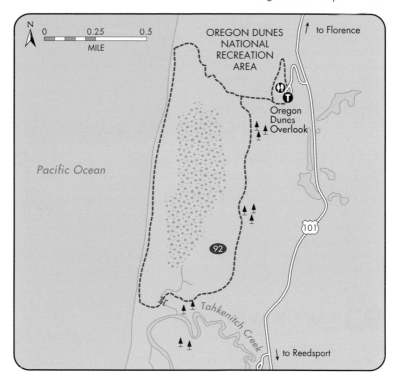

either walk down a winding, sandy trail from the upper viewing deck (on your left, as you face the ocean), or follow the two long switchbacks on the trail to your right, behind the restrooms, leading down the hill from the main covered viewing structure adjacent to the parking lot. Both approaches take you to the middle of an open dune; from here, posts mark the route west across about 0.3 mile of open sand. To reach the beach, bear right with the posts to enter what's called the deflation plain, which the trail crosses with help from small bridges. Climbing over the foredune, the trail reaches the beach at 1 mile. Turn around for a 2-mile out-and-back walk.

Otherwise, head south on the beach for 1.5 miles until you see a trail post in the foredune (if you reach the mouth of Tahkenitch Creek, you've gone almost 1 mile too far). The trail leads up and over the foredune, granting a glimpse of Tahkenitch Creek on your right. Cross a little footbridge 0.2 mile from the beach, then head up into a tall "island" of shore pines. Drop down the other side of the tree island and you'll find yourself above an oxbow in Tahkenitch Creek; if you're willing to wade the creek (not right here, but around to the left, where the bank isn't so steep), the middle of the oxbow makes a fine rustic tent site in summer.

The main route leads across a Sahara-like landscape of open dunes, and turns north; follow the trail posts to skirt west around another tree island, then get back on the open sand. The trail skirts west of the next big tree island; follow the trail posts (not always easy to spot here). Just before reaching the end of the loop in the open sand below the overlook, the trail enters the deflation plain and becomes a narrow, sandy path. Return to the parking area either up the dune on your right or up the trail on the left.

TREE ISLANDS AND TRANSITION FORESTS

The 1-mile-wide plant community found between the Oregon Dunes and the forest stretching up into the Coast Range is a unique mix of trees including Sitka spruce, western hemlock, Douglas fir, and shore pine. Shore pine grows right on the coast but not in the Coast Range forest. Sitka spruce does, but only 2 to 3 miles inland (though it grows as much as 100 miles up the Columbia River). You'll also find huge rhododendron, evergreen huckleberry, and salmonberry growing here. Over time, shifting sands sometimes isolate patches of forest to create "tree islands": steep-sloped miniforests surrounded by open dunes.

93 LAKE MARIE

BEFORE YOU GO
   MAP Download from state parks website
   CONTACT Umpqua Lighthouse State Park
   NOTES Privy in nearby campground
   GPS N43° 39.65' W124° 11.863'
ABOUT THE HIKE
   SEASON Year-round
   DIFFICULTY Easy
   ROUND-TRIP 1-mile loop
   HIGH POINT 170 feet
   ELEVATION GAIN 20 feet

GETTING THERE

Turn off US Highway 101 at the sign to Umpqua Lighthouse State Park, about 4 miles south of Reedsport. Follow signs to trailhead parking at the west end of the lake, off the lighthouse road.

ON THE TRAIL

This short, nearly flat trail through the forest is a good choice for families camping at Umpqua Lighthouse State Park—or anyone looking for an easy hike on this part of the coast. If the day is hot, end with a dip in the little lake's swimming area.

Lake Marie is surrounded by forest and encircled by an easy hiking path.

Walking clockwise from the parking area, the trail starts as a paved path, turning to dirt as it approaches the marshy south end of the lake. It climbs a bit at the west end of the lake, descending again and meeting a spur trail about 0.2 mile before you complete the loop. (The spur leads uphill 0.1 mile before dropping and ending at the open dunes and a view of the ocean.)

If you visit between May and September, when it is open, you might get to look inside Umpqua River Lighthouse, a short drive (or walk) from the trailhead. It is almost identical to the lighthouse at Heceta Head (see Hike 90) and, like it, went into service in 1864. Visit the website (see Resources) for information about guided tours.

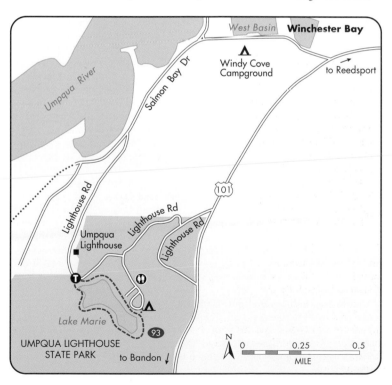

GREAT GETAWAY: CAPE ARAGO

Between the small port town of Charleston and the state parks and estuarine reserve nearby, there is so much to do here that it's hard to know where to start. How about with the climate? It's often rainy, especially in winter, but—less well known—just as often sunny, especially in summer and fall. If the weather does get stormy during your visit, there are kid-scale nature-oriented indoor attractions. And the Cape Arago shoreline is one of the state's most dramatic storm-watching sites!

Lodging and camping. There are a couple of no-frills motels in Charleston. But outdoorsy families may prefer camping at Sunset Bay State Park, which has several yurts as well as tent and RV sites. A second option is nearby Bastendorff Beach Park, run by Coos County, which has a couple of "camping cabins" in addition to tent and RV sites. Both accept reservations.

Hiking and more at three shoreline parks. A trio of state parks is arrayed along Cape Arago Highway just a few miles south of Charleston, and each of the parks has its own charms. Sunset Bay itself is shallow, so the water is warmer (if not actually warm) than on the open ocean; families with their own kayaks can explore the bay that way. The day-use area here is one end of the Shoreline Trail, which links with a large network of trails leading into the forest above.

Sunset Bay is the only one of the three state parks with a campground. Shore Acres State Park occupies the grounds of a historical estate; it preserves the estate's sprawling formal botanical gardens, which get decorated with millions of tiny lights each December. Cape Arago State Park has short trails leading down to beaches and coves on either side of the cape. Stop at Simpson Reef Viewpoint, which is off the access road as you approach the parking area at Cape Arago, in spring or summer to see lots of different seabirds, seals, sea lions, and even—if you're lucky—elephant seals and their babies. Binoculars are helpful here.

Exploring South Slough. South Slough National Estuarine Research Reserve, a few miles south of Charleston on Seven Devils Road, preserves a beautiful and remote arm of Coos Bay. The hiking here is great for families, even if you only go as far as the viewing platform at the estuary's edge. The small interpretive center near the parking area provides kid-size bites of natural history and is open Tuesdays through Saturdays. Check the reserve's online calendar (see Resources) for free or low-cost family-friendly tours and workshops on weekends, including kayak tours of the slough (though bring your own boat).

Charleston, indoors and out. Charleston is an active fishing port; it's fun to watch the boats come and go. Then wander over to the campus of Oregon Institute of Marine Biology, which now hosts the Charleston Marine Life Center, open Wednesdays through Saturdays. Its aquariums, tidepool touch tanks, and other exhibits focused on marine science are geared for kids.

Simpson Beach makes a great goal while hiking the Sunset Bay Shoreline Trail.

94 SUNSET BAY SHORELINE TRAIL

BEFORE YOU GO
   MAP Download from state parks website
   CONTACT Sunset Bay State Park
   NOTES Privy available
   GPS N43° 19.927' W124° 22.438'
ABOUT THE HIKE
   SEASON Year-round
   DIFFICULTY Moderate
   ROUND-TRIP 5 miles out and back
   HIGH POINT 80 feet
   ELEVATION GAIN 150 feet

GETTING THERE

From US Highway 101 in North Bend or Coos Bay, follow signs for Sunset Bay State Park. You'll follow Cape Arago Highway south for 12 miles, past the town of Charleston, until you reach Sunset Bay State Park. The trail begins across a bridge over a creek on the left (south) side of the park near a sign about a balloon trip.

ON THE TRAIL

Three contiguous state parks south of Charleston offer a variety of seashore fun for families, including swimming (or wading) in a protected cove, strolling through formal gardens, and forest camping a few steps from the ocean. What most visitors to this area never see, however, is the dramatic, rocky

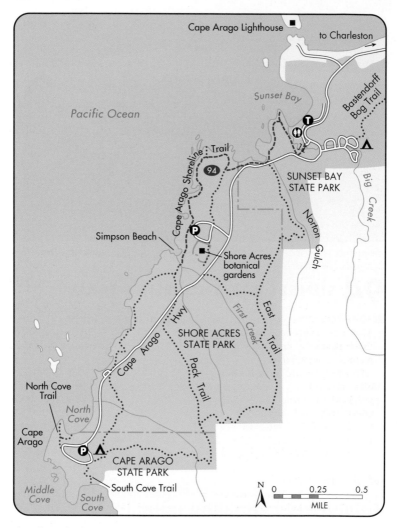

shoreline that's only accessible by trail. So consider pulling on boots (it's muddy in places) and walk a stretch of the Oregon Coast Trail between Sunset Bay State Park and a pocket beach below Shore Acres State Park. The hike from Sunset Bay to Simpson Beach is 5 miles round-trip.

The Shoreline Trail continues all the way to Cape Arago and with a shuttle car, it's possible to arrange a one-way hike of various distances.

To start the featured hike, look for a trail post near the restrooms at the south end of the Sunset Bay State Park parking area. Cross the footbridge over

Big Creek, ascend the headland, and bear right around a big mowed meadow, then continue south along the bluff. At 0.6 mile the trail leads back out to the highway, follows it south a short distance, and resumes at a stile over the guardrail. It continues through woods some distance from the shoreline; at a junction, veer north and west out to the bluff, where you'll view the Cape Arago Lighthouse (on an island, off-limits to the public) to the north and offshore rocks to the south (or continue straight for a shortcut through the forest to Shore Acres State Park).

Within Shore Acres, at about 2.2 miles, consider stopping to explore a large formal garden created by timber baron Louis Simpson. A large gate allows access into the garden, even more elaborate than when the Simpsons lived here. Outside the garden, there's a viewpoint and indoor glass lookout spot. Some of the coast's largest displays of waves crashing into the rocky shoreline can be viewed safely here.

From Shore Acres, follow a paved pathway downhill, following pointers for Simpson Beach. It's a total of 2.5 miles to this beautiful, cliff-encased sand beach. Return as you came for a healthy day's hike.

If you want to continue all the way to the Shell Island viewpoint, leave Simpson Beach, enter the forest, and follow the trail back up onto the bluff. At the trail junction, bear right. (A left turn leads to the highway.) The trail leads out to the shore, back to the highway briefly at 3.3 miles, resumes as a trail, and ends at the viewpoint, 0.5 mile north of the road's end at Cape Arago State Park. From the Cape Arago State Park parking loop at the end of the highway, you can follow trails 0.2 mile down to the cape's North Cove (closed March 1 through July 1) or South Cove (open year-round) for tide pooling, wildlife watching, and beach playing.

Our map focuses on the Shoreline Trail, but these state parks have more trails, including an expanding trail system in the upland forest east of the road in Shore Acres State Park; inquire at the parks about more hiking options here.

95 SOUTH SLOUGH

BEFORE YOU GO
    MAP Download from reserve website
    CONTACT South Slough National Estuarine Research Reserve
    NOTES Dogs prohibited on North Creek Trail loop portion (allowed on leash elsewhere); privy available
    GPS N43° 17.757' W124° 20.105'

ABOUT THE HIKE
    SEASON Year-round
    DIFFICULTY Moderate
    ROUND-TRIP 4-mile loop
    HIGH POINT 340 feet
    ELEVATION GAIN 400 feet

A footbridge spans an arm of Rhodes Marsh on the South Slough loop hike.

GETTING THERE

From US Highway 101 in North Bend, follow signs to west and south about 8 miles on Cape Arago Highway to Charleston. Turn left at the sign to South Slough and follow Seven Devils Road south 4.3 miles to the signed entrance to the research reserve and interpretive center, on the left.

ON THE TRAIL

There is just so much to see at this South Slough, a finger of Coos Bay and the country's first federally designated national estuarine research reserve. For a quick out-and-back hike, drive down to the Hidden Creek Trailhead (off a gravel spur road 0.2 mile from the interpretive center) and follow Hidden Creek Trail 0.7 mile to the observation platform at the edge of the marsh (leashed dogs allowed here). But we suggest you make the most of the drive here and walk this entire loop, which takes you across a skunk cabbage bog on a long wooden boardwalk, up into a tall viewing platform, and across a long footbridge linking the mainland to an old dike. Begin at the interpretive center (see website for hours; Resources) to learn about the complex interactions of estuarine ecology in terms kids can relate to.

From the interpretive center, take the Ten-Minute Loop Trail to connect with the North Creek Trail, which gently descends to the salt marsh, following the contours of the hillside in and out of creek ravines crossed by numerous footbridges (passing a 0.1-mile spur trail to North Creek Spur with a view of the marsh). At 1.5 miles the trail reaches Rhodes Marsh, crossing it on a long footbridge that connects with 0.1-mile Sloughside Trail spur leading north on the top of a narrow levee. Walk it out and back, then follow signs onto the 0.4-mile Tunnel Trail south to a large elevated viewing platform.

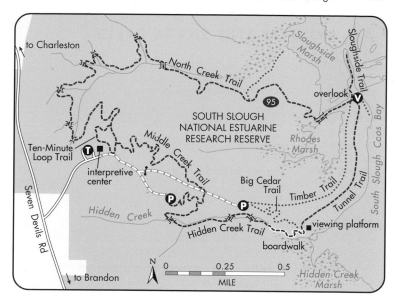

Climb down from the observation platform and zigzag down the trail briefly to join the Hidden Creek Boardwalk leading away from the water's edge and into a gorgeous marsh crowded, at the freshwater upper end, with skunk cabbage blooming in early spring. It becomes Hidden Creek Trail, which heads back up the hillside, crossing and recrossing the musical creek. About 0.5 mile from the observation deck, turn right at the junction with Middle Creek Trail, which leads 0.4 mile up the hill, over a road, and back to the Ten-Minute Loop Trail and your starting point.

WATCH YOUR STEP! CARNIVOROUS PLANTS

Actually, these plants won't harm you; both species of carnivorous plants found on the Oregon Coast stick to a diet of insects. Tiny sundew plants (*Drosera rotundifolia*) can be found near the dikes on the Tunnel Trail at South Slough (Hike 95). The end of the sundew's rounded leaf blades, fanned out close to the ground, are covered by fine hairs tipped with digestive glands. Insects get trapped in the hairs and consumed.

The pitcher plant (*Darlingtonia californica*) also uses its purple-green leaves to lure, capture, and digest the insects it uses to supplement its diet. At six inches to three feet tall, it's much easier to spot, especially where it grows in crowded bogs such as at Darlingtonia State Natural Area, on the east side of US 101 a few miles north of Florence on the central coast. Leave these plants in place of course, stay on trail, and take only pictures.

96 GOLDEN AND SILVER FALLS

BEFORE YOU GO
> **MAP** Download map from state parks website
> **CONTACT** Golden and Silver Falls State Natural Area
> **NOTES** Privy available
> **GPS** N43° 28.946' W123° 55.986'

ABOUT THE HIKE
> **SEASON** Year-round
> **DIFFICULTY** Easy–moderate
> **ROUND-TRIP** 2.9 miles out and back
> **HIGH POINT** 692 feet
> **ELEVATION GAIN** 200 feet

GETTING THERE
From Coos Bay, follow Coos River Highway 241 east to the small town of Allegany. Continue on winding East Fork Road and then Glenn Creek Road,

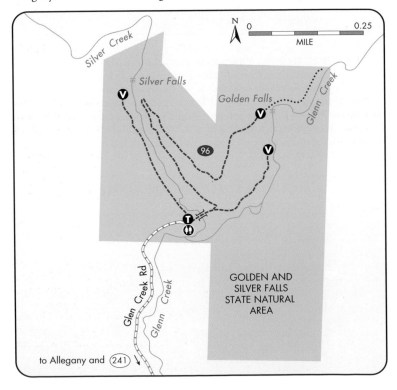

Sometimes hiking can make you feel tired.

heeding the many signs for Golden and Silver Falls State Park. The final stretch follows rough gravel to a parking area and trailhead.

ON THE TRAIL

Two of the most spectacular waterfalls in Oregon roar together in this remote canyon in the Coast Range near Coos Bay. Two very short hikes and one longer one offer views of the waterfalls. Exploring all three trails adds up to a nearly 3-mile round-trip hike.

This small and rarely visited state park is often confused with the more popular Silver Falls State Park (Hike 34); but with two very tall cascades and a fascinating history, it can more than hold its own as a great family hike. Homesteaders lived in the valley above Golden Falls as far back as 1880. To get around the dangerous escarpment that forms the precipice for the falls they used a steep pack trail until 1901, when they blasted a route through the rocky bluff above Golden Falls. Today, that pack trail serves as one of three hiking options here.

After the long and winding drive from Coos Bay—including a narrow gravel road for the final few miles—you'll be thrilled to get out of the car at the moss-covered parking area and trailhead where all three pathways begin. The hike to Silver Falls takes you through Coast Range forest on a hike of 0.6 mile out and back. The 130-foot waterfall spools off a rounded dome like gray hair falling off a balding head. Up next is Golden Falls, which at 165-feet is the more impressive of the two. A hike of 0.5 mile brings you to the roaring base of the waterfall. Finally, the longest trail climbs to the top of Golden Falls and looks down on a hike of 1.8 miles out and back with a climb of around 170 feet.

97 PORT ORFORD HEADS

BEFORE YOU GO
   MAP Download from state parks website
   CONTACT Port Orford Heads State Park
   NOTES Steep drop-offs on portions of trail; no privy
   GPS N42° 44.358' W124° 30.646'
ABOUT THE HIKE
   SEASON Year-round
   DIFFICULTY Easy
   ROUND-TRIP 1.2-mile loop
   HIGH POINT 320 feet
   ELEVATION GAIN 100 feet

GETTING THERE

From the town of Port Orford on US Highway 101, turn west on Ninth Street (north of milepost 301), then left on Coast Guard Hill Road and follow signs to Port Orford Heads State Park. Park in the small parking area at the top of the head, west of the old barracks and tennis court.

ON THE TRAIL

Port Orford Heads have some of the most stunning vistas on the entire coast. And from 1934 to 1970 those viewpoints had a very important practical

Check out the restored lifeboat near the start of the trail at Port Orford Heads.

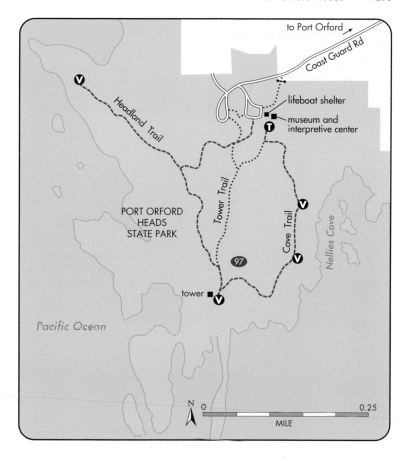

purpose: to spot trouble at sea. The Port Orford Lifeboat Station housed as many as one hundred "surfmen" whose job it was to keep watch over 40 miles of coastline and, when needed, dash down more than 530 steps to a boathouse in Nellies Cove and head out, often in huge storms, in unsinkable 36-foot motor lifeboats. (The surfmen's motto: "You have to go out; you don't have to come back.") Their observation tower, boathouse, and stairs are all gone, but you can see the remnants and the dramatic vistas the surfmen surveyed on a loop hike at Port Orford Heads that starts at the old lifeboat station, now serving as Port Orford Lifeboat Station Museum and Interpretive Center (see website in Resources for schedule details).

An interconnected network of short trails starts at the center. It's just 0.6 mile straight out to the tower viewpoint and back, but in an easy loop of 1.2 miles you can see several more viewpoints. From the shelter housing the

GREAT GETAWAY: THE ANCIENT REDWOODS

Once upon a time, giant redwood forests covered the length of the northwest California and southwest Oregon coast. Today, only five percent of those original forests remain, protected almost entirely by the National and State Parks system. While the most impressive trees are certainly in California—protected in the patchwork of parks—Oregon also has a few places where you can see the world's tallest species of tree.

The redwood area we're focusing on is extreme northwest California at Jedediah Smith Redwood State Park (Hikes 100 and 101) along with Oregon's small collection of giants (Hikes 98 and 99). The two closest towns include Crescent City, California, and Brookings, Oregon. Both towns have all the amenities a family could need. Our favorite time to visit the redwoods, particularly Jedediah Smith, is quieter winter, spring, or fall. The height of summer brings large crowds.

Lodging. Both Crescent City and Brookings have plenty of hotels, bed and breakfasts, and interesting places to spend the night. Closer to the big trees, Hiouchi Motel and Patrick's Creek Lodge offer affordable and interesting lodging.

Camping. Jedediah Smith Redwoods State Park Campground is the main place to camp on a redwood visit. There are eighty-four sites and lots of fun attributes, including a seasonal bridge that crosses the Smith River during summer to Stout Grove (Hike 100). Four heated cabins can be rented as well.

In Oregon, Alfred A. Loeb State Park is the trailhead for Hike 98. It has beautiful scenery along the Chetco River and offers forty-eight electrical sites and three rustic log cabins that can be reserved. A larger campground can be found at Harris Beach State Park.

Biking. Have a hankering to ride two wheels through the redwoods? The locally based outfitter Redwood Rides offers early morning biking tours down Howland Hill Road, the scenic gravel road that bisects the middle of Jed Smith's redwoods.

River running. While the giant trees get most of the attention, Jed Smith also happens to be home to one of the West's most beautiful rivers, the Smith. Bland name notwithstanding, Smith River is California's largest undammed river system and one of the world's clearest streams. Rent an inflatable kayak and float the river's mellow stretches—or even tempt its rapids—with help from Redwood Rides.

Family fun. You can see the redwood canopy up close by taking a gondola ride through the "Trees of Mystery" just south of Crescent City. The attraction just south of Crescent City also has a museum, gift shop, and restaurant.

restored lifeboat at the old lifeboat station, bear left to take the Cove Trail. Pausing at a view looking 280 feet down into Nellies Cove, search for the concrete breakwater and portions of the boathouse foundation and boat carriage rails, and peer back up the cliff to see foundations that once anchored the staircase. Soon you'll reach another great view of the coast and, at 0.4 mile, a dramatic view of Humbug Mountain from the site of the station's observation tower. To return, head inland and uphill on the Tower Trail, then bear left at two trail junctions to link with the Headland Trail, which leads to the park's westernmost viewpoint (watch for the flash from Cape Blanco Lighthouse). Returning, follow the Headland Trail a scant 0.2 mile and bear left to walk another 0.2 mile back to the parking area.

98 REDWOOD NATURE LOOP

BEFORE YOU GO
 MAP Pick up interpretive map at trailhead
 CONTACT Alfred A. Loeb State Park
 NOTES Privy available
 GPS N42° 06.766' W124° 11.225'
ABOUT THE HIKE
 SEASON Year-round
 DIFFICULTY Easy–moderate
 ROUND-TRIP 1.2 to 2.6-mile loop
 HIGH POINT 250 feet
 ELEVATION GAIN 250 feet

GETTING THERE
From US Highway 101 in Brookings—in the middle of town—turn onto North Bank Chetco River Road. Follow signs for Alfred A. Loeb State Park along the paved road for 7 miles and park either at the state park (at the Riverview Trailhead) or continue less than a mile to the Redwood Nature Loop trailhead on the left.

ON THE TRAIL
The world's northernmost grove of old-growth redwoods can be explored on this wonderful hike that runs 1.2 or 2.6 miles depending on where you start. For the shorter option, start at the US Forest Service's Redwood Nature Loop trailhead. For the longer route, start at Loeb State Park and follow Riverview Trail until it connects with the redwood trailhead. Either way, it's tough to go wrong in this enchanted area.

Large redwoods reach for the sky along the Nature Loop.

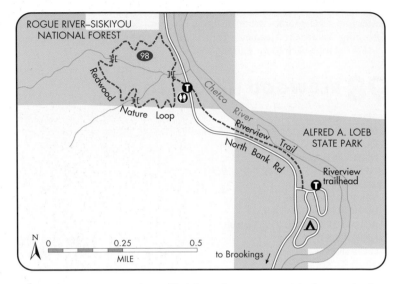

From Loeb State Park, you'll follow the Riverview Trail, a total of 0.7 mile, along the emerald waters of the Chetco River. The upside here is a moss-covered forest of hemlock and Douglas fir and the longer trek. The trail ends on the paved road you drove in on. Simply cross it to the Redwood Nature Loop trailhead, which takes you around and through a lush forest of giant redwoods. Make sure to pick up an interpretive map at the trailhead, which guides you to the rich flora and fauna of this rainforest.

The trail is easy to follow and beautiful, though it can get muddy in winter and spring. The grove's tallest redwood is 296 feet tall and around 800 years old. The trail winds over a footbridge crossing a cascading silver falls twice before returning to the redwood loop (and eventually Loeb State Park) trailheads.

99 OREGON REDWOODS TRAIL

BEFORE YOU GO
   MAP Rogue River–Siskiyou National Forest, Gold Beach Ranger District
   CONTACT Gold Beach Ranger District
   NOTES Privy available
   GPS N42° 00.516' W124° 08.826'
ABOUT THE HIKE
   SEASON Year-round
   DIFFICULTY Easy
   ROUND-TRIP 1.8-mile loop
   HIGH POINT 1027 feet
   ELEVATION GAIN 380 feet

Looking up at the tall trees on Oregon Redwoods Trail makes a person feel small.

GETTING THERE

From Brookings, drive south on US Highway 101 for 5 miles. Turn left on Winchuck Road (following signs for Oregon Redwoods Trail) for 1.5 miles. Turn right across a bridge onto Peavine Ridge Road, continuing for 4 miles of somewhat bumpy gravel road to the trailhead at road's end. The route has many signs pointing people in the correct direction.

ON THE TRAIL

In 1988, the US Forest Service planned two timber sales for one of the last remaining groves of old-growth redwoods on Oregon soil. The sale included plans to cut about 300 trees, to produce a whopping 3 million board feet of lumber, which tells you how big these trees truly are. A story in the *Eugene Register-Guard* newspaper about the sale outraged Oregon's populace, and eventually resulted in the sale being canceled. Today, a trail explores this once-condemned grove of redwoods on a pathway cut out in preparation for the timber sale.

Of the two Oregon redwood hikes in this book, the upside of this one is more redwood trees and a quieter atmosphere. Crowds are never an issue. The trail begins among unimpressive Douglas fir trees from a gravel parking area. Stay right at the loop junction. After 0.4 mile, the trail reaches a junction in the first grove of redwoods. A short while later you'll reach a dead and hollowed out redwood that you can walk inside, a joy for most kids. After playing for a while, keep right to continue on the loop trail.

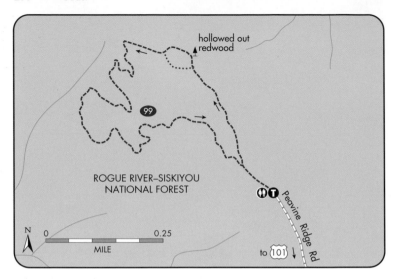

Next the trail drops down into a forested but redwood-free canyon for a while before reaching a second large grove at mile 1.3 and the best and largest grove of redwoods at mile 1.5. More than any other redwood hike in this book, a defining characteristic of this pathway is the quiet in the forest. The lack of other visitors and giant canopy of the trees creates a church-like feeling as you make your way among the giants. Too soon, you'll reach the junction and turn right, following the entrance pathway back to the trailhead.

100 STOUT GROVE

BEFORE YOU GO
> **MAP** Download map from park website
> **CONTACT** National Park Service, Redwood National and State Parks
> **NOTES** Dogs prohibited; privy available at park visitor center
> **GPS** N41° 47.385' W124° 05.092'

ABOUT THE HIKE
> **SEASON** Year-round
> **DIFFICULTY** Easy
> **ROUND-TRIP** 1-mile loop
> **HIGH POINT** 279 feet
> **ELEVATION GAIN** 70 feet

GETTING THERE

From Grants Pass, Oregon, head southwest on Redwood Highway (US Highway 199) across the California border toward Crescent City, California, traveling a total of 70 miles. After passing the small town of Gasquet, continue 10 miles to turn left onto South Fork Road, just before the bridge across Myrtle Creek. You'll immediately cross a bridge over the Smith River and then a second bridge over the South Fork of the Smith River. At the three-way junction, following signs for Stout Grove, turn right and continue 1.5 miles through a residential area. The paved road becomes the gravel Howland Hill Road as it enters the park. Follow this winding,

Show children what a real giant looks like at Jedediah Smith Redwoods State Park.

stunningly beautiful road 0.8 mile to a well-marked trailhead and parking area on the right.

From Crescent City, drive south 1 mile on US 101 and turn left (east–northeast) onto Elk Valley Road; continue 1 mile and turn right (east) onto Howland Hill Road. After 1.5 miles the road becomes unpaved as it enters the park. Continue past multiple trailheads to signs for Stout Grove on the left.

ON THE TRAIL

The easiest way to experience an ancient redwood forest is this short and sweet loop through Stout Grove. Located off scenic Howland Hill Road—a gravel road that bisects the heart of Jedediah Smith Redwoods State Park—this short trail with lots of connections is often crowded on summer weekends. The largest redwood in this grove is 340 feet tall and 16 feet in diameter. Make sure that everyone stays on marked pathways: let the kids know that hiking off-trail can damage the trees' root systems, which are very shallow.

From the parking area, a paved pathway heads downhill to the beginning of the short loop. We recommend heading right to start the loop, hiking below a forest so dense the canopy overhead almost seems like a green roof. After a short trek, a short detour on Riverview Trail takes you to Cedar Creek and back; this forest, too, is well worth exploring and only adds 0.3 mile to the hike. Back at the loop, the trail turns along the Smith River. You'll pass a network of trails connecting to Mill Creek and Hiouchi trails and to a summer plank bridge that crosses the Smith River to Jed Smith campground. Return as you came. The hike is finished far too soon back at the junction with the paved path that returns you to the parking lot.

Riverview Trail

From Stout Grove continue east from the first trail junction along the Smith River to and past Cedar Creek, a total of 0.5 mile, to a trailhead and parking

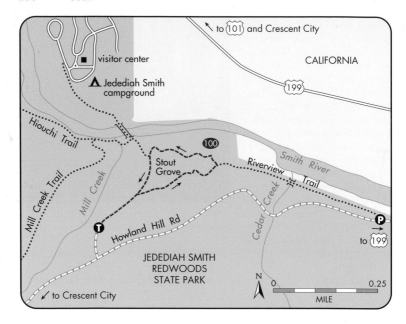

area on Howland Hill Road. Highlights include occasional views of spawning salmon and the Smith River.

Campground and Hiouchi Trail

From the second trail junction at Stout Grove, follow the Hiouchi Trail to the summer plank bridge that crosses the Smith River to the Jed Smith Campground area. In summer, families cross the plank bridge from the campground to explore Stout Grove.

101 BOY SCOUT TREE TRAIL

BEFORE YOU GO
    MAP Download map from park website
    CONTACT National Park Service, Redwood National and State Parks
    NOTES Small parking area and popular trail, so arrive early in summer
    GPS N41° 46.116' W124° 06.614'
ABOUT THE HIKE
    SEASON Year-round
    DIFFICULTY Moderate–challenging
    ROUND-TRIP 5.5 miles out and back
    HIGH POINT 295 feet
    ELEVATION GAIN 910 feet

The trees on Boy Scout Tree Trail at Jedediah Smith Redwoods State Park are enormous.

GETTING THERE

From Grants Pass, Oregon, head southwest on Redwood Highway (US Highway 199) across the California border toward Crescent City, California, for a total of 70 miles. After passing the small town of Gasquet, continue 10 miles. Just before the bridge across Myrtle Creek, turn left onto South Fork Road. You'll immediately cross a bridge over the Smith River and then a second bridge over the South Fork of the Smith River to a three-way junction. Turn right at the junction, following signs for Stout Grove, continuing 1.5 miles through a residential area. The paved road becomes gravel Howland Hill Road as it enters the park. Follow this beautiful road 3.2 miles, past Stout Grove, to a small trailhead on the right.

From Crescent City, drive south 1 mile on US 101 and turn left (east–northeast) onto Elk Valley Road; continue 1 mile and turn right (east) onto Howland Hill Road. After 1.5 miles the road becomes unpaved as it enters the park. Continue to signs and a parking pullout for the Boy Scout Tree Trail.

ON THE TRAIL

Stout Grove may be the most famous hike at Jedediah Smith Redwoods State Park, but most would agree that the best overall hike is the Boy Scout Tree Trail. This longer trek gets you away from the bustle of Howland Hill Road and spreads out the crowds, greatly improving the experience for those seeking a lonelier experience in an ancient forest. The only challenges are a decent amount of dropping and climbing and a muddy trail in wet seasons: both may exhaust youngsters.

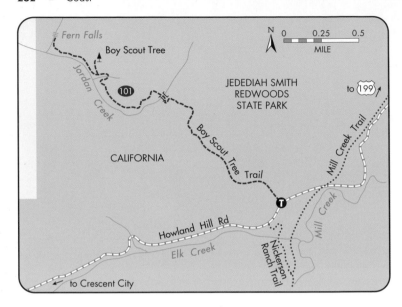

From a small, signed trailhead to the side of the road, the trail sets out through truly monstrous redwoods. You'll cross several footbridges including one over Jordan Creek while hiking through redwood trees with different colored bark—some are chestnut brown, others are ash or even white. The size of the trees varies tremendously as well; this site has not burned in many years, but a fire would burn out smaller trees and parts of the understory.

After hiking 2.5 miles, a side trail leads to the Boy Scout Tree, namesake tree of this trail. This massive tree is what's known as a "fused redwood," where two trees have joined into one massive 40-foot-diameter trunk as though giving the two-finger Boy Scout salute. Past the Boy Scout Tree, the trail enters a brushy area and ends at small Fern Falls, a quiet little waterfall sliding down a rock face. Return as you came.

Opposite: *From the end of Cleetwood Cove Trail (Hike 106), you can dive into the impossibly blue water of Crater Lake.* (Photo courtesy of National Park Service)

SOUTHERN OREGON

102 WOLF CREEK FALLS

BEFORE YOU GO
   MAP Umpqua National Forest, North Umpqua Ranger District
   CONTACT North Umpqua Ranger District
   NOTES Small parking area sometimes fills on weekends
   GPS N43° 14.024' W122° 57.074'

ABOUT THE HIKE
   SEASON Year-round
   DIFFICULTY Easy
   ROUND-TRIP 2.4 miles out and back
   HIGH POINT 1163 feet
   ELEVATION GAIN 350 feet

GETTING THERE

From Interstate 5 in Roseburg, take exit 124 and follow State Highway 138 east. Follow signs for Diamond Lake through downtown Roseburg and continue on Hwy. 138 to the town of Glide at milepost 16. From Glide, turn right onto Little River Road and follow it 10.8 miles to a trailhead sign and parking pullout on the right side of the road.

ON THE TRAIL

There are multiple fun-to-explore waterfalls in the Little River area just south of the main North Umpqua Canyon. Wolf Creek Falls is the most scenic and

A long bridge crosses the Little River at the beginning of the trail to Wolf Creek Falls.

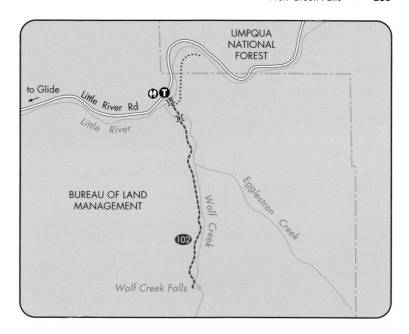

accessible of these treks. It begins with a pretty footbridge and climbs through lush forest to a waterfall that drops in tiers of 75 and 50 feet.

The trail begins at a small parking area and crosses a bridge over Little River, a tributary of the North Umpqua. There are a number of curiosities on this pathway, including a gigantic boulder within the first quarter mile. The trail climbs gradually uphill, although never too steeply, crossing multiple footbridges, as the route parallels Wolf Creek. The sound of falling water marks the beginning of Wolf Creek Falls at mile 1.2. The main section of the waterfall slides down a thick slab of black basalt. Return as you came.

Other Little River Falls

While Wolf Creek Falls is generally open year-round, some of the other falls in the Little River area will be blocked by snow, depending on conditions. Call the North Umpqua Ranger District to check conditions ahead of time. Below are some other falls we recommend for late spring, summer and early fall.

Shadow Falls. This triple waterfall has eroded its way through a rock fracture to form a narrow, natural grotto at the bottom of a 100-foot plunge. The trail totals 1.6 miles. From Glide, follow Little River Road 6.6 miles. Turn right at the covered bridge on Cavitt Creek (Road 82B) and continue 11.6 miles on Road 82B and Forest Road 25 to the trailhead. Follow Trail 1504 to the falls.

Grotto Falls. This waterfall plunges down along Emile Creek. Hike into the grotto behind the falls. The hike is 0.6 mile round-trip. From Glide, take

Little River Road (County Road 17, becoming Forest Road 27) for 16.1 miles to Road 2703 across from Coolwater Campground. Turn left onto Road 2703 for 4.5 miles and stay left on a turnoff for Road 2703-150 for another 2 miles to a trailhead just over a bridge. The route is marked with Grotto Falls signs.

Hemlock Falls. Rocks, ferns, and trees surround this 80-foot falls along Hemlock Creek. The hike is 1.2 miles round-trip. From Glide, follow Little River Road (CR 17, becoming FR 27) for 25.8 miles to Lake in the Woods Campground. The final 7 miles are gravel. Trailhead parking is at the campground entrance. Access to Hemlock Falls Trail is near Campsite 1.

Yakso Falls. Little River drops 70 feet among protruding rocks that spread the water flow out like a silver fan. This hike is a round-trip of 1.4 miles and also begins at Lake in the Woods Campground. Follow the same directions as to Hemlock Falls (above) and park in the campground. The trailhead is just across FR 27 from the campground.

GREAT GETAWAY: NORTH UMPQUA

Sometimes called the "Canyon of Thundering Waters," the North Umpqua area east of Roseburg is home to numerous waterfalls. More than eleven cascades can be reached on trails that are often easy, kid-friendly, and accessible from State Highway 138. We feature many of them here (Hikes 102, 103, 104), but there are lots of others, including: Lemolo, Steamboat, Little, Whitehorse, Warm Springs, and Deadline falls.

Lodging. The gateway to the North Umpqua Canyon is Roseburg, a small city with all the hotels you could need. However, for a more intimate experience with Umpqua—and to have the waterfalls and river right outside your door—consider iconic Steamboat Inn. On the upper side of the canyon is Diamond Lake Resort, which has more affordable rooms but is centered on the fishing and outdoor activities around the lake.

Camping. Numerous campgrounds operated by Umpqua National Forest can be found along Hwy. 138. A few favorites include Susan Creek, Horseshoe Bend, and Boulder Flat.

Rafting. The North Umpqua River is one of the best rafting and inflatable kayaking experiences in Oregon. The river runs all summer and features emerald waters, lush forest, and numerous Class III rapids. A number of local outfitters offer guided trips.

Hot springs. Check out Umpqua Hot Springs, which requires a slippery quarter-mile hike from the trailhead. A heads-up to parents planning to visit with kids: these hot springs have a questionable reputation, and naked hippies may be found here.

Swimming holes. There's nothing better than the swimming holes of the North Umpqua canyon on hot summer days. A few of the best are located up Steamboat Creek Road, just off Hwy. 138 near Steamboat Inn.

Fishing. The North Umpqua River has a famous fly-fishing-only stretch for 34 miles from Rock Creek to the Soda Springs Dam.

The bottom tier of Fall Creek Falls roars into a grotto in the North Umpqua Canyon.

103 FALL CREEK AND SUSAN CREEK FALLS

BEFORE YOU GO
    MAP Umpqua National Forest, North Umpqua Ranger District
    CONTACT North Umpqua Ranger District
    NOTES Can be muddy and slippery in winter and spring; watch for poison oak; privy available
    GPS N43° 18.801' W122° 50.125' (Fall Creek);
           N43° 17.935' W122° 54.343' (Susan Creek)

ABOUT THE HIKE
    SEASON Year-round
    DIFFICULTY Easy–moderate
    ROUND-TRIP 2 miles (Fall Creek); 1.6 miles (Susan Creek) out and back
    HIGH POINT 1673 feet
    ELEVATION GAIN 410 feet (Fall Creek); 110 feet (Susan Creek)

GETTING THERE

From Interstate 5 in Roseburg, take exit 124 for State Highway 138. Follow signs for Diamond Lake through downtown Roseburg and continue on Hwy. 138 east, passing Glide, for 32 miles.

For Fall Creek Falls, just past milepost 32 look for a large parking area on the left. For Susan Creek Falls, at mile marker 28.2, look for the trailhead on the left side of Hwy. 138, just across from Susan Creek's namesake campground.

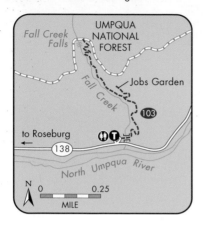

ON THE TRAIL

Two stunning waterfalls with great hikes for kids sit right next to each other in the North Umpqua canyon. Of the two, Fall Creek Falls is the better hike, but if you have extra time, make sure to check out Susan Creek Falls as well.

Fall Creek Falls

It's easy to keep kids interested along this short trail, from the wooden bridge at the trailhead to the viewing platform partway up the falls. Spring brings an array of woodland wildflowers to the trail's borders, further enhancing a hike here.

From the trailhead, immediately cross Fall Creek on a wooden bridge. Just up the trail, squeeze through a crevice in a rock the size of a small house. The trail continues close to the creek, which spills and froths over mossy boulders. It switchbacks uphill briefly; then, at about 0.5 mile, a spur trail takes off to the right, leading in 0.1 mile to Jobs Garden (an area of unusual rock formations). There's plenty of poison oak here, so watch the children and stay on the trail. As the creek flattens, the trail levels out and veers away from it, still staying within earshot.

At mile 1, the trail rejoins the creek, now flat and quiet, just before reaching the falls. Here the creek twists around a corner, then showers down a rock face, falling nearly 100 feet in the process. There's not much to see at the top, though there's a nice intermediate viewpoint along the way. The trail ends at a gravel road atop the falls. Return as you came.

Susan Creek Falls

Follow the trail as it begins through deep forest east of the creek until it ends at the base of the falls after 0.8 mile. Susan Creek Falls tumbles 60 feet into a punchbowl. Look for dippers, or water ouzels—small, dark-gray birds adapted to life in and around mountain streams. They often build nests right on the edge of waterfalls, and they're frequently seen at Susan Creek Falls dipping in the spray and walking under the stream. Return as you came.

104 TOKETEE AND WATSON FALLS

BEFORE YOU GO

   MAP Umpqua National Forest, North Umpqua Ranger District

   CONTACT North Umpqua Ranger District

   NOTES Privies available

   GPS N43° 15.842' W122° 25.655' (Toketee); N43° 14.733' W122° 23.493' (Watson)

ABOUT THE HIKE

   SEASON Year-round, except during low-elevation snowstorms

   DIFFICULTY Easy

   ROUND-TRIP 0.8 mile (Toketee); 1 mile (Watson) out and back

   HIGH POINT 3214 feet

   ELEVATION GAIN 30 feet (Toketee); 310 feet (Watson)

GETTING THERE

From Interstate 5 in Roseburg, take exit 124 for State Highway 138. Follow signs for Diamond Lake through downtown Roseburg and continue east on Hwy. 138, passing the town of Glide.

   For Toketee Falls, at milepost 59, turn left onto Forest Road 34. Veer left at the first junction and go 0.4 mile to a well-marked trailhead and parking area. For Watson Falls, continue on Highway 138 to milepost 61, then turn right (south) onto FR 37. The trailhead parking lot is just down FR 37.

ON THE TRAIL

Trailheads for these two short hikes are just about 2 miles apart; pair them and you'll have just less than 2 miles of hiking and some of southern Oregon's best waterfall views. Toketee Falls (which in Chinook Jargon means "pretty" or "graceful") is probably the most dramatic of the North Umpqua corridor falls, especially viewed as hikers see it—across a chasm from a platform clinging to a cliff. That said, Watson Falls

Watson Falls drops through a snowy forest in the North Umpqua area of Southern Oregon.

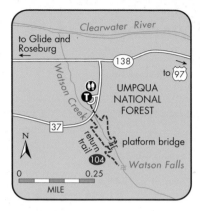

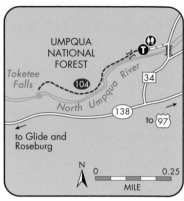

is also a sight to behold after a good rain in winter, spring, or late fall when the waters are running high.

Toketee Falls

That huge, dripping redwood pipe you see next to the trailhead is used to divert water from nearby Toketee Lake and carry it to another pipe, where it drops steeply to a powerhouse to make electricity. Cross a footbridge and walk the level path through the forest, passing several informal picnic sites along the river. The trail then starts to climb a bit on sturdy stone steps. Peek down to the left at the gorgeous deep pools in the creek along the trail. Approaching the end, the trail drops about 100 feet to a viewing platform perched on the side of the canyon. Look across a wide gulf to see the North Umpqua River pouring through a cleft in a wall of columnar basalt and dropping some 90 feet into an emerald pool. Return as you came.

Watson Falls

From the trailhead, signs lead hikers up and across Forest Road 37 and onto a footpath ascending the hillside across the road. The route to the falls is rather steep, sticking close to the creek as it runs noisily over mossy boulders that have rolled down out of the mountains. The first trailside view of the 272-foot falls comes at about 0.25 mile. Keep going to a railed wooden platform zigzagging over the creek near the base of the falls. Continue up the trail on another switchback for a better view of the falls, then up yet another switchback to reach the highest viewpoint, poised about one-third of the way up the falls in a magnificent natural amphitheater of gray rock and pale green moss.

The cataract falls straight down a cliff, pounding a pile of boulders and vaporizing into clouds of mist. To return, follow signs to the "return trail" spur that starts just west of the railed platform bridge. It takes a slightly steeper, quicker route back to the parking area, forming a nice loop.

A stunning view of Crater Lake and Wizard Island from the Watchman at Crater Lake National Park (Photo courtesy of Crater Lake National Park)

105 THE WATCHMAN

BEFORE YOU GO
   MAP Download from park website
   CONTACT Crater Lake National Park
   NOTES Rim Drive closed for snow in winter and often as late as July;
      dogs prohibited
   GPS N42° 56.754' W122° 10.152'
ABOUT THE HIKE
   SEASON Late June–October
   DIFFICULTY Easy–moderate
   ROUND-TRIP 1.6 miles out and back
   HIGH POINT 8056 feet
   ELEVATION GAIN 420 feet

GETTING THERE

From Medford, take State Highway 62 about 70 miles north to the western border of Crater Lake National Park, just past Union Creek. Continue east on

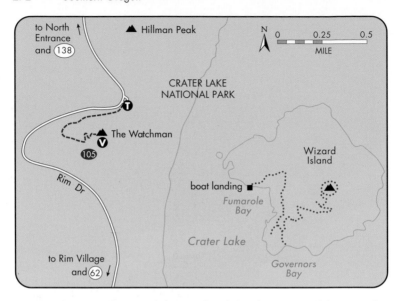

Hwy. 62 about 7 miles. Turn left toward park headquarters and drive 4 miles to Rim Drive. Turn left and drive 3 miles to Rim Village. Continue north for 3.8 miles on Rim Drive. Park in the viewpoint parking area for The Watchman.

From the Willamette Valley or from Bend, follow US Highway 97 to the north entrance of Crater Lake National Park and follow signs toward Rim Village. Continue south on Rim Drive for 3.8 miles to the viewpoint parking area.

ON THE TRAIL

On your family's visit to Crater Lake, don't leave without hiking to a high point overlooking the lake. Several peaks with summit trails dot the lake's rim. The Watchman is the shortest and easiest of the bunch but grants a dynamite bird's-eye view of the deep blue lake and the best view possible of Wizard Island, directly below.

The trail starts just south of the parking area along the rim. Climb a long straightaway that gradually curves behind The Watchman peak. At about 0.5 mile the trail reaches a switchback—the first of a half-dozen switchbacks that come closer and closer together as you near the top. At the summit there's a fire lookout cabin, but no visitors are allowed inside. (With so many visitors, the person staffing the lookout would never get a chance to watch for fires.) Instead, enjoy the view from the rock-walled viewpoint. Return as you came.

Older children seeking more challenge might enjoy Garfield Peak, a 3-mile round-trip (980 feet of elevation gain) that begins just behind Crater Lake Lodge, or Mount Scott, a 5-mile round-trip (1330 feet of elevation gain) directly across the lake from Rim Village.

GREAT GETAWAY: CRATER LAKE AND THE UPPER ROGUE RIVER

Crater Lake, the United States' deepest body of water, is one of the world's most beautiful sights. A volcano that erupted and collapsed on itself 8000 years ago filled with snowmelt and rainwater over the millennia to become a cliff-walled pool of iridescent clarity. The high elevation of this national park—5000 to 8000 feet—means it is fully open only for a few months each year. The Rim Road, which encircles the lake, often doesn't open until mid-June or later. Sharply growing crowds have stressed the park's campground and facilities and, especially for a family vacation, makes planning well in advance crucial. Mazama Village and nearby Rim Village provide most of the essentials, but again, planning is key.

Lodging. Within the national park, there are two options for spending the night indoors: either cabins at Mazama Village or rooms at Crater Lake Lodge. They are reserved quickly and don't come cheap (upward of $200 per night), but offer unmatched access. Less expensive cabins can be had at Union Creek Resort, about a forty-five-minute drive from the park's rim.

Camping. The only campground in Crater Lake National Park is Mazama Campground, home to 214 tent and RV sites that generally open early June to late September. The campground is a standard camping experience that doesn't have any views of the lake. A restaurant and gift shop are also located at Mazama Village, set a long way back from the lake's rim.

Another option is to stay at one of the Forest Service campgrounds along the Upper Rogue River corridor, along State Highway 62, about an hour's drive from the park. Campsites at Farewell Bend, Natural Bridge, and River Bridge are the less-expensive options. They are also more pleasant than the other local campgrounds and have plenty of accessible hikes in their own right.

Boat tour. Perhaps the most memorable adventure at Crater Lake is a boat tour of the lake. Park rangers teach the area's natural and cultural history during the hour-long experience. The best option is getting dropped off on Wizard Island, a spectacular cinder cone in the middle of the lake. A fairly steep 1-mile hike round-trip takes you to the summit of the cone, smack in the middle of the lake. (See map, Hike 105.)

Swimming. Yes, you can swim in Crater Lake. Just be ready to freeze your butt. The temperature below the surface is a frigid 37 degrees; but if you stay on the surface, it's not quite as bad. Remember to breathe! The only access point for swimming is via Cleetwood Cove Trail (Hike 106).

Hikes. Given the popularity and well-established nature of the trails at Crater Lake National Park—and how steep many of them are—we included just two hikes (105 and 106). However, other hikes worth taking with kids include Garfield Peak, Plaikni Falls, and Scott Mountain (with its steep but unmatched views). Maps for these hikes can be found on the national park's website.

Dining. Crater Lake Lodge is home to a fancy, five-star eating experience. Sip beer or nibble snacks beforehand on a balcony overlooking the lake. More affordable options can be found at Rim Village.

106 CLEETWOOD COVE

BEFORE YOU GO

MAP Download map from park website

CONTACT Crater Lake National Park

NOTES Dogs prohibited; privy at trailhead; Rim Drive closed for snow in winter and often as late as June

GPS N42° 58.778' W122° 04.994'

ABOUT THE HIKE

SEASON July–October

DIFFICULTY Moderate

ROUND-TRIP 2 miles

HIGH POINT 6950 feet

ELEVATION GAIN 700 feet

GETTING THERE

From Medford, take State Highway 62 about 70 miles north and, just past Union Creek, turn right at signs for Crater Lake National Park, traveling east on Hwy. 62 about 7 miles. Turn left toward park headquarters and drive 4 miles to Rim Drive, which circles the lake. Turn left (clockwise) and drive 3 miles to Rim Village, continuing north and then east on Rim Drive 10.6 miles more. Park in the large trailhead parking area on the left side of the road.

From the Willamette Valley or from Bend, follow US Highway 97 to the north entrance of Crater Lake National Park and follow signs toward Rim Village, continuing 10.6 miles on Rim Drive to the trailhead.

ON THE TRAIL

Thousands of people drive around the rim of Crater Lake to gaze across its deep, clear blue waters; but far fewer actually dip their toes in it. There's only

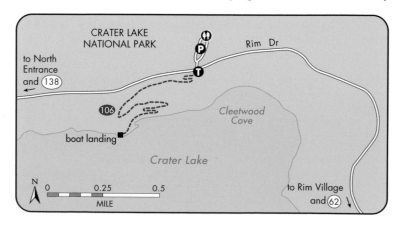

one way to get to the lake, and that's with a hike down Cleetwood Cove Trail. Boat tours to Wizard Island leave from the dock at the trail's end (see "Great Getaway: Crater Lake" for boat details). Even without the boat ride, the hike is worthwhile, especially if it's hot enough to justify a dive or a dip into the bone-chilling lake.

Cross the road to reach the trailhead. The wide trail's descent isn't really steep, but it's steady. Benches are scattered all along the trail. (The prospect of a boat tour motivates a lot of less-than-fit tourists to walk this trail; they make good use of the opportunities to rest on the return.) The lake glimmers along the trail all the way down the long switchbacks.

The trail ends at the little boat dock. Sit on the edge of the dock, dipping your feet, or pick your way along the boulder-strewn shore to find a picnic or wading spot. Bring old sneakers or water shoes for wading, as the rocks can be sharp. As for swimming, floating on the top layer of water isn't so bad; but dip much deeper and it's as cold as anything you've ever experienced.

Amazingly, you're allowed to fish at Crater Lake. Six species of fish were stocked beginning in 1888, and today, rainbow trout and kokanee remain. Because they are not native to the lake, fishing is not only allowed, it's encouraged. No license is required and there is no limit on how many you may catch—the only rule is that you must use artificial bait.

107 NATURAL BRIDGE

BEFORE YOU GO
  MAP Download from USFS website
  CONTACT Rogue River–Siskiyou National Forest, High Cascades Ranger District
  NOTES Privy available
  GPS N42° 53.315' W122° 27.889'
ABOUT THE HIKE
  SEASON May–November
  DIFFICULTY Easy–moderate
  ROUND-TRIP 2.4 miles loop
  HIGH POINT 3280 feet
  ELEVATION GAIN 200 feet

GETTING THERE
From Medford, take State Highway 62 north about 54 miles (after Prospect but 1 mile before Union Creek). Turn left (west) at the sign to Natural Bridge (Forest Road 300) and continue 0.5 mile. Bear left at the Y and park at the day-use area with a bridge and large signboard and viewpoint near the river.

ON THE TRAIL
In its dash from the slopes of Crater Lake to the Pacific Ocean, the Rogue River does a sudden disappearing act, reappearing a short distance downstream. Where does it go? Through a series of lava tubes in the river's channel. An

The Upper Rogue River squeezes through narrow basalt channels and disappears into Natural Bridge.

excellent interpretive trail overlooking Natural Bridge enlightens visitors and steers them safely away from walking on the natural bridge itself. Link that short, paved path with forest trails on either side of the river, throw in a pair of foot-bridges, and what results is a wonderful, generally uncrowded loop hike. The east-bank trail section skirts a busy campground, but the west-bank section is little used. The trail is generally snow-free from April through November, but the road to Natural Bridge is open only mid-May through mid-October.

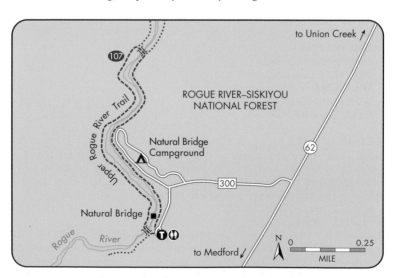

From the trailhead walk past the kiosk with interpretive signs to a paved path leading to a dramatic metal footbridge spanning the churning Rogue River. The path then winds upstream, on the west side of the river, safely fenced off from steep cliffs, with several overlooks and signs explaining the geologic processes that created the scene below you. The paved path ends at a view of Natural Bridge, but the trail—Upper Rogue River Trail—continues as a dirt footpath. It follows a level course, then climbs perhaps 200 feet above the river in deep woods. Look down and see the now peacefully flowing green river between the trees.

After a while you will glimpse tents and trailers parked in the campground across the river, then a wooden footbridge below at mile 1.2. The trail seems to overshoot the footbridge as it drops to river level, but a right turn at a trail junction leads along a quaint, rock-lined path back to the bridge. Cross it and turn right (south). (A left turn leads 1.5 miles to the small outpost of Union Creek.) The north end of the campground is about 0.25 mile from the bridge. The trail here threads between river and campground for 0.5 mile or so; notice the river's initial calm, then its growing sense of urgency, as it narrows and drops toward Natural Bridge. For the last 0.25 mile the trail veers away from the river and into the woods, ending at the viewpoint parking area.

108 BLUE CANYON BASIN

BEFORE YOU GO
   MAP Sky Lakes Wilderness, Rogue River–Siskiyou National Forest
   CONTACT Rogue River–Siskiyou National Forest, High Cascades Ranger District
   NOTES Long, confusing drive to trailhead, but open to low-clearance cars
   GPS N42° 31.783' W122° 17.798'

ABOUT THE HIKE
   SEASON Late June–October (best in Sept., early Oct.)
   DIFFICULTY Moderate
   ROUND-TRIP 4 miles out and back
   HIGH POINT 6258 feet
   ELEVATION GAIN 500 feet

Blue Lake marks the highlight of a hike into Blue Canyon Basin.

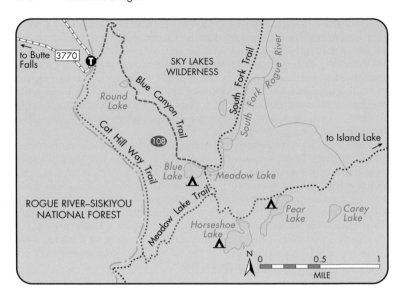

GETTING THERE

From Medford, take State Highway 62 north to milepost 16 and turn right at signs for Butte Falls. Drive 17 miles to town on Butte Falls Highway. Continue on the highway for 1 mile to the Prospect turnoff and turn left, crossing over a bridge. Continue 2 miles and veer right onto gravel Rancheria Road. Stay on Rancheria, which becomes Forest Road 32, for 15 miles. FR 32 merges with FR 37; stay on it for about 1 mile until you see a red gravel road, FR 3770, taking off on the right. Follow FR 3770 for 6 miles to the well-developed Blue Canyon trailhead.

ON THE TRAIL

The Blue Canyon basin is a wonderful place for children to experience a first backpacking trip or just to enjoy the experience of hiking into a wilderness area—in this case, the Sky Lakes Wilderness. It's a short and downhill hike to Blue Lake, the highlight of this journey, but there are many other nearby lakes for exploring, fishing, or tent camping. We suggest a day hike or backpacking trip in late August, September, or early October, after the June and July clouds of mosquitoes have dispersed.

From the trailhead, two trails branch off in opposite directions. Take the left option, Blue Canyon Trail, and not Cat Hill Way Trail (which could be used for a return loop, but makes the trip a bit long). The hike along Blue Canyon Trail drops downhill through an old-growth forest of Shasta red fir, mountain hemlock, and western white pine to reach little Round Lake after 1 mile. Your destination, Blue Lake, sits at mile 2. Nestled below a towering cliff headwall, Blue Lake is the most scenic pool in this area (you'll want to take a swim on hot days in summer); and it's received a little too much love because of it. Many of the former campsites right along the lake are roped off to help the area's vegetation regenerate. Pick a site 200 feet from the water's edge; there are a few to be found. Next day or same day, return as you came.

If you don't find any good campsites at Blue Lake, fear not. You can also stay to the right at a trail junction just past Blue Lake (keeping on the Blue Canyon Trail) and then keep right again at another junction (with the Meadow Lake and Cat Hill Way trails) to head for Horseshoe Lake (mile 2.8) or Pear Lake (mile 3.3). While not quite as scenic as Blue Lake, these two lakes offer more campsites and better fishing.

For a slightly longer hike of 4.4 miles, from Blue Lake continue about a quarter mile to the Meadow Lake Trail junction, turning right (southwest) then right again onto Cat Hill Way Trail to return to the trailhead. The upside of this return loop is close-up views of Mount McLoughlin, a broken shield volcano and the tallest mountain in southern Oregon at 9495 feet. The downside of the loop is a steep trail that's a little bushy and tougher than simply returning on the route you came in on.

109 UPPER TABLE ROCK

BEFORE YOU GO
   MAP Download from BLM website
   CONTACT Bureau of Land Management, Medford District
   NOTES Little shade on hot days; dogs and camping prohibited; privy available
   GPS N42° 27.974' W122° 52.909'
ABOUT THE HIKE
   SEASON Year-round (but best in spring)
   DIFFICULTY Moderate–challenging
   ROUND-TRIP 3.6 miles out and back
   HIGH POINT 2050 feet
   ELEVATION GAIN 780 feet

GETTING THERE

From Interstate 5 in Medford take exit 33 (Central Point) and turn left on Biddle Road 0.8 mile to Table Rock Road. Turn left and drive 5.3 miles. Where the road swings to the left, turn right on Modoc Road. Continue 1.5 miles to the signed trailhead, on the left.

Views across Rogue Valley can be had from Upper Table Rock.

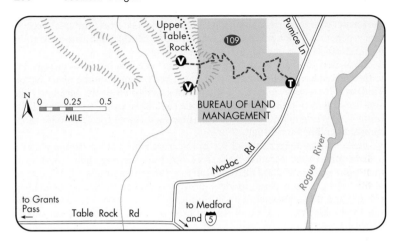

ON THE TRAIL

Anyone who has driven past Medford on I-5 has noticed the pair of flattop mesas just north of the freeway. Both Upper and Lower Table Rock have trails to their summits; the trail that ascends Upper Table Rock is shorter, a little less steep, and a bit more open for views. It's a good wildflower walk in spring, but children will be more intrigued by the summit, which is literally flat enough to land a plane on (there's a grassy airstrip on Lower Table Rock). The summit meadow is a bit boggy in winter and spring; in summer, go early in the day, before the heat becomes oppressive. In all seasons, beware of poison oak and rattlesnakes.

Start up through a tangle of oak and madrona trees. The trail can be rocky in some places, muddy in others. It passes between huge basalt outcrops at 0.2 mile. There's a bench at 0.5 mile inviting hikers to pause and enjoy the view of the Rogue River Valley. There's another bench at 0.9 mile, where the trail enters the forest and obscures the view the rest of the way to the summit, even though the shade is welcome on hot days. The upper part of the trail has some steep pitches. Quite suddenly, at mile 1.4, the trail emerges onto the flat, open expanse at the top of the rock.

Even kids who have a hard time dragging themselves up the trail tend to become converts once they reach the summit, with its unusual open and virtually treeless landscape. It's fun to explore this flat-as-a-pancake world where plenty of wildflowers grow in vernal pools that fill with water in winter. Signs detail the many unique plants that grow here, including the dwarf woolly meadowfoam, which is endemic to the table rocks. The trail hits the summit near one end of the horseshoe-shaped rock; head left to get to the end, or wander to the center of the horseshoe for a dramatic view of the rocky gorge below. The collection of trails include around 0.4 mile of hiking, but it can be more or less depending on energy level. Return as you came.

110 LOWER SKY LAKES BASIN

BEFORE YOU GO

MAP Sky Lakes Wilderness, Rogue River–Siskiyou National Forest

CONTACT Fremont-Winema National Forest, Klamath Ranger District

NOTES Privy available; small campground at trailhead; area was impacted by 2017 wildfire; beware of mosquitoes in early summer

GPS N42° 32.572' W122° 10.848'

ABOUT THE HIKE

SEASON Late June–Oct. (best in Sept., early Oct.)

DIFFICULTY Challenging

ROUND-TRIP 5.6 to 7.7 miles out and back

HIGH POINT 6650 feet

ELEVATION GAIN 860 feet

GETTING THERE

From Medford, follow State Highway 62 northeast for 6 miles into White City. Turn right onto State Highway 140 east, headed toward Klamath Falls. Follow Hwy. 140 for 41 miles, passing Lake of the Woods. At milepost 41, at signs for "Cold Spring Trailhead," turn left onto gravel Forest Road 3651. Follow it 10 miles to the Cold Spring trailhead.

ON THE TRAIL

This longer hike will challenge older children, but also serves as a great avenue for a backpacking trip in a wilderness area. The lower Sky Lakes Basin is home to six lakes that invite fishing, exploring, and swimming. Each lake is unique—some are big circular pools while others are long and thin. All have nice campsites. Many sections of this trail were impacted by the 2017 High Cascades Complex Wildfires. The result is dead and downed trees and less shade.

From the Cold Spring trailhead, the trail leads out through mountain hemlock and lodgepole pine, passing South Rock Creek Trail on the right at mile 0.6. Stay on the main, Cold Spring route. Assuming you've convinced your kids to stay with you this long, at mile 2.8 the good stuff begins. The junction of Sky

Long, thin Isherwood Lake shimmers in the Lower Sky Lakes basin.

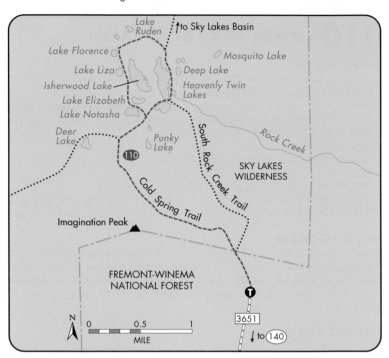

Lakes Trail and Isherwood Loop Trail is where you'll want to look at the map and make a decision about which way to go next.

From the junction, there are four lakes in fairly close proximity. Turn left up Isherwood Loop, and you'll shortly reach lakes Notasha and Elizabeth—both small, nice but unspectacular. Choose to instead stay right on Sky Lakes Trail and you'll quickly reach Big Heavenly and Little Heavenly Twin lakes. The bigger of the two is the most interesting—at 22 acres it has lots of room for exploring and camping. Despite its size, Big Heavenly is fairly shallow, just six feet deep in most places. The lake is usually warm and very pleasant for swimming, so consider making camp along its shores. Hiking to this cluster of lakes makes the hike a total of around 6 to 6.5 miles, depending on how much you look around.

The full loop—visiting all six lakes by following Isherwood Loop and Sky Lakes Trail, then returning on the Cold Spring Trail—makes the hike a total of 7.7 miles. It's certainly worthwhile to do the longer route to visit what's probably the nicest lake, Isherwood Lake. Long and thin, Isherwood is surrounded by old-growth forest and has many fun, private campsites near the lake's sparkling blue water. The best spots are on the northern tip.

For the return trip, consider South Rock Creek Trail. It's rocky, steeper, and generally tougher in places—unlike the smooth superhighway you came in on—but just a bit shorter.

GREAT GETAWAY: ASHLAND

The tourism center for southern Oregon is Ashland, just a stone's throw from the California border and home to the world-famous Oregon Shakespeare Festival. Nestled in the rolling greenish-brown Siskiyou Mountains, Ashland provides an abundance of local wine and beer, restaurants, music, and outdoor recreation, including the Rogue River and Cascade-Siskiyou National Monument.

Make sure to visit nearby Jacksonville, a small touristy spot modeled after the area's mining and Old West history. For a cheaper alternative to Ashland—and closer access to the Rogue River—try the town of Grants Pass to the north.

Lodging. There is no shortage of hotels of various prices to be had in Ashland. Some more nature-y resorts include Green Springs Inn, Ashland Springs Hotel, and Callahans Mountain Lodge. In the Rogue River canyon, Morrison's Lodge or Double Tree Ranch are great choices.

Camping. The area's best camping is near Jacksonville in the wine-rich Applegate Valley, and at Cantrall-Buckley and Jackson campgrounds. To the north, in the Rogue River canyon, Indian Mary and Almeda campgrounds are great choices.

Oregon Shakespeare Festival. Started in 1935, this annual festival in Ashland offers classical and reimagined works by the Western world's most famous playwright. The season runs February to early November and features three stages, one of which is outdoors. The plays draw people from all over the world, and any trip here would be incomplete without taking in at least one production.

Music. Jacksonville hosts one of the best outdoor music festivals on the West Coast—the Britt Festival. The summertime concert festival hosts a number of high profile acts as well as beloved, local musicians at a small, intimate venue. Visitors can bring in beer and wine and sit on the grass.

Parks. Lithia Park in downtown Ashland is one of Oregon's iconic parks. There are walking trails and small pools for wading or swimming—the best being Lower Reservoir on the park's south side. Autumn colors are brilliant in September and October.

Swimming. A handful of reservoirs and lakes surround Ashland. Emigrant Lake is the closest and most popular, although Hyatt and Howard Prairie reservoirs also have inviting waters. Our favorite reservoir is Applegate Lake, about an hour's drive southwest of Ashland, where you can camp, mountain bike, hike, and fish—and swim. A small general store at Hart-Tish Park at Applegate Lake will help you get started (see Resources).

Rafting and inflatable kayaking. Southern Oregon in summer is all about the famous Rogue River. Book a guided raft trip or rent inflatable kayaks. The best and most scenic one-day floats are around the small outpost of Galice, northwest of Grants Pass. Our favorite floats tempt Class II rapids from Hog Creek Boat Ramp to Galice, or slightly larger rapids from Galice to Grave Creek Boat Ramp. Make sure to get solid information about river conditions and levels and be correctly outfitted before putting in on the river. Call any of the many outfitters in Merlin or Galice for information.

Upper Sky Lakes Basin

Frankly, the most spectacular collection of lakes is in the upper basin. Craggy mountains rise above emerald Trapper and Marguerette lakes. Reaching them means bypassing the Isherwood loop to the lower basin and continuing north on Sky Lakes Trail, a total of 5.5 to 6 miles one way (or 11 to 12 miles round-trip) from the Cold Spring trailhead. All campsites must be at least 200 feet from lakeshores.

111 TUNNEL RIDGE

BEFORE YOU GO
MAP Download map from BLM website (search for Sterling Mine Ditch Trail)
CONTACT Bureau of Land Management, Medford District
NOTES No water or privy; watch out for poison oak
GPS N42° 09.503' W122° 54.199'

ABOUT THE HIKE
SEASON Year-round
DIFFICULTY Easy–moderate
ROUND-TRIP 2 to 4.7 miles
HIGH POINT 2872 feet
ELEVATION GAIN 540 feet to 600 feet

GETTING THERE
From Interstate 5 in Grants Pass, follow US Highway 199 south through downtown, across the Caveman Bridge, to a busy intersection where Highway 199 turns southwest toward the redwoods. At this point, follow State Highway 238 southeast toward Murphy into the Applegate Valley. Drive a total of 25.5 miles to the small town of Ruch. From Ruch, follow the Upper Applegate Road (County Road 859) south for 3 miles to Little Applegate Road. Turn left onto Little Applegate Road at a sign for Sterling Mine Ditch Trail and proceed east 10 miles, past the Bear Gulch trailhead, to the Tunnel Ridge trailhead.

ON THE TRAIL
The Sterling Mine Ditch Trail system highlights the botanically diverse Siskiyou Mountains and the fertile Applegate Valley—a well-known destination for wine lovers. Open oak savanna and shaded pine forest make this a particularly inviting hike in the spring, when the sun is shining and the wildflowers—including Indian paintbrush and trillium—are in bloom. The entire trail system is 17 miles, but this hike highlights one of the prettiest slices on a route that can either be a quick 2 miles out and back or include a longer but satisfying 4.7-mile loop.

The trail system was created from the remnants of a mining project. In 1877, miners built the 26-mile Sterling Mine Ditch to redirect water from the Little Applegate River to the Sterling Creek Mine for hydraulic mining. The 100-foot-long tunnel through Tunnel Ridge is the highlight of this ambitious engineering project and the destination of this hike.

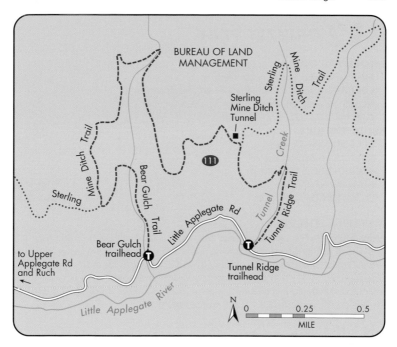

From the Tunnel Ridge trailhead, just above the Little Applegate River, the pathway climbs gradually through a forest of white oak, steepening as it approaches an open meadow at mile 1, with the tunnel and a junction with the Sterling Mine Trail. You can actually crawl inside the tunnel here and kids will have fun exploring an area that makes a nice picnic spot. Return the way you came for a 2-mile hike.

For a longer, rewarding trek option, turn left at the junction and follow the almost perfectly level trail, contouring along Tunnel Ridge for 2 miles. Giant, gnarled madrone trees sit on the edge of the trail and mountain views abound. At the junction with Bear Gulch turnoff, turn left and follow the trail 1 mile down to the Bear Gulch trailhead and the Little Applegate Road. Turn left and trek alongside the road another 0.7 mile back to your car.

Views of the Siskiyou Mountains and Applegate Valley abound from the Sterling Mine Ditch Trail system.

112 GRIZZLY PEAK

BEFORE YOU GO
> **MAP** Download map from BLM website
> **CONTACT** Bureau of Land Management, Medford District
> **NOTES** Hot with little shade during height of summer
> **GPS** N42° 16.323' W122° 36.386'

ABOUT THE HIKE
> **SEASON** May–October
> **DIFFICULTY** Easy–moderate
> **ROUND-TRIP** 5.2-mile loop
> **HIGH POINT** 5920 feet
> **ELEVATION GAIN** 790 feet

GETTING THERE

From Interstate 5 in Ashland, take exit 14 and turn left. In 0.7 mile turn left onto Dead Indian Memorial Highway and follow it out of town. After milepost 6, turn left onto Shale City Road (paved) and drive 3.1 miles to the Grizzly Peak Trail sign (BLM 38-2E-9.2). Turn left and follow the gravel road 0.7 mile to an intersection, which may or may not be marked. Take the uphill road, Road 39-2E-9.2, on the center left, 1.7 miles to the trailhead.

ON THE TRAIL

From downtown Ashland, look across the valley to the northeast, up to twin humps on the horizon scattered with gray snags—the remnants of a forest fire

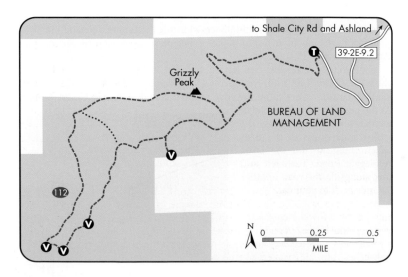

on Grizzly Peak. An ascent to viewpoints on the peak is doable for fit kids and rewarding, with a riot of wildflowers in midsummer and views of the Ashland valley below and Mount Ashland and Mount Shasta beyond. The Antelope Fire burned through here in 2002; the mostly gentle loop trail now winds alternately through lush conifer groves and dramatic burned, but recovering forest.

The trail immediately heads up, ascending 1.1 miles through a Douglas fir, white fir, and hemlock forest to a junction. Go left for a quicker out-and-back hike to the best viewpoint (1 mile ahead). To hike the loop, go right instead, passing the peak's rock-pile summit on your right in a scant 0.2 mile (no view from here). Continue on the nearly level trail through the forest, passing a wide meadow cut by a narrow shortcut trail 0.8 mile from the junction. Continuing, you plunge into the burned area and slowly descend to the first of a series of increasingly dramatic viewpoints on the peak's south side. From the last, best viewpoint the trail heads up, levels off, and reenters the forest; follow it, past a 0.1-mile spur to more views, to the start of the loop and back down to the trailhead.

113 RAINIE FALLS

BEFORE YOU GO
  MAP Download Rogue River Trail Guide from BLM website
  CONTACT Grants Pass Interagency Office, Smullin Visitor Center
  NOTES Hot in summer; be wary of children getting too close to the falls—rocks are slick and falling could be fatal; privy is a steep walk to Grave Creek boat ramp
  GPS N42° 38.924' W123° 35.133'
ABOUT THE HIKE
  SEASON Year-round
  DIFFICULTY Moderate
  ROUND-TRIP 4 miles
  HIGH POINT 790 feet
  ELEVATION GAIN 110 feet

GETTING THERE
From Interstate 5 north of Grants Pass, take exit 61 to Merlin. Continue straight on Merlin-Galice Road for 3.2 miles into Merlin and then another 8.5 miles toward Galice, the rafting outpost and general store. From Galice, continue another 6 miles. Just before a bridge crosses over the river, park along the side of the road. The trail begins on the left side of the river and follows it downstream.

ON THE TRAIL
The Rogue River is among the most famous streams in the world for rafting, but during the past decade, hiking and backpacking have become increasingly popular as well. The Rogue River Trail cuts 40 miles along the wilderness river on one of the best backpacking tours in the state. With children, you're probably not ready for such an adventure, but you can still sample the many charms of this beautiful cliff-walled canyon on a short hike to Rainie Falls. The best

Viewpoint of the Rogue River from Rainie Falls Trail in Southern Oregon

time to visit is September, when you're likely to see salmon leaping up the falls.

The hike to Rainie Falls begins on the opposite side of the river from the official Rogue River Trail. The odd spelling isn't named for weather, but for an old man who used to live near the falls and made his living catching salmon jumping up the falls each autumn. It's now illegal to fish near the falls.

This hike starts out just above and opposite Grave Creek boat ramp. The trail is quite rocky but mostly level, following the river through oak and madrone forest as the mountains loom almost directly overhead. There's a great viewpoint at mile 0.5, and sights of rafters and kayakers running Class III rapids below. Bald eagles and osprey are commonly seen floating on the breeze. After the viewpoint, the trail gradually drops downhill, swinging away from

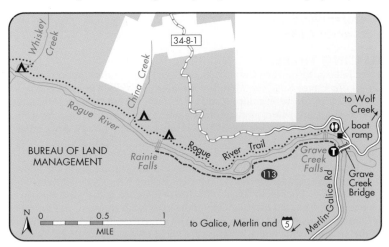

the river at times, until it curves back around to a viewpoint at Rainie Falls. Those expecting a 50-foot cataract will be disappointed—the falls is only about 6 feet tall and more of a roaring rapid than a true waterfall. The water is powerful here, and the riverside boulders often slippery, so keep a close eye (or even arm) on smaller children to keep them away from the edge. A few people have died in this area after falling in.

The upside of this viewpoint is twofold: in summer, you can watch rafters attempt to navigate their way around the falls, either via the fish ladder or middle chute. In autumn, salmon leap up the main falls. Return the way you came.

Rogue River Trail

The official 40-mile Rogue River Trail begins at Grave Creek boat ramp. The views of Rainie Falls from this trail aren't good, but it makes a nice hike or easy backpacking route. An excellent goal is Whiskey Creek campsite and cabin (you cannot stay overnight in the cabin, it's just to visit). This riverside camping spot is 3.5 miles down the trail (7 miles round-trip).

114 BIG TREE LOOP

BEFORE YOU GO
    MAP Download map from park website
    CONTACT National Park Service, Oregon Caves National Monument and Preserve
    NOTES Privies at visitor center and Oregon Caves Chateau; no dogs on walking trails
    GPS N42° 05.879' W123° 24.397'
ABOUT THE HIKE
    SEASON June–October
    DIFFICULTY Challenging
    ROUND-TRIP 3.5 to 4 miles
    HIGH POINT 5080 feet
    ELEVATION GAIN 1150 feet

GETTING THERE

From Interstate 5 in Grants Pass, take exit 58 and head into downtown Grants Pass following Redwood Highway (US Highway 199). At an intersection, turn west (right), following signs for US 199 and drive 30 miles to Cave Junction. Drive through Cave Junction, and turn east (left) onto State Highway 46 for 19 miles to Oregon Caves National Monument and Preserve.

ON THE TRAIL

Hikers in southern Oregon don't tend to think of the trails around Oregon Caves National Monument when choosing a destination, and tourists visiting the caves don't tend to be interested in hiking. That combination makes this interesting and moderately challenging loop trail relatively secluded. This hike, along with a tour of the caves, makes a full day's outing for a family; but an

The Cliff Nature Trail offers wonderful views. (Photo courtesy of Oregon Caves National Monument and Preserve)

out-and-back hike to the huge Douglas fir is only 2.6 miles. Ask at the monument's information office about even shorter loop hikes in the caves area.

Walk up the road toward the cave entrance, then continue up the double staircases, past the ticket booth, and onto an asphalt path. Immediately the trail splits, signaling the start of the loop trail. Turn left for the more gradual approach to the Big Tree.

The trail quickly turns to dirt. The route, fairly steep for the first 0.4 mile, flattens out for a bit where the first of several trailside benches appears. Then the trail makes a turn to the right; notice how the trees are bigger here and the forest cooler. At about 0.7 mile the trail steepens again and heads up steadily. In early July some pink rhododendrons may be in bloom. At 1.3 miles cross a tiny creek and immediately reach the Big Tree—a 12.5-foot diameter Douglas fir with a broken top.

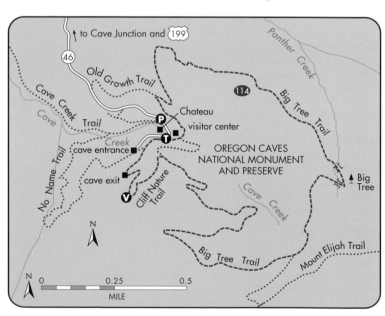

GREAT GETAWAY: OREGON CAVES

The Oregon Caves National Monument and Preserve is home to the largest cave system in the Western United States. But it's also surrounded by the Siskiyou Mountains high country that invites exploring, camping, or staying at a historic lodge.

Discovered in 1874 and designated as a monument in 1909, the Oregon Caves is one of the least-visited national monuments in the West due to its remote location, tucked away in the Illinois Valley just north of the California border. It's mostly visited by families stopping on their way to the redwoods. The monument was expanded in 2014, in large part to try to entice more visitors to come. Those who do make the trip will find adventure above and below ground. There is no fee to hike or explore outside, only to tour the caves.

Lodging. The best place to stay overnight is the Oregon Caves Chateau, a historic, six-story building originally constructed in 1934. Open May to October, reservations are suggested (see Resources). The chateau also serves meals in a cozy dining room. The closest towns with other hotel lodging are Cave Junction and Grants Pass.

Camping. Cave Creek Campground is located just a few miles from Oregon Caves. It offers primitive amenities and cannot accommodate large RVs. Grayback Campground is located 8 miles from the caves, which offers running water and vault toilets. The area is flatter and more accommodating to RVs. The campsites are offered on a first come, first served basis. Lake Selmac Campground is located about 25 miles from Oregon Caves and has ninety-one sites, thirty-nine with full hookups, RV dump station, restrooms, showers, picnic shelters, ball fields, playground, and boat ramps. There is an assistant ranger and seasonal hosts in the park to answer your questions.

Oregon Caves tour. This classic tour brings you into marble caverns, past fossils, twisting columns, unusual insects, bats, and any number of other curiosities. The tour is ninety minutes, led by rangers and considered moderately difficult, with half a mile of walking and some bending down to get through low passageways. Children must be three feet, five inches to go on the tour. A unique way to do the cave tour is by candlelight, an experience offered on Friday and Saturday nights in-season. Dates run May 23 to Sept. 7.

Off-trail cave tour. Only for those aged fifteen and older, this three-hour tour takes those up for an adventure into dark passageways and requires belly-crawling through horizontal fissures as tight as 11 by 19 inches. The tours are only June 19 to August 30 on Fridays and Saturdays. Tour reservations must be made in advance.

Mount Elijah and Bigelow Lake. This alpine meadow and lake basin is home to one of the richest collections of plants and wildlife in the Siskiyou Mountains and is the jewel of the new land added to the national monument and preserve. The problem is the hike is quite difficult, running 9.2 miles to Mount Elijah and around 12 miles to Bigelow Lake meadows, with well over 1000 feet of climbing. The National Park Service is planning to offer an easier, guided route that uses a rough road to reach an alternate trailhead, but that tour hasn't been made official yet.

More than 120 species of plants and wildflowers have been found in the basin, along with many species of butterflies.

POISON OAK MYTHS AND FACTS

Poison oak is a shrub found along many trails in southern Oregon as well as in the southern Willamette Valley and parts of the south coast. It's known by its glossy three-part leaves and the contact dermatitis it causes for those sensitive to the urushiol oil found in its leaves, stalks, and roots. If it doesn't bother you, you're lucky! The rest of us can look forward to an icky, oozing rash lasting ten days to two weeks. The rash is an allergic reaction to the oil. You get it by touching or brushing against any part of these plants or anything that has come in contact with these plants, such as pet fur.

If you've touched poison oak, rinse off as quickly as possible, preferably with cold water, and wash any clothes that may have brushed up against it. There are special soaps marketed to get rid of the urushiol, but thorough rinsing of skin is the most important first step. Wash your dog, too. But don't worry about "contaminating" other people with your rash, nor about spreading it by scratching. It can only be spread by exposure to the urushiol oil.

At mile 2 a side trail leads to Mount Elijah (see Great Getaway: Oregon Caves for details) and at mile 3.3 the path merges with Cliff Nature Trail. This route adds 0.5 mile to the journey but is highly recommended. (If you go right, you'll be back at the trailhead in 0.2 mile but will miss the marble outcrops and vistas.) The nature trail goes over the top of the marble formation containing the caves, with beautiful views into the Illinois Valley. After that, the trail winds down to the base of the marble, passes the cave exit, and returns to the entrance.

115 ILLINOIS RIVER TRAIL

BEFORE YOU GO
MAP Wild Rivers Ranger District
CONTACT Rogue River–Siskiyou National Forest, Wild Rivers Ranger District
NOTES Very rough drive to trailhead; steep cliff edges: only recommended for older children; no privy available
GPS N42° 22.681' W123° 48.262'

ABOUT THE HIKE
SEASON Year-round
DIFFICULTY Easy–moderate
ROUND-TRIP 4.8 miles
HIGH POINT 1058 feet
ELEVATION GAIN 430 feet

GETTING THERE
From Interstate 5, take exit 58 for downtown Grants Pass and follow US Highway 199 south through downtown. After crossing a bridge over the Rogue River, turn right to stay on US 199 for 20 miles to the town of Selma. At a blinking

Kalmiopsis, a small wildflower native to the Kalmiopsis Wilderness, can be found on the Illinois River Trail.

yellow light, turn right onto Illinois River Road (Forest Road 4130; there is a sign). Follow the winding road for 11 miles of pavement and another 8 miles of very rough, bumpy road to its end at the Briggs Creek picnic site. The last few miles are rough on passenger cars and can become muddy in winter and spring. A high-clearance vehicle is strongly recommended.

ON THE TRAIL

The wild, beautiful, and botanically fascinating canyon of the Illinois River offers one of the greatest adventures for families in this book. It's best for older children used to hiking, camping, and exploring wild places.

The drive into the canyon is an adventure in itself, taking you high above the burnt-orange river canyon and then down into it, with some awful sections of road at the end best to negotiate with a rugged high-clearance vehicle. If coming from far away, you may want to consider camping along Illinois River Road at one of the many beautiful campgrounds with close-in swimming holes in summer or early autumn (or face a roaring river in spring). Store Gulch Campground is a favorite but there are many, including Briggs Creek, at the trailhead.

This very cool hike explores just the first 2.4 miles (with options for a longer backpack) of the 31-mile Illinois River Trail; but right away, you feel like you're in a wild place. There is little climbing—the trail is quite level in the section described. This area was burned by the 2002 Biscuit Fire, one of the worst in state history, but is recovering nicely. Rare wildflowers and plants that live nowhere else can be found here.

From the trailhead, cross a long steel bridge over Briggs Creek and begin among blooms of wildflowers. The trail passes into oak and madrone forest

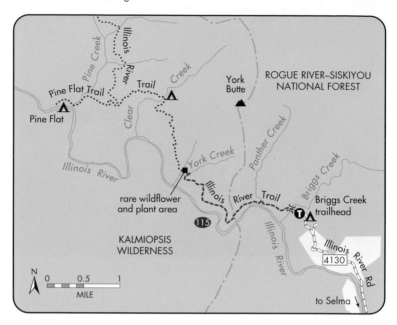

crossed by small clear creeks. After about a mile, the trail opens up above sheer cliffs and rockfalls overlooking the river far below. Make sure your child is happy to stay on trail and doesn't bolt off. The canyon is almost pure serpentine rock here, which gives the canyon walls their orange color. At mile 2.4 the trail crosses the west fork of York Creek. Stop here to enjoy some of the most interesting biology in the world.

A little side trail will lead to large grove of cobra lilies, or Darlingtonia. These carnivorous plants trap unsuspecting flies and spiders with nectar and then force them downward with a combination of slippery wax and pointed hairs. Eventually the victims are entombed and digested.

Smaller, and also nearby, are blooms of *Kalmiopsis leachiana*, a tiny, pink to purple azalea-like flower that blooms nowhere else in the world. There are other rare wildflowers here, including lady slipper orchids. York Creek marks your turnaround point; return as you came.

If you plan on backpacking, continue on for a campsite at Clear Creek (mile 4.1) or, in another couple miles, better sites farther on at Pine Flat. To reach Pine Flat: at a trail junction at mile 4.9 head left onto the Pine Flat Trail, dropping steeply downhill until at mile 6 you reach this wonderful grassy oasis in the middle of wild mountains. The best camping spots are on the meadow's far side along the river.

Opposite: *The Painted Hills (Hike 116), one of the units of the John Day Fossil Beds National Monument, rolls out in multicolored splendor in Oregon's desert.*

EASTERN OREGON

116 PAINTED HILLS

BEFORE YOU GO
> **MAP** Download map from monument website
> **CONTACT** National Park Service, John Day Fossil Beds National Monument
> **NOTES** Can be hot and crowded in summer; privy near trailheads; water available May–Sept.
> **GPS** N44° 39.002' W120° 16.022'

ABOUT THE HIKE
> **SEASON** Year-round
> **DIFFICULTY** Easy
> **ROUND-TRIP** 0.5 to 1.6 miles
> **HIGH POINT** 2092 feet
> **ELEVATION GAIN** 10 to 400 feet

GETTING THERE

From Prineville, drive east on US Highway 26 for 43 miles. Just before reaching the town of Mitchell, turn left on Bridge Creek Road (Burnt Ranch Road) at signs for the Painted Hills. Follow this paved road 5.5 miles. At signs, turn left onto gravel Bear Creek Road and follow it to the many trailheads of the Painted Hills.

ON THE TRAIL

The most popular destination of the John Day Fossil Beds National Monument is the Painted Hills, considered one of the state's seven wonders. There are multiple colored hills here, but the main attraction is a long hillside ornamented with twisting waves of red, gold, and black created by iron and manganese.

The good news for travelers with children is that there are five mostly short trails, each unique in its own way. The bad news is that a rise in visitors during the past few years means that crowds can be large on sunny weekends in spring and early summer, and parking can be a challenge. Get to the trailheads early and midweek if possible. Do not climb on or touch the colored hills. The road

Painted Cove Trail gets you up close with the Painted Hills.

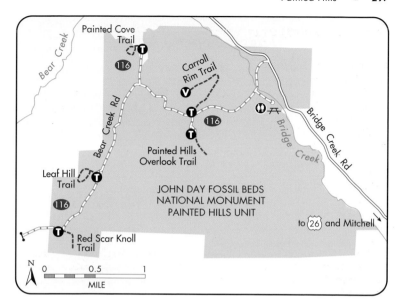

accessing the hikes ends at a locked gate one mile west of the last hike (Red Scar Knoll Trail) the monument boundary. All trails except Carroll Rim are stroller and wheelchair accessible.

Carroll Rim Trail

The longest hike in the Painted Hills, the 0.8-mile (1.6 miles round-trip) Carroll Rim Trail climbs 400 feet to a stunning viewpoint overlooking a panorama of the surrounding landscape of canyon and river. It's also a great place to watch a high desert sunset. The trail is a bit steep, but it is well graded up a series of switchbacks. The often crowded parking area is shared with the Painted Hills Overlook Trail.

Painted Hills Overlook Trail

The most popular (and often crowded) trail is a 0.5-mile round-trip trek that takes you closest to the most impressive of the Painted Hills. Photographers dot the trail, shooting the bright waves of color from every possible angle. Signs inform visitors of what they're seeing, and the trail, with 100 feet of climbing, ends at a high viewpoint of this part of the monument.

Painted Cove Trail

Climbing off-trail in the Painted Hills is prohibited, so it's difficult to get close to them—which is why this is such a cool trail. It gets you up close and personal with the colorful clay hills on a short boardwalk loop of 0.25 mile. Savor every step as you walk into a bright red cove and then back out.

GREAT GETAWAY: JOHN DAY FOSSIL BEDS NATIONAL MONUMENT

Three different units comprise the John Day Fossil Beds National Monument in the dry canyonlands of Eastern Oregon. While the Painted Hills (Hike 116) are famous for their colored cliffs, it's the area's well-preserved fossil record that made this a national monument. Once a lush landscape of lakes and forest, that history is preserved in one of North America's best fossil records of plants and animals dating to 45 million years ago. You can examine fossils both on the trails and at the Thomas Condon Paleontology Center.

The three different units of the monument—Painted Hills, Sheep Rock, and Clarno—are each unique and worth visiting but are spaced far apart. The long drives between units makes planning a trip here important.

Lodging. The largest nearby town is Prineville, which has plenty of supplies and hotels. Closer to the attractions, the small towns of Mitchell (near the Painted Hills Unit), John Day (near the Sheep Rock Unit), and Fossil (near the Clarno Unit) offer restaurants and hotels to spend the night.

The Oregon Hotel in Mitchell is a great option, as are Wilson Ranches Retreat Bed and Breakfast and Hyatt House Bed and Breakfast in Fossil.

Camping. There are many campgrounds in the sprawling landscape between the units. A few close to the action include Shelton Park (thirty-six sites) and Bear Hollow (twenty sites) county parks near Fossil. Mitchell's city park offers four RV hookups with water and electricity (no sewer), along with open lawn tent spaces.

Thomas Condon Paleontology Center. Located inside the Sheep Rock Unit, this 11,000-square-foot facility is a visitors center, a museum, and a working scientific facility for researchers studying the area's fossils. The center's museum displays over 500 fossil specimens along with murals and other exhibits.

John Day River swimming and access. The famous waterway of Eastern Oregon courses through the canyons in this area. Two of the nicer places to access and enjoy the river include Clarno, a unit of the national monument, and Priest Hole, a remote site managed by the BLM just north of the Painted Hills Unit.

You're allowed to collect some fossils at the Wheeler High School fossil beds for a fee. For details, contact Oregon Paleo Lands Center & Gallery at (541) 763-4480 or visit www.oregonpaleolandscenter.com/.

Leaf Hill Trail

The Leaf Hill area has been the site of extensive paleontological research. While you cannot see any fossils along the trail today, an interpretive exhibit shows examples of a few of the fossil leaf imprints that have been found there. There is not much in the way of colorful hills, but this hike is still very worth doing if your kids (and you!) have the energy.

Red Scar Knoll Trail

The multicolored knoll in question looks a bit like a magician's hat, or the world's largest ant colony rising out of the ground. This out-and-back trail gives you another close look at what makes the Painted Hills painted. The trek is just 0.25 of a mile and doesn't require much climbing, so relish each step.

117 SHEEP ROCK

BEFORE YOU GO
MAP Download map from monument website
CONTACT National Park Service, John Day Fossil Beds National Monument
NOTES Privy available at trailhead and visitor center; trail slippery when wet and can be very hot in summer; not recommended for dogs
GPS N44° 35.729' W119° 37.873'

ABOUT THE HIKE
SEASON Year-round
DIFFICULTY Easy–challenging
ROUND-TRIP 1.3 or 4.1 miles
HIGH POINT 2920 feet
ELEVATION GAIN 220 to 800 feet

GETTING THERE
From Prineville, drive east on US Highway 26 for 77 miles, passing the turn-off for the Painted Hills, to a junction with State Highway 19. Turn left and follow Hwy. 19 north for 5.2 miles to the many trailheads and attractions of this area.

ON THE TRAIL
The Sheep Rock Unit is forever playing second fiddle to the more famous Painted Hills in the John Day Fossil Beds National Monument. In reality, the

The John Day Fossil Beds are known for their intact bones of exotic creatures from another time. Visitors can see replica bones along the Island in Time Trail.

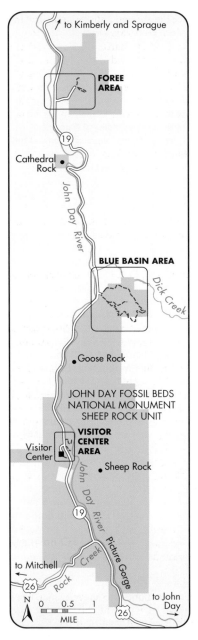

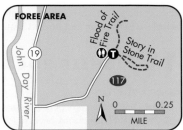

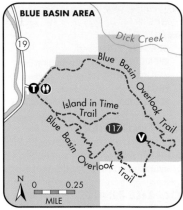

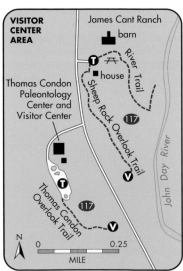

trails that begin at this eastern section of the monument offer a more reward-ing hiking experience and views that are almost as dramatic.

The best way to experience this area is by starting at a wonderful museum, the Thomas Condon Paleontology Center and Visitor Center. You'll find colorful displays of this area's prehistoric animals—a life-size replica of a saber-tooth tiger is just one—along with the well-preserved fossils that made this area famous. Then head onto the trail where the fossils were discovered.

There are multiple trail options starting at the center. Here's a breakdown.

Thomas Condon Overlook Trail
Beginning from the parking lot of the museum, this hike of 0.25 mile starts from the center parking lot and ends at an overlook with a great view of the valley.

River Trail
Beginning from the James Cant Ranch parking lot—a nice shaded place for a picnic—this trail leads to the John Day River on a 0.6-mile hike.

Sheep Rock Overlook Trail
After starting at the front gate to the Cant House, in 0.5 mile the trail ends at an overlook with a great view of the valley and the river.

Blue Basin and Island in Time Trails
The longest and most impressive trail system at the Sheep Rock Unit offers an easier and a more difficult option. They can be combined into one loop totaling 4.1 miles with 800 feet of climbing.

From the Blue Basin Trailhead, head left on the Blue Basin Loop for a 3.25-mile loop. It's the best overall hike in Sheep Rock and climbs to a spec-tacular vista overlooking the John Day River valley and the monument's mul-ticolored canyon lands. Hike the Island in Time Trail on the way back if you still have energy.

For an easier option, hike only the Island in Time Trail on a 1.3-mile trek with 220 feet of elevation gain. This pathway enters an amphitheater carved out of the blue-green claystones of the John Day Formation. The volcanic ash, now turned to stone, contains a rich variety of vertebrate fossils. Interpretive signs and fossil replicas are located along the trail.

Flood of Fire Trail
Beginning at the Foree Area, 5 miles north of Blue Basin, this short hike fol-lows a gravel trail up a small ridge to a viewpoint overlooking the John Day River Valley and a colorful rock formation similar to Cathedral Rock.

Story in Stone Trail
A second short hike at Foree takes you 0.3 mile round-trip above a small basin of blue-green claystone. The formation contains fossils of animals that lived here 25 to 30 million years ago. This mostly level trail is partially paved.

GREAT GETAWAY: WALLOWA MOUNTAINS

There's a good argument that Oregon's most impressive mountain range is not the Cascades—the familiar volcanoes such as Hood and Jefferson—but the Wallowa Mountains in the state's northeast corner. Known as the Oregon Alps, the Wallowa Mountains are home to seventeen mountains towering more than 9000 feet high above the traditional homeland of the Nez Perce Indians.

The Wallowa Valley makes a wonderful place to visit with children, especially the tourist-friendly towns of Enterprise and Joseph. Craft food, art, music, water activities and kid-friendly adventures can all be had in these two small towns about five and a half hours from Portland.

Lodging. There are plenty of hotels, bed and breakfasts, and vacation rentals in the Enterprise and Joseph area, from affordable to extravagant.

Camping. The most popular campground is Wallowa Lake State Park, home to 121 full-hookup sites and eighty-eight tent sites with bathrooms and showers. Smaller Forest Service campsites dot the surrounding areas, with some of the nicest in the Lostine River Canyon south of the town of Lostine.

Wallowa Lake. The centerpiece of the Wallowa Mountain experience is this lake, where anglers, jet skiers, kayakers, and swimmers are found on summer days. The swimming beach with the best views is a county park on the north side of the lake. The south side is home to the state park with a swimming beach and the Wallowa Lake Marina, where everything from paddleboats to a 22-foot pontoon boat can be rented, along with fishing equipment and advice on how to land 'em. The south end of Wallowa Lake also features bumper boats and minigolf.

Wallowa Lake Tramway. Normally, reaching the top of a Wallowa Mountain high peak requires a leg-burning climb that leaves you breathless. The journey to the top of Mount Howard is much different. The Wallowa Lake Tramway whisks visitors from 4450 to 8150 feet in just fifteen minutes. There's 2.5 miles of mountaintop trail to explore and even a restaurant, the Summit Grill, at the top. This experience doesn't come cheap, however, costing more than $33 per person at the time of publication.

Art. A thriving artist community in Joseph specializes in bronze castings, landscape images, and hand-crafted jewelry. Art galleries line the small town, and statues of bald eagles, Native Americans, and cowboys populate the streets downtown.

Restaurants. There are too many good places to eat in the area to name them all, but we list two favorites. Red Horse Coffee Traders in Joseph is home to the best breakfast burritos this side of the Mississippi. Terminal Gravity Brew Pub in Enterprise offers a wonderful outdoor lawn, with a creek running through the middle, where you can sip craft beer and munch dinner options.

Eagle Cap Wilderness. The downside to the Wallowa Mountains is that many of the hikes into the wilderness area are too difficult for the average child. This book features the easiest options we've found in Hikes 118 and 119. But, if you want to push your luck, or if you have an exceptionally determined child, the Eagle Cap is home to stunning alpine lakes.

The Wallowa Mountains tower over the peaceful trails that begin at Iwetemlaykin State Heritage Area.

118 IWETEMLAYKIN TRAIL

BEFORE YOU GO
    MAP Download map from state park website
    CONTACT Wallowa Lake State Park
    NOTES Be careful of cars at trail's start; privy available
    GPS N45° 20.578' W117° 13.410'
ABOUT THE HIKE
    SEASON April–November
    DIFFICULTY Easy
    ROUND-TRIP 2.6 miles
    HIGH POINT 4339 feet
    ELEVATION GAIN 250 feet

GETTING THERE

The Iwetemlaykin State Heritage Area is located between the communities of Joseph and Wallowa Lake and managed by the latter's state park. From Joseph, drive 1.2 miles south of downtown on State Highway 351, and keep your eyes peeled for a sign on the right side of the road leading to a small parking lot.

ON THE TRAIL

The hustle of the Joseph and Wallowa Lake area during the height of summer can be a bit overwhelming, making this trail a perfect place for children to

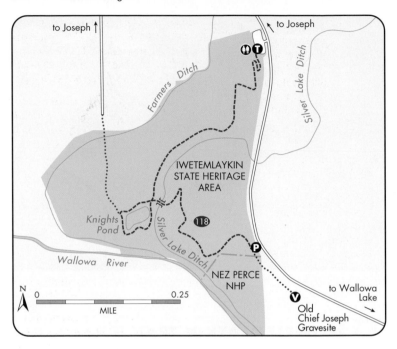

mellow out. Pronounced "ee-weh-TEMM-lye-kinn"—a Nez Perce word for "at the edge of the lake"—the site features an easy trail, spectacular mountain views, and a history lesson.

The roadside state park is a good one for younger children, and the hike can be shortened to 1.3 miles with a shuttle.

From the trailhead, the hike heads up a few switchbacks to spectacular mountain views that stay with you for almost the entire hike. The trail's beginning also details this area's heartbreaking history.

"Here at the south end of the Wallowa Valley, the wal'waama band of the Nez Perce Indians gathered to begin a sorrowful journey: leaving their homeland. In 1877, the wal'waama were driven out of the Wallowa Valley, which had been their homeland since time immemorial," says an interpretive sign.

Beyond the sign, the trail heads across grassland meadow and down through ponderosa forest as the giant mountains loom overhead. At mile 0.8, you'll reach Knights Pond, dug by the area's early settlers. A short loop circles the pond, passing a trail junction that leads to Joseph. The pond is a good place to wade barefooted before continuing. Next, the trail crosses a bridge over Silver Lake Ditch (another nice place to put your feet in the water) before showcasing more mountain views. The trail ends at mile 1.2 at a parking pullout. You could head back the way you came but the better option is walking just up the highway to the gravesite of Old Chief Joseph, father of the more famous Chief Joseph.

One of the many sites that comprise Nez Perce National Historical Park across Oregon, Washington, Idaho, and Montana, Old Chief Joseph's gravesite looks out over Wallowa Lake. More history, including a breakdown of broken treaties, are highlighted. There's also a gravesite of some of the earliest white settlers, including the McFarland and McCully families. Return the way you came or arrange a shuttle to this point.

119 HURRICANE CREEK

BEFORE YOU GO
   MAP Eagle Cap Wilderness, IMUS Geographics
   CONTACT Wallowa National Forest, Wallowa Mountains Ranger District
   NOTES USFS parking fee; privy available
   GPS N45° 18.690' W117° 18.436'
ABOUT THE HIKE
   SEASON Late June–October
   DIFFICULTY Moderate–challenging
   ROUND-TRIP 6 miles
   HIGH POINT 5778 feet
   ELEVATION GAIN 750 feet

GETTING THERE
From State Highway 82 into downtown Enterprise, turn right onto South River Road Street, which becomes Hurricane Creek Road. Follow it for about 9 miles to the trailhead.

ON THE TRAIL
There are precious few trails in the Eagle Cap Wilderness suitable for even motivated and athletic children. The downside of Oregon's largest wilderness area is the trails often require long, steep hikes to reach anything of consequence. Hurricane Creek Trail is the exception to that rule. The trail begins in a

A view up Hurricane Creek with the giant peaks of the Wallowa Mountains towering above

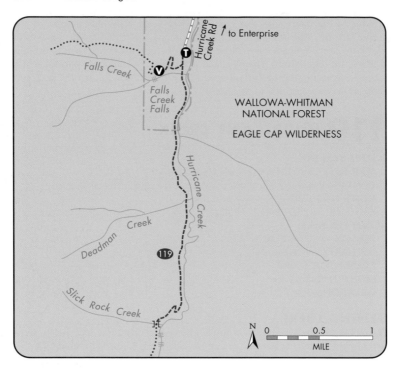

scenic setting and doesn't disappoint, passing waterfalls and beautiful mountain views on a relatively moderate trail. It's a good place to backpack with kids.

The best way to experience this trail is probably to just start hiking and go
as far as your children will tolerate. There's a wonderful nearby waterfall close
in; but a better goal is Slick Rock Gorge 3 miles in.

To visit the waterfall, turn right onto Falls Creek Trail at mile 0.1. Follow
it a short 0.1 mile to where a user trail drops down to the river for a view of
roaring 40-foot Falls Creek Falls. You can get pretty close to the waterfall by
scrambling around on the riverbank, but it's a bit dangerous for younger kids
given the creek's swift current.

After checking out the falls, head back to the main trail to continue alongside Hurricane Creek. There's a good chance you'll need to cross side creeks by
fording or crossing on downed trees. The views are mostly forested at first, but
gradually the trail opens up to reveal some of the Wallowa Mountains' tallest
peaks, including the Matterhorn, a stark white peak in the distance.

Along the way are a handful of creek-side camping spots and meadows
swell for having lunch. Continue on to Slick Rock Creek, where multiple waterfalls tumble into an alpine meadow surrounded by mountains. Beyond, the
trail climbs steeply to the lakes basin and Echo Lake.

GREAT GETAWAY: ANTHONY LAKE AND ELKHORN MOUNTAINS

Few Oregonians from the state's populous west side have even heard of the Elkhorn Mountains. That's a big part of the appeal: the nearby Wallowa Mountains get the bulk of tourists, but the Elkhorn Mountains are quieter. And they offer options that are better with kids (see Hikes 120 and 121). The best base camp for adventure is Anthony Lake. Craggy peaks rise over this beautiful mountain pool home to a campground, guard station, and network of wonderful trails. The Elkhorn Mountains are easy to explore from the 106-mile long Elkhorn Crest Scenic Highway.

Lodging. Hotels and amenities can be found in nearby La Grande and Baker City, both about an hour's drive from Anthony Lake. The best overall place to stay is Anthony Lake Guard Station: a log cabin built by the Civilian Conservation Corps in the 1930s. You can rent the cabin from the US Forest Service; make sure to book your stay six months in advance on Recreation.gov.

Camping. Anthony Lake Campground, on the lake's northern side, is the largest in the area, although the sites are fairly small. The walk-in campgrounds on the southern side, past the guard station, offer more room but require carrying in your gear. Nearby campgrounds include Rocky Ford and Mud Lake; but a favorite is the North Fork John Day campground, 16 miles west of Anthony Lake.

Anthony Lake watersports. Bring a kayak or other watercraft to Anthony Lake if you can. The lake has plentiful quiet nooks and crannies to explore. Only electric motors are allowed.

Fishing at Anthony Lake. The lake is stocked during the summer with rainbow trout. The best fishing is usually in the early part of summer. A spinner and bait seems to work well if the fish are biting.

Elkhorn Scenic Byway. This 106-mile byway (Highway 73) begins and ends in Baker City, and travels through mining ghost towns, Old West tourist stops, a reservoir, and the natural scenery of the Elkhorn Mountains. It's a great place for you and the kids to choose your own adventure.

Sumpter. This former mining boomtown along the byway features a Wild West theme with museums, historic sites, and fun old buildings that house modern saloons.

Phillips Lake. Located on the south end of the Elkhorn Scenic Byway's loop, this reservoir offers camping, boating, fishing, and swimming.

Elkhorn Crest Trail. One of the best backpacking trails in Oregon travels from Anthony Lake to Marble Pass for 23 miles across the high alpine country of the Elkhorns. Home to lakes, wildflowers, and mountain goats, this spectacular backpacking trip is doable with older children ready for a challenge. The best route starts at Marble Pass and travels downhill to Anthony Lake. Hire Range Tour and Shuttle Company (see Resources) to drive your shuttle, because the road leading to Marble Pass is among the worst in the state.

120 ANTHONY AND HOFFER LAKES

BEFORE YOU GO
MAP Wallowa-Whitman National Forest
CONTACT Wallowa-Whitman National Forest
NOTES USFS parking fee; privy available
GPS N44° 57.677' W118° 13.914'

ABOUT THE HIKE
SEASON July–October
DIFFICULTY Easy–moderate
ROUND-TRIP 2.4 miles out and back
HIGH POINT 7485 feet
ELEVATION GAIN 380 feet

GETTING THERE
From Interstate 84 between La Grande and Baker City, take exit 285 in North Powder, following the ski area signs on State Highway 237 for 4 miles to Ellis Road. Turn left on Ellis and go about 1 mile to take a right on Anthony Lake Highway, which becomes Forest Road 73. Continue for 16 miles, passing the Elkhorn Crest trailhead, to the campground entrance on your left. Follow the entrance road, and at the fork go right along the lake's southern shore to park at a gazebo just across from the Anthony Lake Guard Station. (If all spaces are filled, there are other small picnic areas along the road that work for parking, as well as a larger lot for walk-in campsites at road's end.

ON THE TRAIL
Nestled in the heart of the Elkhorn Mountains, Anthony Lake makes a perfect base camp for families on a multiday vacation. Craggy mountains rise above a lake surrounded by campsites and picnic areas.

The craggy Elkhorn Mountains rise above Anthony Lake.

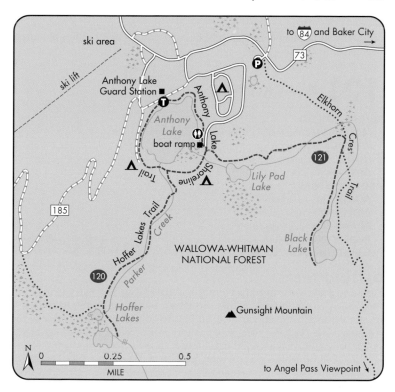

This hike showcases Anthony Lake before shooting off through the forest to the quieter and more scenic Hoffer Lakes. You can start this hike at any of the picnic areas around Anthony Lake, but a good place is at a gazebo just across from the Anthony Lake Guard Station, a log cabin that can be rented out (see Great Getaway: Anthony Lake and Elkhorn Mountains). Both have that wonderful charm of having been built in the 1930s by the Civilian Conservation Corps.

Start by heading right along the Anthony Lake Shoreline Trail. You'll enjoy spectacular views of craggy Gunsight Mountain and Angel Peak looming above the lake before reaching a parking area for walk-in campsites near the lake's southern shore. Follow the trail past the campsites to a junction with Hoffer Lakes Trail. Turn right at a signboard and follow this jumbly, rocky trail 0.6 mile along Parker Creek to the first of the two Hoffer Lakes, alpine pools nestled right up against Lees and Angel peaks.

Follow a trail left toward the larger of the two lakes to a campsite with lots of room for running around (assuming nobody is camping there). Wildflowers and a small creek dropping into the lake invite exploring. Once you've had enough, return the way you came until you reach the junction at Anthony

Lake. To complete your hike, turn right, this time following the eastern and northern shoreline on a trail that reaches a boat ramp in 0.3 mile and returns to your car in another 0.3 mile.

121 BLACK LAKE

BEFORE YOU GO
    MAP Wallowa-Whitman National Forest
    CONTACT Wallowa-Whitman National Forest
    NOTES USFS parking fee; privy available
    GPS N44° 57.546' W118° 13.747'
ABOUT THE HIKE
    SEASON July–October
    DIFFICULTY Easy–moderate
    ROUND-TRIP 2.3 miles
    HIGH POINT 7345 feet
    ELEVATION GAIN 250 feet

GETTING THERE

From Interstate 84 between La Grande and Baker City, take exit 285 in North Powder. In North Powder, follow the ski area signs on State Highway 237 for 4 miles to Ellis Road. Turn left on Ellis Road and go about 1 mile to the Anthony Lake Highway (which becomes Forest Road 73). Continue for 16 miles, passing the Elkhorn Crest trailhead, to the campground entrance on your left. Following the entrance road, turn left and drive past the lake's official campground to the boat ramp and a large parking area. The trail begins from the left.

ON THE TRAIL

The scenery is less dramatic than that of Hike 120, but this pleasant trek to another alpine lake is more than worthwhile for kids during a stay at Anthony Lake. Although the suggested trailhead is the boat ramp—the shortest route to Black Lake—it would be easy to start this hike from Anthony Lake's many picnic areas or campgrounds. Just follow the Anthony Lake Shoreline Trail, which circles the lake on a 1-mile circuit, until you reach the boat ramp.

Either way, from the boat ramp, follow Black Lake Trail and in very short order you'll reach aptly named Lily Pad Lake. This shallow marshy pool is covered with yellow water lily blossoms all summer and backed by Gunsight Peak. The trail travels 0.5 mile to a junction with the Elkhorn Crest Trail. Turn right and follow it, but only for a few hundred feet. Black Lake Trail resumes on the right and climbs gradually 0.6 mile to the lake's eastern shore. Black Lake is pretty, but doesn't have the spectacular scenery of Anthony or Hoffer Lakes. It makes up for it, however, with good fishing and some nice backcountry campsites scattered around the lake. Return the way you came.

Celebrating upon reaching Black Lake in the Elkhorn Mountains

Angel Pass and Dutch Flat Lake

Continue on the Elkhorn Crest Trail—a 23-mile national recreation trail—and you'll reach Angel Pass Viewpoint and Dutch Flat Lake. With well over 1000 feet of climbing, these hikes aren't for most kids; but the views are stunning. It's 8.2 miles round-trip to Angel Pass Viewpoint and 10.4 miles and around 1700 feet of elevation gain to reach Dutch Flat Lake.

RESOURCES

MANAGING AGENCIES

Baskett Slough National Wildlife Refuge
(541) 757-7236
www.fws.gov/refuge/baskett_slough

Bureau of Land Management
www.blm.gov/contact/oregon-washington
  Medford District
  (541) 618-2200
  Northwest Oregon District
  (503) 375-5646
  Roseburg District
  North Umpqua Waterfalls
  http://tinyurl.com/3g6wpdn
  Smullin Rogue River Visitor Center
  (541) 479-3735

Beacon Rock State Park
(509) 427-8265
http://parks.state.wa.us/474/
  Beacon-Rock

Cape Perpetua Visitor Center
(541) 547-3289
www.fs.usda.gov/siuslaw

City of Cannon Beach
(503) 436-1581
www.ci.cannon-beach.or.us

City of Eugene
(541) 682-4800
www.eugene-or.gov

Columbia Hills State Park
(509) 767-1159
www.parks.state.wa.us/489/
  Columbia-Hills

Columbia River Gorge National Scenic Area
(541) 308-1700
www.fs.usda.gov/crgnsa

Crater Lake National Park
(541) 594-2211
www.nps.gov/crla

Deschutes National Forest
(541) 383-5300
www.fs.usda.gov/deschutes
  Bend/Fort Rock Ranger District
  (541) 383-5300
  Newberry National Volcanic Monument
  (541) 593-2421
  Sisters Ranger District
  (541) 549-7700

Fremont-Winema National Forest
www.fs.usda.gov/main/fremont-winema
  Klamath Ranger District
  (541) 883-6714

Grants Pass Interagency Office
(541) 471-6500
http://tinyurl.com/y9gj7z6k

John Day Fossil Beds National Monument
(541) 987-2333
www.nps.gov/joda

Lincoln County Parks
(541) 265-5747
www.co.lincoln.or.us

Linn County Parks Department
(541) 967-3917

Lava Lands Visitor Center
Newberry National Volcanic
Monument
Within boundaries of Deschutes NF
(541) 593-2421
www.fs.usda.gov/deschutes

**Lewis and Clark National Historical
Park**
(503) 861-2471
www.nps.gov/lewi

Memaloose State Park
(541) 478-3008
http://oregonstateparks.org

Mount Hood National Forest
(503) 668-1700
www.fs.fed.us/r6/mthood
   Clackamas River Ranger District
   (503) 630-6861
   Hood River Ranger District
   (541) 352-6002
   Zigzag Ranger District
   503-622-3191

Mount Pisgah Arboretum
(541) 747-3817
www.mountpisgaharboretum.com

The Nature Conservancy
Portland office
(503) 802-8100
www.nature.org/oregon

**Oregon Caves National Monument
and Preserve**
(541) 592-2100
www.nps.gov/orca

**Oregon Dunes National Recreation
Area**
(541) 271-3611
www.fs.fed.us/r6

Oregon State Parks
(800) 551.6949
http://oregonstateparks.org

Oxbow Regional Park
(503) 663-4708
www.oregonmetro.gov/parks/oxbow-
regional-park

Recreation.gov
For permits on federal lands
(877) 444-6777

Redwood National and State Parks
(707) 465-2039
www.nps.gov/redw/index.htm

Ridgefield National Wildlife Refuge
(360) 887-4106
www.fws.gov/refuge/ridgefield

**Rogue River–Siskiyou National
Forest**
(541) 618-2113
www.fs.usda.gov/rogue-siskiyou
   Gold Beach Ranger District
   (541) 247-3600
   Hart-Tish Park
   (541) 899-9220
   High Cascades Ranger District
   (541) 560-3400
   Star Ranger District
   (541) 899-3800
   Wild Rivers Ranger District
   (541) 592-4000

Santiam State Forest
503-859-2151
www.oregon.gov/ODF/Recreation

Siuslaw National Forest
(541) 750-7000
www.fs.fed.us/r6/siuslaw
   Hebo Ranger District
   (503) 392-5100

Mapleton Ranger District
(541) 902-8526
Waldport Ranger District
(541) 563-3211

South Slough National Estuarine Research Reserve
(541) 888-5558
www.oregon.gov/dsl/SS

Steigerwald Lake National Wildlife Refuge
(360) 835-8767
www.fws.gov/refuge/steigerwald_lake

Tillamook County campground reservations
http://reservations.co.tillamook.or.us

Umpqua National Forest
(541) 672-6601
www.fs.usda.gov/Umpqua
    Cottage Grove Ranger District
    (541) 767-5000
    North Umpqua Ranger District
    (541) 496-3532

Wallowa-Whitman National Forest
(541) 523-6391
www.fs.usda.gov/wallowa-whitman

Willamette National Forest
www.fs.usda.gov/willamette
(541) 225-6300
    Detroit Ranger District
    (503) 854-3366
    McKenzie River Ranger District
    (541) 822-3381
    Middle Fork Ranger District
    (541) 782-2283
    Sweet Home Ranger District
    (541) 367-5168

SERVICES
Adventure Maps Inc.
www.adventuremaps.net

Breitenbush Hot Springs Retreat and Conference Center
(503) 854-3320
www.breitenbush.com

Camp Dakota
(503) 873-7432
www.campdakota.com

City of Joseph
www.josephoregon.org

Columbia Gorge Express
www.columbiagorgeexpress.com

Multnomah Falls Lodge
(503) 695-2376
www.multnomahfallslodge.com

National Forest Map Store
www.nationalforestmapstore.com

Opal Creek Ancient Forest Center
(503) 892-2782
www.opalcreek.org

Oregon Caves Chateau
(541) 592-3400
www.oregoncaveschateau.com

Range Tour and Shuttle Company
(541) 519-8028
http://rangetour.com

Redwood Rides
(707) 951-6559
www.redwoodrides.com

Tillamook Forest Center
(503) 815-6800
tillamookforestcenter.org

Wallowa Valley Arts Council
For Wallowa Mountains getaway
www.josephoregonartists.com

INDEX

ABOUT THE AUTHORS

Zach Urness has been an outdoor writer and reporter in Oregon for the past decade. He's currently the outdoors editor at the *Statesman Journal* in Salem and a regular contributor to *USA Today* and the television show *Oregon Field Guide*. He is author of the book *Hiking Southern Oregon* and loves exploring Oregon with his wife, Robyn, and two daughters, Lucy and Rollie. When not hiking, Urness loves whitewater kayaking, fishing, and reading in a hammock, preferably alongside a mountain lake.

Journalist and outdoorswoman **Bonnie Henderson** has lived in Oregon nearly all her life. She spent most childhood vacations hiking and backpacking in the wilderness areas of the Northwest; her own son accompanied her on many scouting trips for earlier versions of this book, first in a baby backpack and later on his own two feet. She is thrilled to be collaborating with Zach to update *Best Hikes with Kids: Oregon* for a new generation. She is the author of another guidebook, *Day Hiking: Oregon Coast*, as well as two other books, *Strand* and *The Next Tsunami*. Visit her website at www.bonniehendersonwrites.com

MOUNTAINEERS BOOKS

SKIPSTONE   BRAIDED RIVER

recreation • lifestyle • conservation

MOUNTAINEERS BOOKS including its two imprints, Skipstone and Braided River, is a leading publisher of quality outdoor recreation, sustainability, and conservation titles. As a 501(c)(3) nonprofit, we are committed to supporting the environmental and educational goals of our organization by providing expert information on human-powered adventure, sustainable practices at home and on the trail, and preservation of wilderness.

Our publications are made possible through the generosity of donors, and through sales of more than 800 titles on outdoor recreation, sustainable lifestyle, and conservation. To donate, purchase books, or learn more, visit us online:

MOUNTAINEERS BOOKS

1001 SW Klickitat Way, Suite 201 • Seattle, WA 98134

800-553-4453 • mbooks@mountaineersbooks.org • www.mountaineersbooks.org

Leave No Trace strives to educate visitors about the nature of their recreational impacts and offers techniques to prevent and minimize such impacts. Leave No Trace is best understood as an educational and ethical program, not as a set of rules and regulations. For more information, visit www.lnt.org or call 800-332-4100.

OTHER MOUNTAINEERS BOOKS TITLES YOU MAY ENJOY!

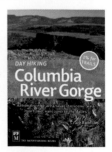